THE WRITER'S TOOLBOX

A Writing & Grammar Handbook
for Christian Schools®

Grace Collins Hargis

D1042668

🕮 BJU PRESS

THE WRITER'S TOOLBOX: A WRITING AND GRAMMAR HANDBOOK for Christian Schools®

Author
Grace Collins Hargis, Ph.D.
Chairman of the Departments of Linguistics and English Education,
Bob Jones University

Adapter/Reviser
Kimberly Y. Stegall, M.Ed.

Advisor
Ronald A. Horton, Ph.D.
Chairman of the Division of English, Language, and Literature,
Bob Jones University

Editor: Kelly Cooper
Designer: Duane A. Nichols
Compositor: Nancy C. Lohr

Contributing Writers
Dana Denise Gage, M.A.
Denise L. Patton
Elizabeth Rose, M.Ed.

Produced in cooperation with the Bob Jones University School of Education and the Department of English.

for Christian Schools is a registered trademark of Bob Jones University Press.

© 2000 Bob Jones University Press
Greenville, SC 29614

Printed in the United States of America

ISBN 1-57924-391-6

15 14 13 12 11 10 9 8 7 6 5 4

Table of Contents

Part 2: Usage Tools

Preface

One of the most amazing gifts God has given us is the gift of language. With no noticeable effort, we can use our language to talk about a game we participated in, to understand directions for a fire drill, to read a story about missionaries in Mexico, or even to imagine how it would be to float in air like a fish in water. That is, through language we can tell—or learn—about old things and new things, and things that have never been. And most of the time we give no thought to the sounds and words and sentences we use to do all of this.

Sometimes, though, we do have questions about what and how to speak or write. THE WRITER'S TOOLBOX: A WRITING AND GRAMMAR HANDBOOK for Christian Schools® seeks to answer many of those questions simply and accurately. Of course, the complexity of any language requires that there be some compromise between these two goals. The working principles have been these: to keep the terms as simple and familiar as possible; to present accurately the facts and concepts that will be the most helpful tools for practical use in the improvement of writing; and to reveal the basic order and system of the language.

Some students will come to this text from a different approach to teaching grammar such as was presented in ENGLISH HANDBOOK for Christian Schools® and the student worktexts of the first editions of WRITING AND GRAMMAR for Christian Schools®. This system, simply stated, further divided various parts of the traditional parts of speech to distinguish between related yet different classes of words. (In the first editions, *verbs* are divided into *verbs* and *auxiliaries; adverbs* are divided into *adverbs* and *qualifiers;* and *adjectives* are divided into *adjectives* and *determiners.*) Indeed, when those first edition books were written, the trend in language arts appeared to be toward this system of grammar study. However, since that time most grammarians and English teachers have remained consistent to the more familiar and traditional study of grammar, which describes only eight parts of speech: noun, pronoun, verb, adjective, adverb, preposition, conjunction, and interjection. In this handbook, as well as in our second editions of the seventh through twelfth grade writing and grammar worktexts, we have returned to the study of eight parts of speech as well as a more separate and flexible organization of the grammar, usage, and composition topics. For those who used the ENGLISH HANDBOOK successfully, the terms *auxiliary, qualifier,* and *determiner* are included in this handbook as subcategories or further divisions of the three previously mentioned parts of speech.

God's gift of language is well worth studying in its own right. Every language is both powerful and flexible, allowing for generous amounts of creativity. Languages also reflect God's nature in being reasonable and orderly.

The basic structure of the orderliness of English is presented in *Grammar Tools*. A knowledge of grammatical structure will not automatically make you a better writer, but it will certainly help you understand a great deal of good advice about writing.

Some of that good advice will come from your teachers and other sources, and some of it will be found in part two of this handbook. In *Usage Tools* you will learn more about avoiding errors and making wise use of the many choices that English gives us. The final section of the book, *Composition Tools,* contains other helps toward good writing. A major goal of all of these materials is to help writers express ideas with greater clarity, strength, and confidence.

PART ONE

Grammar Tools

Eight Parts of Speech

Sentences are made up of words, but not just any words in any place. In order for sentences to make sense, the right kinds of words must appear in the right places. These "kinds of words" are what we call the *parts of speech*. Thinking about the different kinds of words and learning labels for them is basic to learning something about how our language works.

This task of assigning labels would be much simpler if every word in every situation acted as one part of speech and no more. However, words have a tendency to switch categories, depending on their function in the sentence. Notice how the word *downtown* functions differently in each of the following sentences.

The renovation of *downtown* has taken five years. (noun)

Many *downtown* stores have been given facelifts. (adjective)

Lots of shoppers head *downtown* for lunch-hour errands. (adverb)

So our study of language must focus not only on the individual parts of speech but also on their various functions within the sentence.

Function Versus Part of Speech

In any sentence we can ask two very different questions about the words: What part of speech is this word? How does this word function in this sentence? For example, we can ask both questions about the individual words in the sentence "A wise man prepares for the future."

Part of Speech		Function in the Sentence
adjective (article)	A	modifier (of *man*)
adjective	wise	modifier (of *man*)
noun	man	simple subject
verb	prepares	simple predicate
preposition	for	relater (of *prepares* and *future*)
adjective (article)	the	modifier (of *future*)
noun	future	object of the preposition *(for)*

Words of the same part of speech can often be used in different ways. The two nouns in the sample sentence above have different functions—*man* is the simple subject and *future* is the object of the preposition. How do we know the part of speech and the function of a word? We know its part of speech by applying tests like those that are found in Chapter 1. We know its function in a particular sentence by recognizing how it fits into its own group of words (its phrase or clause) within the sentence and then often by recognizing how that group of words is related to the rest of the sentence. For instance, if a word is an object, it is an object of something. If it is a modifier, it is a modifier of something.

Function, then, is what a word does in the sentence. And whatever it does, it does in relation to the rest of the sentence.

Nouns

A **noun** names a person, place, thing, or idea; it is a "something" or "someone" word. Nouns function in sentences as subjects, direct objects, indirect objects, objects of the preposition, predicate nouns, and so on.

My *brother* broke his *arm*.

He was traveling to *Montana*.

He is a *carpenter*.

Tests of Function

Words that can follow the articles *a, an,* and *the* or the demonstratives *this, that, these,* and *those* to form simple statements are nouns.

a *car*	this *truck*
an *aardvark*	that *ship*
the *computer*	these *students*
	those *antiques*

Words that can act as doers or topics to make simple statements are nouns.

A *bird* flies.	This *man* finished first.
An *orange* squirts juice.	That *book* is ruined.
The *lamp* broke.	These *pictures* fell.
	Those *statements* appear false.

Clues from Form

Words that can be made plural by adding *s* or *es* or in some other way are nouns.

Singular	Plural
robot	robots
tax	taxes
man	men

Words that can be made possessive by adding an apostrophe or an apostrophe and an *s* are nouns.

Simple	Possessive
armchair	armchair's
armchairs	armchairs'

In our analysis, form is secondary to function. Not all nouns change in the plural form *(one deer, many deer)*. Also, a noun in its possessive form usually leaves its noun function behind. However, words that have a possessive form are nouns in their original state.

Kinds of Nouns

Nouns can be categorized in several different ways. An understanding of these divisions will give you a sense of what is included in the concept *noun*.

Common and Proper Nouns

All nouns are either common or proper.

COMMON NOUNS   general words for persons, places, things, or ideas: *father, city, apple, truth*

PROPER NOUNS   specific names for certain persons, places, or things: *Abraham Lincoln, Chicago,* the *White House*

Count and Noncount Nouns

Every common noun is either count or noncount.

COUNT NOUNS   can be made plural (can be counted): *the bean, the beans, some beans, five beans, plenty of beans*

NONCOUNT NOUNS   cannot be made plural (cannot be counted): *rice, some rice, plenty of rice*

We cannot say "the rices" or "five rices." If we want to talk about the individual grains, we have to use a phrase like "five grains of rice." Most count nouns are concrete; most noncount nouns are abstract.

A few words can be used as either count or noncount nouns (but always with a difference in meaning).

AS NONCOUNT	The baby drank some milk (a lot of milk, much milk).
AS COUNT	The daycare worker said, "I handed out eleven milks to the children."

Collective Nouns

Collective nouns are words like *family, committee, jury,* and *team* that refer to groups. Because a collective noun refers to a group, even when it is singular in form it can be treated as a plural.

TREATED AS SINGULAR	Our soccer team *is* playing an away game tonight.
TREATED AS PLURAL	Our soccer team *are* divided about which jerseys to order.

In the first example the focus is on the team as a whole, but in the second it is on the individual members of the team. When using a collective noun, be sure to consider carefully your meaning.

Concrete and Abstract Nouns

All common nouns can be considered either concrete or abstract in meaning.

CONCRETE NOUNS	refer to physical, material things, most of which can be seen, heard, touched, tasted, or smelled (most are count nouns): *rock, flower, cup, steak*
ABSTRACT NOUNS	refer to mental, nonmaterial things, most of which cannot be known through the senses (all are noncount nouns): *love, kindness, joy, self-control*

Idiomatic Use of Count and Noncount Nouns

Count and noncount nouns sometimes take different kinds of words as modifiers. Although we say "a bean" and "five beans," we do not say "a rice" or "five rices." Neither would we ask to be served "some bean" as we would ask for "some rice." Special idiomatic combinations with count and noncount nouns appear below.

Singular count nouns only	each every either neither	adult, bean, child, idea, senator
Plural count nouns only	many few/fewer/fewest a few several a number of the majority of	adults, beans, children, ideas, senators
Noncount nouns only	much little/less/least a little a great deal of a small/ large amount of a piece/grain/etc. of	rice, water, relief, love

The words and phrases listed above as modifiers are restricted to that one type of singular or plural, count or noncount noun. Notice the result of breaking these restrictions:

UNIDIOMATIC *A small amount* of children came, and even less adults.

CORRECTED *A small number* of children came, and even fewer adults.
Few children came, and even *fewer* adults.

The changes are necessary because the words *children* and *adults* are plural count nouns rather than noncount nouns.

The following is an error involving a noncount noun:

UNIDIOMATIC *The majority* of the water had already drained by that time.

CORRECTED *Most* of the water had already drained by that time.

"The majority of" (meaning more than half of the individuals in a group) logically requires either a plural count noun like *senators* or a collective noun like *senate*. In this case, we can substitute "most of," which can be used with any type of noun.

Pronouns

Pronouns are substitutes for nouns. If you had to repeat a noun each time you referred to something, your writing and speaking would certainly be monotonous. Taking the place of nouns, pronouns prevent boredom, improve efficiency, and strengthen coherence.

The word for which a pronoun stands and to which a pronoun points is its antecedent. Usually an antecedent comes before the pronoun, but the antecedent can follow the pronoun when the connection is clear and the distance between the two is short.

The *man* walked up to the desk, and *he* demanded to see the manager.

Before *she* answered the question, *Nylsa* took a deep breath.

Kinds of Pronouns

There are nine types of pronouns, each with a specific function. Recognizing the various types of pronouns will help you choose the best type to use in your speaking and writing.

Personal Pronouns

Of the various types of pronouns, the most common are the personal pronouns: *I, we, you, it, she, he,* and *they,* along with their other forms. **Personal pronouns** refer to persons, places, or things. These pronouns also show differences in what is known as *person.* First person is the speaker or writer; second person is the person spoken or written to; third person is the person or thing spoken or written about. Third person singular designates forms for masculine *(he, him, his),* feminine *(she, her, hers),* and neuter *(it, its).*

Singular			
	Subjective	**Objective**	**Possessive**
First Person	I	me	my, mine
Second Person	you	you	your, yours
Third Person			
neuter	it	it	its
masculine	he	him	his
feminine	she	her	her, hers

Plural			
	Subjective	**Objective**	**Possessive**
First Person	we	us	our, ours
Second Person	you	you	your, yours
Third Person	they	them	their, theirs

Personal pronouns show person, number, gender, and case. For more information on these pronouns, see Chapters 6 and 7.

Indefinite Pronouns

Indefinite pronouns refer to nonspecific persons, places, or things; therefore, these pronouns usually do not have antecedents. The following list names some of the most common indefinite pronouns.

someone	anyone	no one	everyone	none
something	anything	nothing	everything	each
somebody	anybody	nobody	everybody	some
any	all	most	both	one

Knowing whether an indefinite pronoun is singular or plural can be important both for subject-verb agreement and for pronoun-antecedent agreement (Ch. 5).

Demonstrative Pronouns

A **demonstrative pronoun** points out the position of whatever it refers to. *This* and *these* stand for things that are near in space or time; and *that* and *those* stand for things that are farther away.

> *This* is the week when Grandma will come.
>
> *That* was a good visit we had last month.

These words are pronouns only when they replace nouns, not when they are modifiers. (When they modify nouns, they are adjectives.)

Relative Pronouns

A **relative pronoun** has a noun function (S, DO, etc.) in a dependent clause, and at the same time it relates that clause to the rest of the sentence.

who	whom	whose	which	that

The relative pronoun functions as part of an adjective clause, and its antecedent is the word that the whole clause modifies.

S

It was Paul *who* was arrested in Acts 21-22.

DO

He got permission to speak to the great crowd *that* he saw before him.

Rule 1. Use *who/whom/whose* to stand for persons, and use *which* for things and most animals. Use *that* for either type of word.

PERSONS   I know the man [*who* called last night].
            I know the man [*that* called last night].

THINGS   The first house, [*which* is very convenient],
            is actually less expensive.
            They rented the house [*that* I like best].

Rule 2. Use *that* only in restrictive clauses. (Restrictive clauses, described in Chapter 3, are those that are needed to specifically identify the particular item or items named by the noun.)

RESTRICTIVE   I know the man [*that* called last night].
                They rented the house [*that* I like best].

Who and *which* can be used in either restrictive or nonrestrictive clauses.

RESTRICTIVE   Jane is the person [*who* told me that story].
                The brown gloves [*which* you gave me] are my best
                ones.

NONRESTRICTIVE Jane Jackson, [*who* told me that story], said that it
                really happened.
                Those brown gloves, [*which* you gave me last year], are
                still my best ones.

As a matter of style, however, some writers prefer not to overuse *which* in restrictive clauses.

ACCEPTABLE   The brown gloves [*which* you gave me] are my
                best ones.

PERHAPS BETTER The brown gloves [*that* you gave me] are my best
                ones.

Indefinite Relative Pronouns

An **indefinite relative pronoun** is a relative pronoun that does not have an antecedent and does not occur in an adjective clause. Usually it is part of a noun clause, though one is occasionally found in an adverb clause.

		Archaic
who (whom, whose)	whoever (whomever, whosever)	whosoever (etc.)
which	whichever	whichsoever
what	whatever	whatsoever

The indefinite relative pronouns, as opposed to the regular relative pronouns and the interrogative pronouns, usually seem to be doing double duty. For example, in *I know who just left,* the *who* seems to mean "the person who" or "the identity of the person who." Similarly, in *I like whatever you like,* the *whatever* means "anything that" or "everything which." Thus these indefinite relative pronouns have a meaning that is both indefinite ("anything, everything") and relative ("that, which").

In noun clauses

[*Whoever* just left] didn't shut the door.

Anyone can see [*whose* this is].

She gave the sales pitch to [*whoever* answered the phone].

In adverb clauses

[*Whatever* you do], don't try to go downtown during rush hour.

[*Whoever* comes], we will try to do our best.

Interrogative Pronouns

An **interrogative pronoun** asks a question the answer to which would be a noun or a pronoun. These pronouns may be used in direct or indirect questions.

who	whom	whose	which	what

Who will speak at the meeting tonight?

She asked *what* he will talk about.

Whose car should we take downtown?

Sometimes, for special emphasis, *ever* is added to the basic interrogative pronoun.

No way, Rita! *Whoever* told you that?

Whatever made you think that?

Reflexive and Intensive Pronouns

Reflexive and intensive pronouns end in *self* or *selves*. **Reflexive pronouns** are used as objects (or sometimes predicate nouns) but always refer to the same person or things as the subject of the sentence.

Bayley hurt *himself* on the sharp corner of the table.

Cami gave *herself* a haircut.

We listened to *ourselves* on the recording.

Intensive pronouns intensify, or emphasize, some noun or pronoun already in the sentence. Grammatically, an intensive pronoun functions as an appositive; it renames the preceding noun or pronoun.

I *myself* don't know the answer yet.

The author *herself* signed my copy of the novel.

Sometimes the intensive pronoun does not appear right after the noun it emphasizes, but later on in the sentence.

I don't know the answer *myself.*

The author signed my copy of the novel *herself.*

Reciprocal Pronouns

The **reciprocal pronouns** express a mutual relationship between or among the persons mentioned in the subject. There are two reciprocal pronouns: *each other* and *one another.*

DO

On the bus ride home, the players teased *each other* about the goof-ups in the game.

DO

They amused *one another* with stories about past games.

The reciprocal pronouns are used mostly as direct objects, but they can also be indirect objects and objects of prepositions.

IO

The committee gave *one another* the benefit of the doubt.

OP

The Johnsons always choose thoughtful gifts for *each other.*

The reciprocal pronouns can also be made into possessive adjectives, which modify nouns.

Let's try to stay out of *each other's* way.

Those children like to play with *one another's* toys.

Reciprocal pronouns should not be used as subjects of clauses.

> **UNACCEPTABLE** They knew [what *each other* would do].
> **CORRECTED** *Each* knew [what *the other* would do].

Verbs

Probably there is no more important word in the sentence than the verb. Verbs give life to most sentences, and they connect with other words in important ways. For example, in "Joey's foot crushed the dry leaves," *crushed* not only describes the type of action but also tells two other things: what Joey's foot did and what happened to the leaves. Without the verb there is no sentence. Understanding verbs—both the types and various forms they can take—helps us use them wisely and correctly.

Tests of Function

Verbs express action or state of being and are the main words in the predicate of any sentence or clause. Many **action verbs** have movement and excitement.

The athlete *ran* a mile in six minutes.

The computer *crashes* regularly.

The action expressed by an action verb may also be a mental action that cannot be observed with the senses.

Rosa *deliberated* over her next move in the chess game.

Hank *remembers* everything that he reads.

State-of-being verbs explain a condition and are frequently followed by complements.

The mountains *are* lovely.

Garden flowers *smell* sweet.

13

Since verbs combine with nouns and pronouns to form sentences, the following test frame can be used to test for verbs.

> He/It/They _____.
> He/It/They _____ him/it/them.

Clues from Form

Verbs are complicated because they have so many forms and functions. It is sometimes difficult to analyze verbs and their relationships to other words in a sentence. This is because verbs can show time, person, number, voice, and mood.

> Tense—I run.
>
> Person—He runs; you run.
>
> Number—She runs; they run.
>
> Voice—We run that trail; the trail was run on by us.
>
> Mood—I ran; if I were running . . .

Verbs appear as single words or in phrases. The **complete verb** can include one or more auxiliaries (or helping verbs) as well as the main verb.

> The vase broke.
>
> The vase will break.
>
> The vase does break.
>
> The vase is breaking.
>
> The vase has broken.
>
> The vase will have broken.
>
> The vase will have been broken.

Although some of the above sentences would most likely never be spoken (or written!), sometimes several auxiliaries are needed to express a shade of meaning. Be aware of all auxiliaries that work with the main verb.

Forms of *be* and *have* are the most common auxiliaries. However, the list below includes other frequently used auxiliaries.

can	may	will	shall	do
could	might	would	should	must

Verb-Adverb Combinations

A **verb-adverb combination** (VAC) is made up of two words, a verb and a following adverb. The two words often work together to produce a meaning different from the meanings of the two words alone.

back up   bring about
 ("support")   ("cause to happen")
break off   look over
 ("put an end to")   ("inspect casually")

English is rich in such combinations. Many of them express briefly a concept that might otherwise sound complicated. For instance, notice the two uses of *in* in the two sentences below.

He turned in the street.

He turned in his paper.

The first sentence contains a prepositional phrase.

 S InV

He *turned* in the street. (Where did he turn? *in the street*)

The second sentence contains a verb-adverb combination, *turn in,* meaning "submit."

 S TrV (Adv) DO

He *turned in* his paper. (What did he turn in? *his paper*)

The two words of a VAC appear either (1) together in the sentence or (2) with the adverb moved to a position right after the direct object. The best way to tell the difference between a verb-adverb combination and a verb followed by a prepositional phrase is to apply a movement test: the adverb of a VAC can be moved so that it comes after the direct object.

  ORIGINAL He *turned in* his paper yesterday.

 TEST APPLIED He *turned* his paper *in* yesterday.

  CONCLUSION Since *in* can be moved, *turn in* is a verb-adverb
        combination.

If the sentence cannot pass the movement test without a change of meaning, the word in question is a preposition, not an adverb. However, if the complete direct object is long, the sentence will sound better with the adverb next to the verb.

AWKWARD Yesterday he *turned* the very first term paper of his life *in.*

BETTER Yesterday he *turned in* the very first term paper of his life.

Sometimes even with a relatively short noun phrase as direct object, the sentence still sounds better with the VAC adverb next to the verb. Notice that *up* sounds rather weak at the end of the sentence.

ACCEPTABLE Last week they *drew* a new contract *up.*
BETTER Last week they *drew up* a new contract.

Adjectives

Adjectives modify nouns or noun elements. That is, an adjective expands, limits, or describes a noun or pronoun.

Bethel Christian Academy, *private* and *nondenominational,* attracts many students from area churches.

Many students choose *private* and *nondenominational* schools.

The italicized adjectives in the first sentence expand the idea of Bethel Christian Academy to include the ideas of private and nondenominational. In the second sentence those same adjectives limit the noun *schools* to a specific type of school: one which is private and nondenominational. The adjectives focus the statement.

Tests of Function

Most adjectives modify a following noun.

Terri is a *kind* person.

The book has a *stiff* binding.

Some adjectives modify a preceding indefinite pronoun.

After a long run, I need something *cool* to drink.

She would like nothing *better* than a puppy.

Adjectives can also appear in the predicate describing the subject in some way.

The art exhibit is *popular.*

The paintings appear almost *real.*

Two other adjective positions are after the noun and as an objective complement. An adjective that is part of a longer modifying phrase comes after the noun it modifies.

The class president came up with an idea *agreeable* to all of us.

We had the money *necessary* for our senior trip.

Two adjectives joined by a conjunction can come either before or after the noun.

Dazed but *undaunted* the violinist continued playing after he tripped on an electrical cord.

A toddler, *happy* and *unaware,* ate the flowers his mother had picked.

An adjective can appear after the direct object, describing the direct object because of the action of the verb. This type of adjective is known as an objective complement. (See pp. 35-36.)

They painted the study *cocoa brown.*

Coach Boole believed his players *capable* of winning.

Test for adjectives by trying words in these locations.

the _____ man   the _____ idea   the _____ situation
The man is _____.   The idea is _____.   The situation is _____.

Clues from Form

Most adjectives form degrees of comparison. In the positive degree no comparison is made.

Roland is *tall.*
Her attitude was *unselfish.*

The comparative degree is a comparison of two things.

Jack is *taller* than Roland.
Her mother was even *more unselfish.*

The superlative degree is a comparison of three or more things.

> Jessica is the *tallest* in the class.
>
> This time Grandma was the *most unselfish*.

Many adjectives take *er* and *est,* and other adjectives take *more* and *most*. Nearly all one-syllable adjectives are compared with *er* and *est*. Some two-syllable adjectives take *er* and *est,* especially adjectives that end in *y, ly,* and *le*. Otherwise, you can expect the adjective to be compared with *more* and *most*.

Positive	Comparative	Superlative
short	shorter	shortest
quick	quicker	quickest
busy	busier	busiest
friendly	friendlier	friendliest
simple	simpler	simplest
unselfish	more unselfish	most unselfish
observant	more observant	most observant

Other Types of Adjectives

One common type of adjective is the **article.** English has two types: indefinite and definite. *A* and *an* are the **indefinite articles;** *the* is the **definite article.** *A* and *an* show that a singular noun refers to something not named in particular or not mentioned before. (A plural noun used indefinitely has no article: "He collects stamps.") *The* shows that the noun refers to something already known or already mentioned.

> Travis wore *a* sweater.
>
> Travis wore *the* sweater with holes in it.

Many words whose primary function is other than adjectival must be recognized as adjectives when they are functioning as such. Nouns sometimes function as adjectives.

> The museum is surrounded by an *iron* fence.
>
> *Stone* gargoyles are mounted along the roofline.

A **modifying noun** is an individual noun used to modify another noun. Modifying nouns follow any other adjectives that may be present in the phrase.

> his warm wool jacket

Notice the part-of-speech differences between the adjective *warm* and the modifying noun *wool*. *Warm* passes the adjective tests given on page 17.

1. *Warm* usually modifies a noun.
2. *Warm* can be compared using *er/est* or *more/most: warmer, warmest.*
3. *Warm* can fill both blanks in the test frame: The *warm* thing is very *warm.*

Wool does not pass the set of adjective tests, but instead has the characteristics given on pages 4-5 for nouns.

1. *Wool* names a thing.
2. *Wool* can be made possessive by a change in form: *wool's strength*
3. *Wool* can function as subject, direct object, and so on: *Wool is warmer than cotton.*

Wool and *warm* are different parts of speech, but the two words have the same function in the phrase *his warm wool jacket*—both words are modifiers. Therefore we call the word *wool* a modifying noun or an adjective.

Different types of pronouns often function as adjectives. Indefinite pronouns act as indefinite adjectives only when they modify nouns.

> He ate *some* ripe strawberries but *no* plums. (BUT: He ate *some.*)
> *Each* plum tree produced much fruit this summer.

Demonstrative pronouns act as adjectives when they precede a noun.

> *This* dog does many tricks.
> *That* cat has fleas.

Three interrogatives act as adjectives when they precede a noun: *which, what,* and *whose.*

> *Which* book is yours?
> *What* idea did they have?
> *Whose* plan was that?

When possessives modify nouns, they are adjectives. Other possessives are not adjectives. (See p. 89 for information on independent possessives.) A possessive used as an adjective always modifies a following noun.

> *John's* large Thermos would not fit into *my* lunchbox.
> *Today's* lesson is about fractions.
> Ellyn broke in *her* new boots.

Certain verb forms can also function as adjectives: the participle and the infinitive. (See Ch. 3.)

> The *skydiving* team successfully completed its first jump. (present participle)
> Two *melted* peanut butter cups were added to the batter. (past participle)
> Loren searched for a good play *to read*. (infinitive)

What Is a Determiner?

Determiners are adjectives that point out, or limit, a following noun and that come before other types of adjectives that may modify the same noun. Determiners signal that a noun (or a word used as a noun) is coming in the sentence. Although they are adjectives, determiners cannot be compared using *er/est* or *more/most*. Noun/pronoun possessives, articles, and indefinite and demonstrative pronouns that come immediately before a noun are determiners.

det. adj. adj.
the green glass bottle

det. adj.
that ceramic mug

det. adj.
his best friend

det. adj.
any flower seeds

det. adj. adj.
Larry's large brown belt

det. adj.
this large book

Adverbs

Adverbs modify verbs, adjectives, or other adverbs. Adverbs may also modify verbals acting as nouns. Adverbs that modify verbs add information about the action or state of being expressed by the verb. They tell where, when, why, how, or how much about the verb. These types of adverbs are usually quite movable within the sentence.

> He will come *soon*.
> He will *soon* come.
> He *soon* will come.
> *Soon* he will come.

Adverbs that modify adjectives and other adverbs strengthen or weaken the idea of the words they modify. They generally tell how much. Many grammarians identify this type of adverb as a **qualifier.**

The book was *very* rare.

A *really* old man was seen crossing the road.

Joanie's little brother played *rather* poorly at the recital.

The sugar and flour were *almost* gone.

Some Meanings of the Adverb

Manner (including extent and number)	slowly, well, somehow; very, completely, almost, quite, even; once, twice
Place (including direction and order)	here, below, outside, somewhere, everywhere, nowhere; down, northward; first, second
Time (including frequency)	now, later, sometimes, never; often, usually, seldom, sometimes
Negative only (pure negative meaning)	not
Result and logical conclusion	therefore, accordingly, consequently, hence, thus
Cause	why

A sentence can have several adverbs, often with each one coming from a different meaning group.

The rescue team worked *slowly here yesterday.*

Other Types of Adverbs

Conjunctive adverbs such as *however* and *therefore* serve as links between independent clauses.

The builder had been working for nearly twelve hours; *therefore,* he needed a break.

Ron's family prefers orange juice; *however,* they often drink grapefruit juice for breakfast.

Relative adverbs *(when, where, why)* introduce adjective clauses that modify nouns of time, place, or reason. (See p. 52.)

> Cindy showed her friends the place *where* she'd lost her ring.
>
> This is the time *when* anyone can enter.

Indefinite relative adverbs *(when, where, why, how)* introduce noun clauses and have no antecedent.

> I know *when* it happened.
>
> Morgan realized *why* God allowed the tragedy.

Other indefinite relative adverbs *(whenever, wherever, however)* introduce adverb clauses.

> *However* he managed it, Todd completed the marathon.
>
> *Wherever* Abraham went, he built an altar.

Interrogative adverbs *(when, where, why, how)* ask direct or indirect questions.

> *When* did she leave?
>
> She asked *where* he went.

Clues from Form

Many adverbs end in *ly.* However, some adjectives end in *ly* also. Be aware that a noun plus *ly* forms an adjective (as in *manly, friendly*); an adjective plus *ly* forms an adverb.

happy + *ly* = happily   careful + *ly* = carefully   quiet + *ly* = quietly

Like adjectives, most adverbs can form degrees of comparison. (See pp. 98-101.)

Positive	Comparative	Superlative
soon	sooner	soonest
fast	faster	fastest
often	more often	most often

Prepositions

A **preposition** is a word that relates its object (normally a noun or a pronoun) to another word in the sentence. The two words are related most often by time, place, or possession.

The pen *on the table* writes well.

In this sentence the preposition *on* shows the relationship between the table and the pen—the pen is *on* the table, not *by* it or *under* it.

There are nearly fifty common one-word prepositions in English, but nine of them are used more than the others: *of, in, to, for, with, on, at, by, from.* Some prepositions consist of more than one word. For example, *according to, along with, as for, as well as, because of, in spite of,* and *instead of* are all multiword prepositions.

> *According to* the dictionary *limicolous* means "living in mud."
>
> Casey did well on the test *in spite of* a headache.

All prepositions appear in phrases:

of the books	*in* the swimming pool	*to* a defender
for five seconds	*with* liberty and justice	*on* a whim
at the last minute	*by* her father	*from* an admirer

A preposition's object comes at the end of the **prepositional phrase.** Modifiers may come between the preposition and its object.

> near *a perfectly quiet and sunny picnic* spot

Remember that a word is not a preposition if it does not have an object.

> My mother is working *in* the house. (preposition)
>
> The swimmer fell *in.* (adverb)

Prepositional phrases act as adverbs or adjectives. When a prepositional phrase modifies a noun or a pronoun, the prepositional phrase always follows the word modified.

> The bench *at the piano* contains music.
>
> A daisy *on the windowsill* brightened the whole kitchen.

An adverbial prepositional phrase may appear in different places in the sentence, although changing the position of the prepositional phrase may slightly affect the meaning of the sentence.

> The daisy looked cheerful *in the kitchen.*
>
> *In the kitchen* the daisy looked cheerful.

Meanings of Prepositions

Prepositions cover a great many areas of meaning. Here are a few of the most common areas. Other prepositions could be added to these lists.

LOCATION	above, across, against, around, at, behind, below, beneath, beside, between, beyond, by, in, in front of, inside, on, outside, over, past, toward(s), under, upon, within
DIRECTION	down, from, into, off, onto, out, out of, through, to, up
TIME (INCLUDING DURATION)	after, at, before, between, by, during, for, in, on, past, since, until, till, up to
AGENCY OR MEANS	by, by means of, with, of (archaic)
CAUSE	because of, due to, in view of, on account of
ASSOCIATION	about, according to, along with, among, around, as for, besides, for, like, of, with
OPPOSITION OR EXCEPTION	against, apart from, but (meaning except), despite, except, except for, in spite of, instead of, without

Idiomatic Use of Prepositions

Many verbs and adjectives, and even some nouns, must be followed by particular prepositions. Most of these combinations, of course, we know from long observation. Some of the others can be discovered in a dictionary entry by observing the phrases that illustrate particular meanings. The reference list below includes many of the prepositional combinations that can be problems.

accuse (someone) of
adhere to
agree with (someone), to (a proposal),
   on (a plan)
alarmed at
angry with (someone), at (something);
   (Informal: mad at)
between (one) and (another)
capable of
compare with (something similar), to
   (something of a different sort)
comply with (a requirement)
concur with (someone), in (an opinion)
conform to

consist of
consistent with
contend with (someone), for (a principle)
convince (someone) of (a need or
   truth)
die of *or* from (a disease), by (vio-
   lence), to (self, worldly pleasures)
differ with (someone) about or over
   (something), from (something)
different from (something)
disapprove of
equal to
familiar to (someone), with (something)

find fault with
ignorant of
impatient with (someone), at (the delay), for (success)
in search of
independent of
indifferent to
infer from (evidence)inferior to
influence of (one thing) on (another)
married to
oblivious of *or* to
part with (something), from (someone)
persuade to (do something)
prefer (this) to (that)
preferable to

prior to
refrain from
required of (someone)
responsible to (someone), for (something)
result from (a cause), in (an effect); a result of (a cause)
rewarded by (someone), for (an action), with (a good result)
similar to
succeed in
superior to
wait for (someone) at (a place), on (a customer)

Conjunctions

A **conjunction** is a connecting word that joins words or groups of words in a sentence. **Coordinating conjunctions** join sentence parts of the same type. The common coordinating conjunctions are *and, nor, but, or, for,* and *yet.* Coordinating conjunctions join single words, phrases, or clauses.

VERBS The puppies scampered *and* played.

ADJECTIVES He was exhausted *but* happy.

PREPOSITIONAL PHRASE She could not find the book at home *or* at the library.

INDEPENDENT CLAUSE "My yoke is easy, *and* my burden is light" (Matthew 11:30).

DEPENDENT CLAUSE Because the weather was seasonable *and* because we were eager to be outside, our family went to the park for a picnic.

Correlative conjunctions join equal sentence parts and work together in pairs to relate the two parts.

either/or   neither/nor
both/and   not only/but also

Either I will go at 4:00 *or* we'll both go at 5:00.

The teacher gave it to *both* Jan *and* me.

His so-called friends *neither* called him *nor* wrote him while he was sick.

Correlative conjunctions have three special uses:

1. to provide emphasis
2. to let the reader know that a second thing will be added to the first
3. to make clear exactly which things are being joined in the sentence

CONFUSING   ~~John and Mary~~ or ~~Joe~~ will do it.

CLEAR   **Either** John and Mary **or** Joe will do it.
John and **either** ~~Mary~~ **or** ~~Joe~~ will do it.

Subordinating conjunctions join a dependent clause to an independent clause. A subordinating conjunction is part of the dependent clause, but its only function in that clause is to introduce it. A list of common subordinating conjunctions follows.

if	although	unless
because	since	when
where	before	after

If our car is running smoothly, we will make the trip west this summer.

We are eager to see Yellowstone National Park *since* we've heard so much about it.

There are also phrasal subordinating conjunctions such as *so that, even though,* and *as if.*

We may pull a trailer *so that* we can camp along the way.

Subordinating Conjunctions for Adverb Clauses

Most subordinating conjunctions introduce adverb clauses. Many of these subordinating conjunctions appear in the following table, grouped by areas of meaning.

Time	when, while, as, before, after, since, now that, once, until, till, every time (that), whenever	*When* she heard that the famine was over, Naomi decided to go back to Judah.
Place	where, wherever, whither (archaic)	Ruth told Naomi, "*Whither* thou goest, I will go."

Cause	because, since, as, inasmuch as, whereas (legal language)	*Because* Ruth returned with Naomi, she was blessed by God through the kindness of Boaz.
Condition	if, on condition that, provided that, unless	*If* Ruth had remained in Moab, she would have missed God's best for her life.
Contrast	whereas, while	*Whereas* most of the people feared Haman, Esther chose to fear only her God.
Manner	as, as if, as though, however	Haman was invited to dinner *as though* he were a friend of the king and Queen Esther.
Purpose	so that, so (less formal), that, in order that, lest (archaic)	God used Esther's courage to defeat Haman's plan *in order that* He might preserve His people.
Concession	although, even though, though, even if	*Even though* the situation looked hopeless, God gave deliverance.
Comparison and Degree	that, (as . . .) as, (so . . .) as (The word in parentheses is not part of the subordinating conjunction. It is an adverb modifier of the word after it and is modified by the clause introduced by *as*.)	Haman was not so powerful *as* he thought.
Result	so that, (so . . .) that, (such . . .) that (The word in parentheses is not part of the subordinating conjunction. It is an adverb modifier and is modified by the clause introduced by *that*.)	Queen Esther's story is such a powerful one *that* many people consider it one of their favorite biblical accounts.

Subordinating Conjunctions for Noun Clauses

The most common way of beginning a noun clause is with the subordinating conjunction *that*. Like other subordinating conjunctions, *that* is simply an introductory word. It has no other function in the clause. (The subordinating conjunction *that* should not be confused with the relative pronoun *that*. Relative pronouns, used in adjective clauses, are covered on pp. 51-52.)

Did you know [*that* the Agricultural Revolution preceded the Industrial Revolution]?

Here the noun clause is the direct object of *did know*. *That* may sometimes be understood.

I knew [*that* we would win].
I knew [we would win]. (*that* understood)

An additional subordinating conjunction is *whether. Whether* introduces noun clauses involving a choice. *If* is sometimes informally substituted for *whether*.

[*Whether* he will win] is not the question now.
I wasn't sure [*if/whether* he would come].

Interjections

An **interjection** is a word that can stand alone punctuated as a sentence, or it can appear along with a regular sentence in which it takes no real part. An interjection is not a necessary part of any regular sentence. Interjections often express strong feeling, agreement or disagreement, greeting or leave-taking, politeness, or hesitation.

ouch	whew	yes	okay	no
please	thanks	uh	well	oh

Sometimes a phrase may fulfill the same function as a single interjection: *Sure thing! Good morning; thank you; you know.*

An interjection can be set off by commas, or it can stand alone followed by an exclamation mark or possibly a period.

Okay, you may eat your fourth cookie.
We were told, *well*, that we didn't have enough cash to make the purchase.

Basic Sentence Analysis

The basic purpose of any language is to express meaning—to say something to someone. Words (and sometimes parts of words) have little bits of meaning attached to them, but we need more than that. To express ideas, or thoughts, we need to combine words into sentences. The sentence is the most important thing that we build with words.

What Are Sentences?

There are several ways of explaining what a sentence is. One way would be to say, for example, that everything on this page that ends with a period or a question mark is a sentence. That is true, but it's not much of a definition. After all, people do make mistakes in where they put periods.

Another way is to say that **a sentence expresses a complete thought,** or a whole thought. That is not very exact, but it may help. Smaller groups of words (phrases) like "in the house" and "as fast as possible" seem to express pieces of thoughts rather than whole thoughts.

We can also notice that **a sentence sounds complete.** At the end of a spoken sentence a person's voice usually falls and then pauses briefly. At the end of some questions the voice goes up instead and then pauses. However, in a conversation, something less than a sentence (a fragment) can have that same "complete" sound; so this test is not foolproof.

There is a definition that you can actually use to test whether a group of words is a sentence: *A sentence is a group of words that has a subject and a predicate and nothing that makes it part of another sentence.* First, a sentence has a **subject,** something the sentence is about. Then it has a **predicate,** that is, a verb and perhaps other words that say something about the subject. A fragment may have a verb but no subject, a subject but no verb, or neither a subject nor a verb. Still another kind of fragment has a subject and a verb, but also something that makes it part of another sentence. Here are some examples: *whether he will go, that it will rain, what he likes, because they said so.* In these examples the first word changes the word group from a possible sentence to a part of another sentence.

Finding Verbs, Subjects, and Complements

Finding the verb (or simple predicate) is the first step in sentence analysis. Since verbs may have auxiliaries, be sure to find all parts of a verb before identifying the complete verb. (Do not identify verbals as part of the complete verb.)

The crowd *cheered* enthusiastically.

From the balcony, we *could hear* the roar.

With binoculars we *might have been* able to see the parade.

   (Note that *to see* is a verbal and not part of the verb phrase.)

The second step of sentence analysis is locating the subject of the sentence. To find the subject in most sentences, you can ask yourself who or what is described or did the action of the verb. The subject is the doer of the action, is acted upon, or is described by the verb. The subject may be a noun, a pronoun, or a group of words acting as a noun.

Mrs. Hodges quoted John 3:16 in German.

Many in the class did not understand her.

Of course, in a request or command, the subject may be an understood *you.* When we give a command, we usually leave the subject (the doer) unmentioned but clearly understood. For instance, when we say "Shut the door, please," the subject *you* is understood. If we include this understood *you,* we can still say that the normal sentence has both a subject and a predicate.

(You) Make Scripture memory a part of your regular Bible study.

Remember that any part of the sentence may be compound. Be sure to identify the complete subject and complete verb in your sentence analysis.

The box looked suspicious.

The box *looked* and *smelled* suspicious.

The *box* and the *envelope* looked suspicious.

The third step in sentence analysis is locating any verb complements. After finding the verb and the subject, say the subject and the verb and ask yourself *who?* or *what?* If your sentence has a reasonable answer to that question, the sentence has a complement.

The box looked suspicious.

   (box + looked + whom/what? ➔ suspicious)

The box arrived yesterday.

(box + arrived + whom/what? ➔ no complement)

The fourth step in sentence analysis is identifying the type of complement. For this purpose we need to recognize sentence patterns.

Basic Sentence Patterns

Using the subject, the verb, and the complement, there are only a few ways that a simple sentence in English can be put together; we call these ways the **basic sentence patterns** of English. All simple sentences are based on these few sentence patterns—and all other sentences are built from simple sentences. If you can recognize at least the first five of these patterns, you have the basis for understanding some of the most important things about how sentences work.

Here is a listing of the five most common patterns with examples and pattern diagrams:

Pattern	Example	Diagram
S-InV	Joe laughed.	S | InV
S-LV-PN	Brownie is Joe's dog.	S | LV \ PN
S-LV-PA	She looked funny.	S | LV \ PA
S-TrV-DO	Muddy leaves covered her back.	S | TrV | DO
S-TrV-IO-DO	Joe gave Brownie a bath.	S | TrV | DO \ IO

S-InV

The two essential parts of S-InV are a **subject** (S) and a verb. We call the verb an **intransitive verb** (InV) because it needs nothing to complete it—that is, the sentence can be complete with just the subject and the verb. Here are some examples:

S		InV	
Joe		laughed.	
He		was laughing	(at his friend.)
Michelle	(nearly)	fell	(down the stairs.)
Everyone		talked	(loudly.)

Some of these sentences have adverbial words or phrases as modifiers, shown here in parentheses; but the sentences would still be complete and correct if these were left out. Remember to ignore modifying words and phrases when you are identifying a sentence pattern.

S-LV-PN

The three parts of S-LV-PN are the subject (S), the **linking verb** (LV), and the **predicate noun** (PN). The predicate noun is a noun (or pronoun) in the predicate that renames or identifies the subject. That is, the subject and the predicate noun always refer to the same person or thing. They are linked by the verb, which can be thought of as something like an equal sign.

S	LV (=)	PN

In the examples that follow, notice that the predicate noun always renames the subject:

S	LV		PN
Flipper	is		his pet goldfish.
My older brother	has become		a good mechanic.
Sandra	was	(always)	a faithful friend.
An orange	is		a citrus fruit.

The third sentence shows that there can be adverbial modifiers along with the pattern parts.

S-LV-PA

The pattern S-LV-PA has three main parts: a subject, a linking verb, and a **predicate adjective.** The predicate adjective is an adjective that appears in the predicate but describes the subject. (It describes the subject but does not directly modify it.) As in the pattern S-LV-PN, the verb is something like an equal sign: it serves mainly to link the subject with an important word in the predicate.

S	LV (=)	PA

In the examples that follow, notice that the predicate adjective describes the subject, not anything in the predicate:

S		LV		PA
Julie		looked		uncomfortable.
My teacher		is	(usually)	early.
Gracious people	(never)	seem		rushed.
That plan		sounds		good.

Again we see that adverbial modifiers can be added without changing the pattern.

Because predicate adjectives and predicate nouns both are completers of the information about the subject, they can be called **subjective complements.**

S-TrV-DO

Some sentences have a word that receives the action of the verb; we call that word the **direct object** of the verb. The direct object always refers to something different from the subject, except when the direct object is a reflexive pronoun ending in *self* or *selves*. Because the verb in this pattern has a receiver of action (the direct object), it is called a **transitive verb.** The most common pattern involving transitive verbs and direct objects is S-TrV-DO.

S	TrV	DO	
Sand	covered	the porch.	
Mr. Anderson	has (not) read	that book	(yet).
Susan	saw	me	(at the mall).
Douglas	saw	himself	(in the picture).

In the first three sentences, the subject and the direct object refer to different things. As the last sentence shows, if we ever want to have a direct object that refers to the same thing as the subject, we make that direct object a reflexive pronoun.

S-TrV-IO-DO

Sometimes a sentence with a direct object also has an **indirect object.** An indirect object comes before the direct object and tells *to whom* or *for whom* the action is done. An indirect object does not follow a preposition. As in the pattern S-TrV-DO, the verb here is transitive, since there is a receiver of action (the direct object).

S	TrV	IO	DO
Loni	gave	her doll	a bath.
Tom's mother	will get	him	some stationery.
She	will buy	herself	a new pen.
Our friends	gave	their children	a basketball goal.

As with all patterns, adverbial modifiers can be added.

A sentence that has an indirect object can usually be restated with a prepositional phrase replacing the indirect object. In that case, the sentence pattern changes even though the meaning does not.

S-TrV-IO-DO	Loni gave her doll a bath.
S-TrV-DO	Loni gave a bath (to her doll).

Remember that an object of a preposition cannot function as anything else at the same time. Also remember that in today's English the indirect object always comes before the direct object.

S-*be*-Advl

A sixth kind of sentence contains either a prepositional phrase or an adverb after some form of the verb *be*.

S	*Be*		Advl	
Mara	is	(already)	in the house.	
The mailman	was		here	(then).
The game	will be		after lunch.	
The meeting	is		now.	

Advl in this pattern stands for *adverbial*, to include adverbs such as *here* and *now* and adverbial prepositional phrases such as *in the house. Be* is named in the pattern because no other verb is ever used in it. Notice that the word or phrase after *be* seems to be telling us something about the subject, since *be* has no real meaning of its own.

The adverbs and prepositional phrases in the sentences above normally have meanings of place and time. However, occasionally a prepositional phrase unrelated to place or time occurs after *be: This space is for the disabled. His death was with honor. Her bravery was without equal.* These could be considered examples of either S-LV-PA or S-*be*-Advl, according to one's preference. Probably a good rule of thumb, though, is to consider them examples of S-*be*-Advl unless *seem* could substitute for *be*. By that rule only the last of these (referring to chart sentences above) would be S-LV-PA.

In summary, the last element of the pattern is called *Advl* to recognize its adverb-like qualities, but it is included as part of the sentence pattern because it is not an ordinary, optional modifier of the verb.

When the third element of this pattern is a prepositional phrase, parentheses will help make the labeling clear:

S *be*   Advl
Mara is already (in the house).

The interrogative adverbs *where* and *when* can be used in this pattern, as well as along with other patterns.

> S *be* Advl   Advl *be* S
> Mara is where? ➔ Where is Mara?

> S InV Advl   Advl   S InV
> She went where? ➔ Where did she go?

Some sentences with the pattern S-*be*-Advl can be stated in a different way.

> S *be*   Advl   *be* S   Advl
> A boy is (at the door). ➔ There is a boy (at the door).

> S   *be* Advl   *be*   S   Advl
> Two boys are here. ➔ There are two boys here.

The sentences on the right mean the same thing as the original sentences on the left. The same word is the subject in both versions: the verb agrees with the subject even when the subject and the verb are inverted.

    In the inverted sentences, the empty word *there* stands where the subject would usually be. *There*, sometimes called an **expletive,** is simply a placeholder for the delayed subject.

    We often use the inverted form of this pattern when we want to introduce a new topic, and we may even leave out the adverbial part.

>   *be*   S   Advl
> Once upon a time, there was a wicked king (in a faraway country).

The inversion seems to allow a greater focus on the subject.

S-TrV-DO-OC

    Certain sentences with direct objects have an element—usually a noun or an adjective—after the direct object to complete the idea of what the verb does to the direct object.

S	TrV	DO	OC
We	can make	the meeting	longer.
The club	considered	Tanya	very capable.
We	elected	her	president.
We	declared	her	the winner.

In all of these sentences the last element either describes or renames the direct object. Just as predicate adjectives and predicate nouns can be called *subjective* complements (because they complete the information about the subject), the adjectives and nouns here are called *objective* complements. **Objective complements** complete the information about the direct object as a result of the action of the verb. The verb in the pattern S-TrV-DO-OC is transitive because it is followed by a direct object.

Remember that an indirect object answers the question *to whom?* or *for whom?* about the verb and comes before the direct object; an objective complement renames or describes the direct object and comes after it. Indirect objects and objective complements never occur in the same sentence pattern.

IO AND DO **DIFFERENT**	S TrV IO DO The teacher told his students a strange story.
NOUN OC **RENAMES DO**	S TrV DO OC The teacher called his students fine people.
ADJ OC **DESCRIBES DO**	S TrV DO OC The teacher called his students brilliant.

Classifying Verbs

An important way of classifying verbs is based on the sentence patterns just presented. As the sentence pattern labels show, each sentence pattern uses just one type of verb. Therefore, if we recognize the sentence pattern, we know the verb type.

There are just three basic types of verbs: **transitive, intransitive,** and **linking.** Some verbs can be only one of these, but other verbs can fit into several sentence patterns and thus can fall into more than one category.

Transitive Verbs

Transitive verbs are those that occur in the patterns that have direct objects.

S TrV   DO
We called the fire department.

S TrV IO   DO
We gave them the address.

Because the direct object "receives" the action of the verb, we can say that a transitive verb is "a verb that has a receiver of action." Only transitive verbs can be made passive. (See p. 115.)

Intransitive Verbs

Intransitive verbs are verbs that are used in the one pattern that does not require anything after the verb: S-InV.

> S   InV
> The sirens blew loudly.

Intransitive verbs, then, have no receiver of action. Indeed, they have no completer at all.

Linking Verbs

A linking verb is a verb used in either of these two patterns: S-LV-PN, S-LV-PA. The verb links the subject with the predicate noun or predicate adjective:

> S   LV   PN
> The building was an old store.

> S   LV   PA
> It looked empty.

Verbs of More Than One Type

Many verbs—indeed, probably most verbs—can be used in several sentence patterns, so they can fall under more than one verb type. As an example, consider the verb *sound:*

> **TRANSITIVE**   They *sounded* the alarm.
> **INTRANSITIVE**   The siren *sounds* at noon every day.
> **LINKING**   She *sounds* happy.

Sound is slightly unusual in being used in all three ways, but many verbs can be either transitive or intransitive. *Eat* and *read* are two examples.

> **TRANSITIVE**   Jessica *ate* her hamburger slowly.
> Have you *read* today's headline yet?

> **INTRANSITIVE**   We *ate* late today.
> She can *read* fast.

Some verbs can be either linking or intransitive. Most notable of these are five verbs of the senses: *look, taste, smell, feel,* and *sound.*

LINKING   You *looked* busy yesterday.
INTRANSITIVE   They *looked* at the drawing.

Three of these verbs of the senses can also be transitive: *He tasted (smelled, felt) the peach.*

Phrases and Clauses

One of the primary building blocks of the sentence is the phrase. A **phrase** is a word group that does not contain both a subject and a verb. These word groups often function as nouns, adjectives, and adverbs in the sentence and can be divided into two types: **verbal phrases** and **nonverbal phrases.**

Nonverbal Phrases

Prepositional Phrase

The **prepositional phrase** is one of the most common types of phrases. A prepositional phrase consists of a preposition, its object, and any modifiers of the object. Each prepositional phrase acts as either an adjective or an adverb. (See Ch. 1.)

Neither a preposition nor a prepositional phrase ever has a function other than adjective or adverb in a sentence; therefore, it is important to identify and set aside prepositional phrases just for correct sentence analysis and in certain usage situations.

      S   InV
Someone (on the phone) is asking (about our newspaper advertisement).

     S TrV   DO
Do you like the red jacket (on the end)?

     S   LV   PN
A rack (of clothes) is the only prop (in the new play).

      S   LV PN
Two pieces (of pie) are all I can eat.

It is not unusual for one prepositional phrase to modify a word in another prepositional phrase.

OP   OP

He walked (to the door) (of the cage).

To the door and *of the cage* are prepositional phrases; the simple object of each preposition is marked with *OP.* Notice, though, how the two phrases work together: Where did he walk? To <u>the door of the cage.</u> The second prepositional phrase modifies a word in the first phrase. Sometimes one prepositional phrase follows another without the second one modifying the first.

> Our butterfly bush gives us an abundance (of cut flowers) (over the summer).

Over the summer modifies *gives,* not *flowers,* and could be moved in the sentence without a change of meaning.

> (Over the summer) our butterfly bush gives us an abundance (of cut flowers).

Absolute Phrase

An **absolute phrase** consists of a noun modified by a participial phrase. (See pp. 42-44.) We call it an absolute phrase because it is more or less independent (absolute) in the sentence. The absolute phrase loosely modifies the rest of the sentence.

Usually a clause can be reduced to an absolute phrase by dropping the subordinating word and changing the verb to a participle.

ADVERB CLAUSE	*Because no rain fell in June,* this month's water bill is high.
ABSOLUTE PHRASE	*No rain having fallen in June,* this month's water bill is high.

Although most absolute phrases consist of a noun modified by a participial phrase, occasionally the participle can be omitted.

ADVERB CLAUSE	*When the sun was low in the west,* the desert air quickly grew cool.
ABSOLUTE PHRASE	*The sun being low in the west,* the desert air quickly grew cool.
ABSOLUTE PHRASE	*The sun low in the west,* the desert air quickly grew cool.

In its shortest version, then, the absolute phrase consists of a noun and its modifiers with at least one modifier after the noun. This kind of absolute phrase too is considered to modify the rest of the sentence.

Appositive Phrase

Sometimes a noun and its modifiers or a single noun comes right after another noun that it renames and further identifies. It is the second noun that functions as an **appositive** and together with its modifiers is called an **appositive phrase.**

> S   (App)   TrV   DO
> The Marcinkos, *my nearest neighbors,* have a beautiful yard.

A noun performing any of the main sentence functions can have an appositive after it.

> S   InV   OP   (App)
> My little sister plays with Danielle, *the girl next door.*

> S   TrV IO   (App)   DO
> They gave Tiny, *Danielle's dog,* her first bath.

Sometimes an appositive does not immediately follow the noun it renames; but it could, if the sentence were restated.

> I bought some flowers yesterday, *big red roses.*

> Yesterday I bought some flowers, *big red roses.*

Although most appositives are nouns, some appositives are intensive pronouns. (See p. 12.)

> The author *himself* signed the book.
> Liz finished the wallpapering *herself.*

Even less frequently a personal pronoun may be an appositive.

> The three girls, Noelle, Joanie, and *I,* knocked on the neighbor's door.
> Two contestants, Cam Linh and *he,* were awarded special honors.

Notice that, except for the intensive pronouns, all of the appositive phrases given above are set off by commas. This is the usual punctuation for appositives. However, no commas are used with a "close appositive"—a short appositive that is more important than the noun or pronoun before it. There are two kinds of close appositives:

NOUN RENAMING	S	(App)	TrV	IO (App)	DO
A PERSONAL	We girls have found you boys a good job.				
PRONOUN					

SHORT PROPER	S	InV	OP	(App)
NAME NEEDED	Tom was talking to his friend Peter Ames then.			
TO IDENTIFY THE	*(Surely Tom has more than one friend!)*			
ONE DISCUSSED				

Do not confuse appositives and predicate nouns. Both of these rename a noun or pronoun that comes earlier in the sentence, but predicate nouns, you remember, occur in just one pattern: S-LV-PN. Therefore, a predicate noun always renames the subject of the sentence, with a linking verb in between:

S   LV   PN
Peter was a fisherman.

Though an appositive may rename a subject, there will not be a linking verb between the two:

S   (App)   InV
Peter, a fisherman, started toward the Lord on the water.
S   (App)   LV   PN
Peter, a fisherman, later became a leading apostle.

Verbal Phrases

Verbals are special verb forms that allow a verb to be used as if it were a noun, an adjective, or an adverb. The three kinds of verbals are **participles, gerunds,** and **infinitives.** Often verbals occur with their own modifiers and objects. These verbals plus any modifiers or objects are called **verbal phrases.** Verbals never function as simple predicates in the sentences in which they appear.

Participle and Participial Phrase

Participles are verbal adjectives. The simplest participles are formed from the present participle of the verb plus an ending (usually *ing* or *ed/d*).

laugh + ing/ed = laughing/laughed

Present Participle

The present participle consists of the first principal part of the verb with *ing* added to it. As an adjective, a participle modifies a noun or a pronoun.

The laughing children didn't hear their mother.

Like a regular adjective, a participle by itself usually comes before the noun it modifies.

Because the participle is made from a verb, it too can have adverbial modifiers or complements or both. The participle and its modifiers and complements together make up a **participial phrase** (or "participle phrase"). A participial phrase often follows the noun it modifies.

The children laughing at the joke didn't hear their mother.

The man giving the speech had a pleasant voice.

Who were the ones talking loudly?

Remember that the *ing* form of the verb can be used either as part of a progressive verb or as a participle, an adjective.

PROGRESSIVE VERB   He was laughing softly.

PARTICIPLE   The laughing doll sounded eerie.

Past (passive) Participle

The so-called past participle is the same as the third principal part of the verb. (This is the form that is used with *have* to make the perfect tenses.) When it is a true participle (adjective), however, it usually has a passive meaning. Passive participles are possible only for transitive verbs.

The broken window lets in the cold air.

(The window was broken by someone.)

A passive participle can be part of a participial phrase.

The window, broken by Al's home-run ball, still has not been repaired.

Perfect Participle

Having can be used with the third principal part of the verb to make a perfect participle.

Having arrived early, I arranged the chairs.

The perfect participle is used to express an action before that of the main verb. (I arrived, and then I arranged the chairs.) By contrast, the present participle expresses action simultaneous with that of the main verb.

<u>Arriving</u> early, I turned into the snowy driveway carefully.

Other Participles

The most common participles are the present participle, the past participle, and the perfect participle. However, others are possible. They are recognizable because the first word ends with *ing* and the whole phrase is used as an adjective.

The door <u>being opened</u> is the door to Mr. Davis's office.

<u>Being seen</u> through a keyhole, the treasure looked rather small.

<u>Having been seen</u> as he picked up the costume, he knew the secret was out.

The first two examples can be called progressive passive participles, and the last one is a perfect passive participle. The names, however, are less important than their usefulness in certain sentences. For instance, see pages 213-14 and 216-17 on reducing clauses to participles.

Gerund and Gerund Phrase

A **gerund** is a verbal noun.

Present Gerund

The present gerund has the same form as the present participle—the *ing* form of the verb. As a verbal noun, the gerund is used in the same ways nouns are used.

      S   LV   PN
<u>Swimming</u> is good exercise.

S TrV   DO
I like <u>swimming</u>.

Like other verbals, gerunds can have both adverbial modifiers and complements.

                             PN
His favorite relaxation is <u>swimming slowly to the point and back</u>.

OP

I need to give the afternoon to <u>answering letters</u>.

As a verbal noun, a gerund sometimes has regular noun modifiers.

DO

We did <u>our best swimming</u> in the first race.

The whole **gerund phrase** performs the function marked.

Since a gerund is a verbal noun, it can be used by itself as a modifying noun.

ModN

GERUND   Matt had the boys in his class over for a *swimming* party.

Though it may look like a participle, a gerund as a modifying noun has a different meaning and a different "sound" from the participle. In this example it was a party *for* swimming. Notice the difference:

Part

PARTICIPLE   We watched the *swimming* turtle.

Here the turtle is doing the swimming. Note two other examples: *After she obtained her fishing license, Rachel bought a pair of waders.* (gerund as modifying noun) *The fishing bear cub caught two trout in fifteen minutes.* (participle)

Perfect Gerund

Having can be used with the third principal part of the verb to make the perfect gerund: for instance, *having met.*

What a name-dropper! His specialty is <u>having met all the important people</u>. (perfect gerund)

The action of the perfect gerund always takes place before that of the main verb. On the other hand, the action of the present gerund is at the same time as that of the main verb.

His specialty is <u>meeting all the important people</u>. (present gerund)

Other Gerunds

Besides the present gerund and the perfect gerund, other types of gerunds are possible. Following are two examples, both with a possessive "subject."

His <u>being seen</u> was good, because they were able to help him right away.

His <u>having been seen</u> is fortunate; now we know where to look for him.

Both of these gerunds are passive. The second one is a perfect passive gerund: it is now fortunate that he *was seen*.

All gerunds are used as verbal nouns, and all begin with a word ending in *ing*.

Infinitive and Infinitive Phrase

Unlike participles and gerunds, which act as only one part of speech, the **infinitive** is a verbal that can be used as a noun, as an adjective, or as an adverb.

Simple Infinitive

The simple infinitive of a verb is made up of the word *to* followed by the first principal part (basic form) of the verb: *to run, to see, to be,* and so on. We call the *to* here the "sign of the infinitive." Remember that *to* plus the first principal part of a verb is never a prepositional phrase, but always an infinitive. (*To the house* and *to church* are prepositional phrases, but *to go* is an infinitive.) Infinitives can be used in the same ways as nouns, adjectives, and adverbs.

DO
Jeremy likes to sing. (infinitive as noun)

Harry is the person to ask. (infinitive as adjective)

I'll go there to see. (infinitive as adverb)

In all of these cases we have a verb form being used as one of the other major parts of speech, not as the simple predicate.

Even though infinitives have functions other than verb functions, they are still made from verbs and can be modified by adverbs or by prepositional phrases.

DO
I want to go *quickly*.

DO
I want to go *into the house*.

Because they are made from verbs, they may also have objects or other complements.

S TrV DO (IO) (DO)
I want to give you a choice.

S TrV DO (PA)
I want to be nice.

The infinitive and its modifiers and complements together make up the whole **infinitive phrase.** Infinitive phrases are very common in English.

DO
Jeremy likes to sing old hymns.

Adj
Meredith is the person to ask about that.

Adv
I'll go there to see for myself.

Passive Infinitive

The simple infinitive, discussed above, has an active meaning.

I want to choose the next song. (I will *choose* it.)

However, because transitive verbs can be made passive, they can also have passive infinitives.

I want to be chosen. (I *will be chosen;* they will choose me.)

The passive infinitive is made up of the following parts:
1.   the sign of the infinitive *(to)*
2.   the passive auxiliary *(be)*
3.   the third principal part of the true verb *(chosen)*

Passive infinitives can be used in the same ways as other infinitives.

Perfect Infinitive

Have, the auxiliary that makes the perfect tenses, can also be part of an infinitive. An infinitive with *have* is called a perfect infinitive.

I am very glad to have met you.

A perfect infinitive always makes it clear that the action of the infinitive took place before the action of the main verb of the clause. Thus the example means, "I am glad now that I met you earlier." By contrast, "I am very glad to meet you" puts the being glad and the meeting in the same (present) time.

Use a perfect infinitive only when you intend to put the time of the infinitive before that of the main verb.

> **WRONG**   I would have liked to have gone.

> **RIGHT**   I would have liked to go. *(both in past time)*
> I would like to have gone. *(liking present, going past)*

A sentence with *have* in both the main verb and the infinitive is probably wrong.

Perfect Passive and Other Infinitives

Just as there are passive infinitives and perfect infinitives, there are also perfect passive infinitives.

I am happy <u>to have been chosen</u>. (I am happy that I was chosen.)

Have makes it perfect, and the time is before that of the main verb. *Been,* from *be,* makes it passive, and so the implied subject ("I") is acted upon.

Progressive infinitives are another possibility:

I'll try <u>to be waiting</u> for you at five o'clock.

Progressive infinitives emphasize the continuing nature of an action.

Finally, you will sometimes see an infinitive without a *to*. If the infinitive would also sound right with the *to,* the *to* will be used in more formal English.

> **CORRECT**   What he did was *jump* the fence.
> **MORE FORMAL**   What he did was *to jump* the fence.

Sometimes, though, the *to* would sound odd.

> **CORRECT AT**   With his background, he can do nothing except
> **ANY LEVEL**   *succeed.*

"Subjects" of Verbals

Because verbals (participles, gerunds, and infinitives) are made from verbs, there is always a "subject" understood. In most cases that means that there is an understood doer of the action. Let's look at some examples:

> **PARTICIPIAL**   Ramona, *walking along behind,* saw something odd.
> **PHRASE**

UNDERSTOOD MEANING	Ramona saw something odd. *Ramona* was walking along behind.
GERUND PHRASE	Jack likes *winning races.*
UNDERSTOOD MEANING	Jack likes something. *Jack* wins races.
INFINITIVE PHRASE	I want *to go home now.*
UNDERSTOOD MEANING	I want something: *I* go home now.

Notice that in all of these the understood "subject" of the verbal is the same as the subject of the verb *(I want, I go; Jack likes, Jack wins; etc.).* Therefore, the understood subjects of these verbals are not stated in the sentence.

With gerunds and infinitives, though, it is also possible to have a different "subject" for the verbal. This "subject" must appear in the sentence. (The quotation marks around *subject* are a reminder that we are speaking of a subject only in meaning, not in its grammatical form.)

GERUND PHRASE	Jack likes *my winning races.*
UNDERSTOOD MEANING	Jack likes something: I win races.
INFINITIVE PHRASE	I want *him to go home now.*
UNDERSTOOD MEANING	I want something: *He* goes home now.

In the first sentence, *my* modifies the gerund *winning* as its "subject." In the second example, *him* is the "subject" of the infinitive. It is part of the infinitive phrase. "Subjects" of the infinitives are in the objective case. (See p. 92.) "Subjects" of gerunds are correct in the possessive case. (See pp. 91-92.)

Clauses

A **clause** is a group of words that has both a subject and a verb. Phrases may include a verb form, but only clauses have both a subject and a verb that go together. Clauses are one of two types: independent or dependent.

Independent Clause

An **independent clause** is a clause that can stand alone as a sentence. The sentence may be a statement, a question, or a command.

A goalie stops the ball.

Does a goalie stop the ball?

Stop the ball!

Dependent Clause

A **dependent clause** is like a simple sentence in having a subject and a predicate, but it is subordinate to an independent clause. It cannot stand alone as a sentence.

There are three kinds of dependent clauses, based on how the clause is used in the larger sentence:

Adjective clause	Modifies a noun or pronoun
Adverb clause	Usually modifies a verb
Noun clause	Used as a subject, direct object, etc.

Adjective Clause

An **adjective clause** is a dependent clause that modifies a noun or a pronoun. Suppose that we want to express the following two ideas in a single sentence, with the first idea as more important:

Jean talked to *a girl.*

   who

~~The girl~~ had stopped to watch her paint.

The word *girl* expresses the link between the two ideas. Therefore, we may join the sentence ideas by substituting either *who* or *that* for *the girl* in the second sentence.

S   InV

Jean talked to a girl *who/that* had stopped to watch her paint.

The clause tells us something about the girl. Notice three things about the clause:

1. Because it still has a subject and a predicate, it is still a clause.
2. Because the clause can no longer stand alone as a sentence, it is now a dependent clause.
3. Because the dependent clause modifies a noun (as adjectives usually do), it is an adjective clause.

Here is another example. As before, the main sentence idea is in the first sentence.

Jean was repainting *the fence.*

which

Her father had just repaired ~~the fence~~.

Again we substitute a relative pronoun for the repeated noun. Because a fence is a thing, not a person, our choice is between *which* and *that.*

DO   S   TrV

Jean was repainting the fence *that/which* her father had just repaired.

This time the order of the words in the adjective clause has been adjusted. The adjustment is needed because a relative pronoun usually comes at the beginning of its clause, no matter what word it has substituted for.

A relative pronoun can also be substituted for an object of a preposition.

This was *the girl.*

whom

Jean had given a tract to ~~the girl~~ last Saturday.

(This was the girl *whom* Jean had given a tract to last Saturday.)

In somewhat formal English *whom* (the objective form of *who*) substitutes for *the girl* in the second sentence, and the whole prepositional phrase *(to whom)* is moved to the beginning of the clause.

S   TrV   DO

This was the girl [*to whom* Jean had given a tract last Saturday].

In relaxed conversation, the relative pronoun *that* could be the substitute for *the girl.* If so, *that* alone is brought to the beginning, leaving *to* behind.

$$\text{OP} \quad \text{S} \qquad \text{TrV} \quad \text{DO}$$

This was the girl [*that* Jean had given a tract to last Saturday].

Finally, *whose* (possessive form of the relative pronoun *who*) can substitute for a possessive word or phrase.

Jean had been praying for *Susan.*
whose
~~Susan's~~ mother had just been saved.

Since *whose mother* is already at the beginning, no reordering is needed.

Jean had been praying for Susan, [*whose* mother had just been saved].

One final point is that sometimes the relative pronoun *that* is omitted (simply "understood") when it is the direct object or the object of the preposition.

Jean was repainting the fence [her father had just repaired].
    (*that* understood, DO)
This was the girl [Jean had given a tract to last Saturday].
    (*that* understood, OP)

Most adjective clauses contain relative pronouns *(who, whom, which, whose, that).* However, when we attach extra information to a noun of time, place, or reason, a relative adverb *(when, where, why)* often works better than a relative pronoun would. (See p. 22 for more information on relative adverbs.)

Jim had prayed for *a quiet place.*

                                where
    He could talk to the Lord ~~in that place~~.
    ▲_____|

If the second sentence becomes the adjective clause, we substitute *where* for *in that place* and move the *where* to the beginning of its clause.

Jim had prayed for a quiet place [*where* he could talk to the Lord].

Because *where* substitutes for an adverbial prepositional phrase *(in that place,* modifying *talk), where* is an adverb. And because the adverb *where* relates to *a quiet place* in the main clause, it is a relative adverb.

Adverb Clause

An **adverb clause** is a dependent clause that usually modifies a verb. Sometimes we have two similar sentence ideas whose relation we want to make clear.

Whales have lungs instead of gills.

Whales come to the surface for air.

In this pair, the fact in the first sentence is the *cause* of the fact in the second. To express this, we can use *because* with the first sentence idea, joining it to the second.

Because whales have lungs instead of gills, they come to the surface for air.

The word *because* tells us that one fact causes the other, and it changes the clause to which it is added.

1. The word *because* makes the clause a dependent clause—a clause that cannot stand alone as a sentence.
2. The clause tells why the whales come to the surface, that is, why they come. Because this dependent clause modifies a verb (as adverbs do), it is an adverb clause.

Adverb clauses are introduced by **subordinating conjunctions,** words like *because, since, if, while, after,* and *although.* (See pp. 26-27 for more information on subordinating conjunctions.) The subordinating conjunction is part of the adverb clause. This kind of conjunction is called "subordinating" because it joins a dependent clause (a "subordinate clause") to an independent clause. The table below shows those and other subordinating conjunctions.

after	because	if	unless	where
although	before	since	until	while
as	even if	so	when	
as if	even though	though	whenever	

An adverb clause often comes at the beginning of the sentence, as in the example earlier. When the adverb clause does come first, it is followed by a comma. When the adverb clause comes at the end of the sentence, it may or may not be set off by a comma, depending on the meaning intended. Often there is no comma.

Whales come to the surface for air *because they have lungs instead of gills.*

Whales come to the surface for air, since they have lungs instead of gills.

In the first example the adverb clause seems to give important information, but in the second sentence (with a comma) the clause sounds more like an afterthought. (See pp. 134-35 for information on restrictive and nonrestrictive clauses.)

Here are a few more sample sentences with the adverb clauses in italics:

If one whale is in distress, the other whales often try to help.

Whales usually try to help *when another whale is in distress.*

A mother whale nurses her calf *until it can survive on its own.*

Although some kinds of whales have teeth, baleen whales are toothless.

The first three examples here are the most common type, in which the adverb clause fairly clearly modifies the verb of the main clause. The last example shows that sometimes the adverb clause seems to modify the whole main clause; we still call it an adverb clause.

Noun Clause

A **noun clause** is a dependent clause that functions in the sentence as if it were a noun. Noun clauses begin with subordinating conjunctions, indefinite relative pronouns, or indefinite relative adverbs. (See Ch. 1 for more information on subordinating conjunctions, indefinite relative pronouns, and indefinite relative adverbs.)

Noun Clauses with *That*

Previous sections present adjective and adverb clauses, which are modifiers. Sometimes, however, sentence ideas are related to each other in a more integral way.

S TrV   DO
I know something.

     S TrV   DO
Good men hate the way of the wicked.

If the *something* of the first sentence refers to the second sentence idea, then we can show that fact by inserting the second sentence idea in place of *something.*

S TrV DO
I know that good men hate the way of the wicked.

Notice two things about the clause:

1. The added word *that* is a sign that this clause is now a dependent clause, one used as part of another sentence and not a sentence by itself.

2. Just as the word *something* was the direct object of *know,* so now this dependent clause is the direct object of *know.* And since "direct object" is a noun function, we call this kind of dependent clause a noun clause. A noun clause is any clause that performs a noun function—S, DO, IO, OP, and so on.
The word *that,* which introduces most noun clauses, is part of the noun clause. Because it introduces a dependent (or "subordinate") clause, it is called a subordinating conjunction. A subordinating conjunction does nothing within its clause except to introduce it.

Probably noun clauses are most often used as direct objects. But noun clauses can be used in other ways too.

      S   LV   PA

Something is also true.

        S TrV   DO

Wicked men hate good men.

Again, if *something* refers to the second sentence idea, then we can let that idea substitute for *something.* As before, we add *that* to introduce the noun clause.

  S   (S) (TrV)   (DO)LV   PA

That wicked men hate good men is also true.

This time the noun clause acts as the subject of the sentence. The noun clause, of course, still has its own subject and verb, as shown by the parenthesized labels.

When a noun clause is the subject of a sentence, we often turn the sentence around, putting the subject last. (That way the reader or hearer does not have to hold the whole noun-clause subject in mind before he knows what is being said about it.)

  LV   PA S   (S) (TrV)   (DO)

It is also true that wicked men hate good men.

The meaning has not changed. The idea in the noun clause is still the thing that "is also true." The noun clause is still the subject, but the word *it* has been added as a "placeholder" for the subject. This *it* is also called an **expletive** (or subject substitute).

55

Noun Clauses with Other Words

Although most noun clauses begin with the subordinating conjunction *that,* certain other words can also begin noun clauses. The first of these is another subordinating conjunction, *whether.*

In the following pair of sentence ideas, the "something" of the first sentence refers to the question asked by the second.

DO

Please find out something.

Can Jill come with us?

We can make the second sentence into a noun clause, substituting it for *something.* Since the second sentence idea involves a choice (a yes/no question), we add *whether* to it when we make it into a noun clause.

DO   (S)   (InV)

Please find out whether Jill can come with us.

Compare the noun clause that does not have an implied choice: "I found out [that Jill can come with us]." *Whether* is like *that* in being a **subordinating conjunction;** it introduces a dependent clause and does nothing else in the clause. In informal English, the subordinating conjunction *if* sometimes substitutes for *whether,* but only when the noun clause is used as a direct object, as it is here.

Some other words that can be used in noun clauses are the **indefinite relative pronouns.** Below are four examples:

Pair of Sentence Ideas   **Sentence with Noun Clause**

DO
You haven't told me *something.*

DO
You haven't told me *who* came.

who
~~Someone~~ came.

DO
We have just learned *something.*

DO
We have just learned *what* happened.

what
~~Something~~ happened.

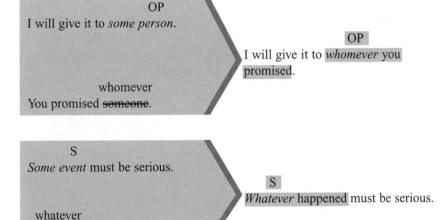

OP
I will give it to *some person*.

OP
I will give it to *whomever* you promised.

whomever
You promised ~~someone~~.

S
Some event must be serious.

S
Whatever happened must be serious.

whatever
~~Something~~ happened.

In all these examples, the italicized word of the first sentence is replaced by the sentence idea below it. Instead of the crossed-out indefinite pronoun, the new noun clause contains an indefinite relative pronoun. We use the term *relative* because the pronoun helps relate the clause to the main clause. Indefinite relative pronouns are covered on page 11.

Finally, **indefinite relative adverbs** can be used in noun clauses.

Pair of Sentence Ideas   **Sentence with Noun Clause**

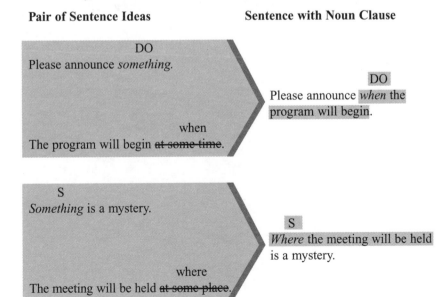

DO
Please announce *something*.

DO
Please announce *when* the program will begin.

when
The program will begin ~~at some time~~.

S
Something is a mystery.

S
Where the meeting will be held is a mystery.

where
The meeting will be held ~~at some place~~.

DO
No one explained *something*.

DO
No one explained *why* the time was changed.

why
The time was changed ~~for some reason~~.

DO
Tell me *something*.

DO
Tell me *how* we can find the house.

how
We can find the house ~~in some way~~.

In every case the second sentence idea substitutes for the italicized word in the first sentence. As the second sentence in each pair becomes a noun clause, a single word replaces an adverbial prepositional phrase. The replacement word is an indefinite relative adverb because it is used adverbially in its own clause. Indefinite relative adverbs are discussed further on page 22.

Sentence Types

A sentence can be classified according to whether it contains one or more than one independent clause and according to whether it contains any dependent clauses. Classifying your own sentences in this way can help you decide whether you have used a pleasing mixture in a piece of writing. It can also be a way to study the style of a good writer in order to learn from it.

Simple Sentences

A **simple sentence** consists of one independent clause only. (An independent clause, you remember, contains one subject-predicate pair, even though the subject or the predicate—or both—may be compound.)

Most shad fishing is done at night.
The fishers and their helpers work with gill nets.

Compound Sentences

A **compound sentence** consists of two or more independent clauses. The independent clauses are usually joined by a comma and a coordinating conjunction, although on occasion a semicolon (or even a colon) alone may be used.

The nets are extremely heavy; the fishermen work hard.
The fish cannot see the nets at night, and *they are easily snared in them.*

In the second sentence above, the two independent clauses are italicized. Notice that the coordinating conjunction is not part of either clause.

Complex Sentences

A **complex sentence** consists of one independent clause and at least one dependent clause. (Remember that although an independent clause can stand on its own as a sentence, a dependent clause cannot; it is *dependent* on another clause.)

> *Shad return each year to the river* [in which they were hatched].
> [Because the fishing is seasonal] and [because the men can work at night], *most of the shad fishermen work full-time at other jobs.*

The independent clauses are italicized, and the dependent clauses are enclosed in brackets. Notice that the relative pronoun *which* and the subordinating conjunction *because* are inside the dependent clauses.

Compound-Complex Sentences

A **compound-complex sentence** contains at least two independent clauses (like a compound sentence) and at least one dependent clause (like a complex sentence).

> *Fishways,* [which allow the shad to pass dams in the rivers], *have been built,* and *an increase in the shad population is likely.*

The two independent clauses are italicized, and the dependent clause is enclosed in brackets. (The clauses are all marked separately, even though a dependent clause is also part of the independent clause to which it is attached.) Compound-complex sentences cannot have fewer clauses than this, but they can easily have more.

Sentence Fragments

To be acceptable, a sentence needs to be complete, not a fragment. A **fragment** is a group of words wrongly punctuated as if it were a complete sentence. In most circumstances the sentence fragment is regarded as a serious error. There are three basic types of fragments.

Fragments Caused by Missing Elements

Except for imperative sentences (which have understood subjects), all normal sentences have both subject and verb. The absence of either a subject or a verb produces a fragment.

NO SUBJECT   The Maya Indians are known for their architectural accomplishments. And also are famous for their advanced mathematical ideas.

CORRECTION   The Maya Indians are known for their architectural accomplishments and also for their advanced mathematical ideas.

NO VERB	The Mayas were a small people. The men only about 5'1" and the women about 4'8".
CORRECTION	The Mayas were a small people. The men averaged about 5'1" and the women about 4'8".
NO VERB	Their greatest empire existed from A.D. 800 to 950. The empire collapsing at that time.
CORRECTION	Their greatest empire existed from A.D. 800 to 950, when it suddenly collapsed.
NO SUBJECT OR VERB	The Mayas were accomplished in several other areas. Especially in the fields of agriculture and astronomy.
CORRECTION	The Mayas were accomplished in several other areas, especially in the fields of agriculture and astronomy.

Notice that a fragment may be corrected by joining it to the adjacent sentence or by supplying the missing elements.

Fragments Caused by Subordinating Words

To be a sentence, a group of words must be able to stand on its own; that is, it must be (or contain) an independent clause. A subordinating word turns a would-be sentence into a fragment. Examples of subordinating words are the relative pronoun *which* and the subordinating conjunction *although*.

FRAGMENT (DEPENDENT CLAUSE)	The Mayas maintained some semblance of an empire until the coming of Cortés. Which resulted in their final overthrow by the Spaniards.
CORRECTION	The Mayas maintained some semblance of an empire until the coming of Cortés, which resulted in their final overthrow by the Spaniards.

As can be seen here, one way to correct a dependent clause fragment is to connect it to the related sentence. Another way is to revise the fragment so that it does not contain a subordinating word:

ALTERNATE CORRECTION	The Mayas maintained some semblance of an empire until the coming of Cortés. His arrival resulted in the final overthrow of the Mayas by the Spaniards.

Fragments Caused by Wrong Punctuation

Remember that a fragment is an incomplete sentence wrongly punctuated as if it were a complete sentence. With most fragments, the wrong punctuation is a period. But a wrongly used semicolon can also create a fragment, or even a pair of fragments.

The correct uses of the semicolon are given on pages 138-40. Most often the semicolon appears between independent clauses, with or without a conjunctive adverb in the second clause.

Independent Clause; Independent Clause

If what precedes or follows the semicolon is not an independent clause, it is a fragment.

FRAGMENT   Some of the Mayas; however, never did submit to the Spaniards.

CORRECTION   Some of the Mayas, however, never did submit to the Spaniards.

Permissible Fragments

Fragments are common (and acceptable) in conversation, particularly in answer to questions.

"Thank you for coming. See you!"

"Loreen is an excellent seamstress. Or used to be."

"Yes—which is more than anyone needs."

Although written fragments look like mistakes, skillful authors do sometimes use a fragment effectively. (See p. 205 for more information on using fragments effectively.)

Comma Splices

It is important that what we punctuate as a single sentence really *be* a single sentence—not two sentences masquerading as one. A **comma splice** consists of two sentences incorrectly joined by only a comma.

COMMA SPLICE   Peace is not the absence of conflict, it is the ability to cope with conflict.

There are three main ways to correct comma splices:

TWO SENTENCES   Peace is not the absence of conflict. It is the ability to cope with conflict.

COORDINATING CONJUNCTION	Peace is not the absence of conflict, but it is the ability to cope with conflict.
SEMICOLON	Peace is not the absence of conflict; it is the ability to cope with conflict.

Sometimes another possibility is to make one of the clauses into a phrase or a dependent clause: *Peace is not the absence of conflict but the ability to cope with conflict.*

Fused Sentences

A fused sentence consists of two sentences incorrectly joined without any punctuation at all. A fused sentence is a serious sentence error.

FUSED SENTENCE	Peace is not obtained by throwing rocks at hornets such action only produces irritation.

Fused sentences are corrected in the same three main ways as comma splices:

TWO SENTENCES	Peace is not obtained by throwing rocks at hornets. Such action only produces irritation.
COORDINATING CONJUNCTION	Peace is not obtained by throwing rocks at hornets, for such action only produces irritation.
SEMICOLON	Peace is not obtained by throwing rocks at hornets; such action only produces irritation.

Furthermore, sometimes one of the clauses can be made into a dependent clause: Peace is not obtained by throwing rocks at hornets, *since such action only produces irritation.*

Be careful not to try to correct a fused sentence by inserting only a comma—the resulting comma splice would be no improvement.

What Do Sentences Do?

Sentences can also be classified by their purpose, that is, by what they do.

1. A **declarative** sentence makes a statement.
   Sam caught the ball.
   He will probably catch the ball again.

2. An **interrogative** sentence asks a question.
   Can Sam catch the ball?
   Why did he catch it?
   Who will catch the ball?
   He caught it, didn't he? (tag question)

3. An **imperative** sentence gives a command or a request.
   Please try to catch the ball.
   Quick, catch the ball!

4. An **exclamatory** sentence exclaims about something, express-
   ing strong feeling.
   He actually caught the ball!
   What a catch that was!

You will notice that the end punctuation of these four types follows a
pattern. (See Chapter 10 for more information on punctuation of various
sentence types.)

PART TWO

Usage Tools

Agreement

Subject-Verb Agreement

Subject-verb agreement is a bit like housekeeping. When we do it right, no one notices; but if we do it wrong, nearly everyone notices. For example:

> Subject-verb agreement are a bit like housekeeping. When we does it right, no one notice; but if we does it wrong, nearly everyone notice.

Then, too, nearly anyone can run a dust cloth, except perhaps around those fragile knickknacks on the high shelf. Likewise, most of us do fine with subject-verb agreement about 95 percent of the time. This section should help with that other 5 percent.

Subject-verb agreement is the correct use of singular subjects with singular verbs and of plural subjects with plural verbs. Sometimes the verb changes in form in order to "agree" (or match up) with certain characteristics of the subject. More specifically, the first word of the complete verb agrees with the person and number of the subject.

If the subject is a noun or a third-person pronoun, the only question is whether the subject is singular or plural.

Pl   Pl
The wild geese *fly* overhead, and they *seem* to call to us.

Sing   Sing
The first goose *flies* strongly, and he *seems* to pull the others.

Except for the irregular word *be,* it is mainly the present tense that shows agreement.

67

The verb words that show agreement can be summarized under three headings. (*A boy* and *boys* stand for all singular and plural noun subjects.)

	Present	**Past**
Be (as a main verb or as the first auxiliary)		
First-person singular *(I)*	am	was
Third-person singular *(a boy; it/he/she)*	is	was
Other *(boys; you/we/they)*	are	were
Have (as main verb or as the first auxiliary)		
Third-person singular *(a boy; it/he/she)*	has	
Other *(boys; I/you/we/they)*	have	
All other true verbs (using *look* as typical)		
Third-person singular *(a boy; it/he/she)*	looks	
Other *(boys; I/you/we/they)*	look	

Identifying the Subject

One problem in subject-verb agreement is that sometimes we may lose track of which word is the subject.

Ignoring Intervening Phrases after the Subject

Do not be distracted from the real subject by a modifier or other phrase between the subject and the verb. These sentences are correct:

> S   LV PA
>
> The *reasons* for the surprising answer to my question *were* not clear.

> S   TrV-P
>
> A *collection* of answers to commonly asked questions *is being written*.

To check sentences like these, look for the simple subject and try it with the first word of the complete verb (*reasons were; collection is*).

Ignoring a Predicate Noun of a Different Number

Usually both the subject and the predicate noun are singular, or both are plural. However, sometimes only one is plural.

```
        S   LV      PN
```
The first *prize was* two tickets to the next concert.

```
   S              LV        PN
```
Two *tickets* to the concert were the first prize.

Even though sentences with predicate nouns can often be turned around (as these two sentences show), in today's English we consider the subject to be the one before the verb. The verb agrees with the subject, not the predicate noun *(prize was, tickets were)*.

Ignoring the Expletive **There**

As you have learned, the sentence pattern S-*be*-Advl can be turned around, with the word *there* taking the position usually filled by the subject.

```
   S    be      Advl              be   S          Advl
```
Rabbits are in that cage.   →   There *are* rabbits in that cage.

```
   S   be Advl                    be   S   Advl
```
A visitor is here.   →   There *is* a visitor here.

Sentences in which a form of *be* is an auxiliary can be changed in a similar way.

```
        S       InV                      S     InV
```
Some dogs *are* barking.   →   There *are* some dogs barking.

In either form of such sentences, the verb agrees with the real subject *(rabbits are, visitor is, dogs are)*. In other words, we ignore *there* and look for the real subject.

On the other hand, the verb is always singular after *it,* the other expletive that can stand in for a subject.

```
   LV PA   S (entire clause)
```
It is good [that we finished before dark].

```
   LV      PN    S (entire clause)
```
It was a disgrace [for me to forget that]!

```
   be      S      Advl
```
It was the Palmers at the door.

69

Ignoring Negative Phrases with the Subject

One way to show a strong contrast is to use *not* with a contrasting word or phrase right after the word in question.

> We were jogging, not walking.
>
> Joyce, not Susan, is the one to ask about that.

When the word with *not* is a noun (as in the second example), we can call it a negative appositive. Negative appositives do not affect subject-verb agreement at all.

> *Exercise,* not the things we eat, *has* the greatest effect on what we weigh. *(Exercise has)*
>
> *Detergents* and *soap,* but never bleach, *are* safe to use on the counter top. *(Detergents and soap are)*

The second example shows that negative words other than *not* can also be used in negative appositives.

Another way to make a point strongly is to use a negative subject before the positive subject, in a construction with *not . . . but.* Here also the verb agrees with the positive subject.

> Not I but you are the real winner. *(you are)*
>
> Not slides but a film is what she showed yesterday. *(film is)*

With either construction, ignore the negative phrase and make the verb agree with the positive subject.

Identifying the Subject as Singular or Plural

Once the subject is clearly identified, subject-verb agreement is usually easy. However, a few kinds of subjects demand special attention.

Nouns of Plural Form

Certain nouns have only one form, a form that appears to be plural. Many of these words are used in only one way, either as singular or as plural nouns.

          S

ALWAYS SINGULAR   The *news* is good today.

          S

ALWAYS PLURAL   The *pliers* are in the toolbox.
    (one or more tools)

Some of the nouns that always require a plural verb can also be used with *pair of* to make clear how many items are meant. In that case, the subject is *pair* instead of the plural noun.

      S

A *pair* of pliers is in the toolbox.

      S

Two *pairs* of pliers are in the toolbox.

Below are some common plural-form nouns, listed according to whether they require a singular verb or a plural verb. (Check other words in your dictionary.)

Singular	Plural	
billiards	clothes	shears
checkers	eyeglasses, glasses	spectacles
measles	goggles	soapsuds, suds
molasses	pants, slacks (etc.)	thanks
news	pliers	tights
Niagara Falls (etc.)	proceeds	tweezers
United States	riches	

The plural-sounding names of teams and organizations, such as the Yankees and the Boy Scouts, usually require a plural verb.

Words ending in *ics* fall into both groups, depending on the meaning intended:

Singular	Plural
Fields of Study	Activities, Products, Characteristics
acoustics	acoustics
acrobatics	acrobatics
athletics	athletics
ceramics	ceramics*
civics	
economics	economics
electronics	
ethics	ethics*
mathematics	
physics	
politics	politics
statistics	statistics*
tactics	tactics*

*A related singular word also exists.

71

Here is an *ics* word used both ways:

> Acoustics *is* a very technical science.
> The acoustics in this auditorium *are* better than we expected.

A good dictionary will distinguish between the singular meaning and the plural meaning of words like these.

Collective Nouns

Collective nouns are nouns like *club* and *team* that refer to groups. In American English these words usually take a singular verb.

> The committee has made its decision.
> Our team is ahead so far.

(Collective nouns take plural verbs much more often in British English than in American English.)

Words That Can Be Understood as Singular or Plural

Certain words may be understood as either singular or plural, depending on what modifies them.

Treat them as—
Singular
when followed by *of* phrase   Part of the cake is left.
with singular object   (It is left.)

Plural
when followed by *of* phrase   Part of the cakes for the sale are here
with plural object   already. (They are here.)

This rule governs the words below:

all	more	part
any	most	some
half	none	ten percent
(and other fractions)		(and other percents)

All of these words subdivide either a group or a single thing. For that reason they are exceptions to the general rule that the verb agrees only with the simple subject.

Here are a few more examples:

Singular Use	**Plural Use**
Half of it was used.	Half of them were used.
Two-thirds of it is left.	Two-thirds of them are left.

Most of it is good.	Most of them are good.
I wanted the cream, but part was gone.	I wanted the cookies, but part were gone.

The last pair shows that the *of* phrase can be understood.

The negative word *none* follows the rule only part of the time. *None* is always singular when followed by an *of* phrase with a singular object.

> None of the cake *is* left.

None may be plural when followed by an *of* phrase with a plural object, if the meaning seems to be plural.

> None of the cakes *are* left.
>
> None of the cakes *is/are* just what I wanted.

To most people the two versions of the last sentence could be equally logical and equally correct. However, in formal English some prefer to use *none* as singular only.

Finally, the word *number* has its own rule:

ALWAYS SINGULAR   *The number* of local candidates was fairly large.
ALWAYS PLURAL   *A number* of the local candidates were present.

In sentences like the second one, there is a strong plural meaning, since *a number* means something like "several."

Titles, Quotations, and Amounts as Singular

Even though key words in the title of a work may be plural, the **title** is treated as singular because it names a single work.

> "Three Blind Mice" is easy for children to sing.
>
> *The Gleaners* was painted by Millet in 1857.
>
> "Birches" is one of Robert Frost's best-known poems.

A **quoted (or cited) noun or phrase** is also a single item, even though it may contain a plural.

> To him, "all good books" means just the ones he enjoys.
>
> *Stories* is a plural noun.

Similarly, **amounts** are treated as singular: measured amounts, amounts of money, and periods of time.

> Two tablespoons of oil *is* enough.
>
> Ten dollars *is* the usual fee.
>
> Two days *is* a long time to wait.

In all of these, the verb is singular because the subject refers to a single amount or time period.

Relative Pronouns

Relative pronouns *(who, which, that)* do not change form for singular and plural, but we treat them as if they did—as if a relative pronoun has the same number as its antecedent. Therefore, when a relative pronoun is a subject, in effect the verb agrees with the pronoun's antecedent.

S   TrV   DO

She is the *person* who *has* read the book.

S   TrV   DO

They are the *ones* who *have* read the book.

In the first example, the antecedent of the relative pronoun *who* is *person,* so the verb is singular *(person has).* In the second, both the antecedent and the verb are plural.

Occasionally we have to look carefully to find the antecedent:

I bought a book of *stories* that *were* of different types.

I bought a *book* of stories that *was* falling apart.

Sentences with "the one of the" or "one of the" before a noun and a relative pronoun are sometimes a problem.

I bought *the* only one of the books that was long enough.

(I bought the one that was long enough.)

Here the antecedent of *that* is *one*—he bought one, the one that was long enough. The clue is "the . . . one" which suggests a singular verb. The next sentence is different.

I bought one of the books that *were* long enough.

This time several *books* were long enough, and he bought one of them. Usually a plural verb is used after "one of the," when no *the* precedes *one.*

Compound Subjects

The rules for subject-verb agreement with compound subjects depend on whether *and* or *or* is used.

Compound Subjects with And

A compound subject with *and* is normally plural—the two or more things add up to more than one.

> John and Mary *have* the paper. (they have)

Similar to *and* is the correlative *both—and.*

> Both Sue and I *are waiting* to read it. (we are)

A compound subject with *both—and* is always plural, because *both—and* always joins separate things.

If the two words joined by *and* refer to the same thing, the subject is considered to be singular, and the verb is singular.

> Our friend and neighbor *was* a great help when we had the flu.

Also, if the things named are considered part of a single thing or a single concept, the verb is singular.

> Peaches and cream *is* my favorite dessert.
> That crackling and banging *was* deafening.

Usually, however, *and* joins separate things and requires a plural verb.

Compound Subjects with Or

For compound subjects with *or* (also *either—or, neither—nor*), the simple subject closer to the first verb is the one that determines the form of the verb.

> Esther or Carwin *has* my copy of *The Mystery of Edwin Drood.* (Carwin has)
> *Are* you or I or Sam going to do it? (are you)
> Either Ross or his sisters *were* there, it seems. (sisters were)

Or always involves a choice of things, not an adding up. Therefore we make the verb agree with the closer noun or pronoun.

Pronoun-Antecedent Agreement

An earlier word or phrase that a pronoun relates to is the **antecedent** of that pronoun.

Uncle Henry wrote that he and Aunt Enna will come next month.

The antecedent of the pronoun *he* is *Uncle Henry.*

Pronouns must agree with their antecedents in number and gender. Agreement in **number** means that singular pronouns are used with singular antecedents and that plural pronouns are used with plural antecedents.

My aunt and uncle usually travel in *their* camper.

Agreement in **gender** means mainly the correct use of the singular pronouns *it* (neuter), *he* (masculine), *she* (feminine). (See p. 88 for details of this use.) Gender agreement can also include the correct use of *who* (for persons only) and *which* (for things only).

Was it your uncle *who* first took you fishing?

Yes, and my aunt taught me all *she* knows about frying perch.

Not all pronouns have an antecedent. First- and second-person pronouns refer to speakers and listeners, who usually have not been mentioned earlier. Certain other pronouns, such as indefinite pronouns, also lack antecedents. But those that have antecedents must agree with them in number and gender (and person, which is usually not a problem).

Most questions of pronoun-antecedent agreement involve a choice among the third-person personal pronouns, including the possessive-pronoun adjectives.

Making Third-Person Pronouns Agree with Their Antecedents

1. Find the antecedent. Do so by asking yourself which earlier word the pronoun represents.
2. Decide whether the antecedent is singular or plural. (The four usual problem areas are dealt with below.) If the antecedent is plural, use the appropriate form of *they.*
3. If the antecedent is singular, decide whether *it, he,* or *she* is called for, according to the gender. If the gender is uncertain, look at the guidelines found below.

Note that agreement does not involve case; a pronoun is in the subjective, possessive, or objective case strictly according to the way it is used in its own clause. (See Ch. 7.)

Singular Indefinite Pronouns

The following indefinite pronouns are always singular:

someone	somebody	something
anyone	anybody	anything
everyone	everybody	everything
no one	nobody	nothing

either	each	much
neither	one	little
another		less

In careful English, a singular pronoun is used when one of these indefinite pronouns is the antecedent.

Someone on the boys' team forgot *his* baseball glove.

On the girls' side of the gym, *everyone* has *her* own locker.

Everyone brought *his* own lunch on the class field trip.

In all the confusion *no one* could find *his* place.

To *each his* own.

One should do *his* best and trust God for the rest.

Because we need a singular pronoun, as in these sentences, we are forced to make decisions about gender. That is, do we use a form of *it* or *he* or *she?* In the first two sentences above, the gender is clear from the rest of the sentence, and we have no trouble choosing *his* and *her*. In the final four sentences, however, the indefinite pronouns could logically cover males or females or both. Notice that in all four sentences *his* is used. There is a general rule for agreement with indefinite pronoun antecedents of uncertain gender: use the masculine singular pronoun whenever the antecedent does not clearly refer to females.

Everyone brought *his* notebook with *him.*

It is understood in such a case that both males and females are probably involved. Use of both masculine and feminine pronouns is also permissible, but it is often awkward.

Everyone brought *his* or *her* notebook with *him* or *her.*

Sometimes we can reword the sentence to avoid personal pronouns entirely.

Everyone brought a notebook along.

Normally, though, it is best to go ahead and use the traditional masculine pronoun to include either or both sexes. What is not acceptable, especially in written English, is to use *their* instead of *his* in such a case.

Singular Nouns Modified by Indefinite Determiners

Very similar to agreement with indefinite pronouns is agreement with nouns modified by indefinite determiners (a special kind of adjective, see p. 20.). Notice the similarity in the following pairs.

Someone forgot to bring his baseball glove.
Some boy forgot to bring his baseball glove.

Anyone can understand that, if he tries.
Any intelligent person can understand that, if he tries.

I needed *something,* and she gave it to me.
I needed *some help,* and she gave it to me.

Just as most indefinite pronouns are always singular, so also a singular noun modified by an indefinite determiner is always singular.

Here again are the indefinite determiners that commonly modify nouns:

Modify Singular or Plural	Modify Singular Nouns Only
some	each
any	either
no	neither
enough	another
most	much

When any of these modify singular nouns, any further references must be singular.

The rule seems obvious, but—as with indefinite pronouns—sometimes the unclear gender misleads us into using a form of *they* instead of a singular pronoun form. The singular pronoun is correct:

Each person took *his* seat before the meeting began.

As with indefinite pronouns, use the masculine singular pronoun whenever the antecedent does not clearly refer to females. If the gender is clear, use the appropriate pronoun:

Each mother brought *her* own supplies.
Neither idea has much to recommend *it.*

Compound Antecedents Joined by *Or*

Compound antecedents are considered singular or plural according to the same rules as those given on pages 74-75 for compound subjects. Usually only antecedents joined by *or* raise any questions.

As with subject-verb agreement, pronoun-antecedent agreement is with the **nearer** of the elements joined by *or, either—or,* or *neither—nor.*

Either Sheri or Darla will give her report after yours.

When the two antecedents are different in number or gender, the rule still holds.

I haven't decided whether to ask Grace or her friends to do what they can.

Sometimes, though, the result seems awkward.

Either Monique or Ron will give his report next.

Then the only graceful solution may be to reword the sentence.

Either Monique will give her report next, or Ron will give his.

Either sentence, however, is preferable to the incorrect use of *their* with a singular antecedent.

Collective Nouns

Collective nouns—words that refer to groups—most often are used with singular verbs. When they are used with singular verbs, any later pronoun references must also be singular.

Sing   Sing
The committee *has* made *its* decision.

Pl   Pl
The committee *are* arguing among *themselves.*

The first sentence illustrates the more frequent singular use of the word, but that sentence could have been in the plural (and in British usage it probably would have been):

The committee *have* made their decision.

The essential matter here is consistency—if the verb is plural, the pronoun must be plural.

Of course, some verb forms (such as the simple past) cannot show agreement with the collective noun. In that case we are simply guided by the meanings: a singular pronoun for the group as a whole, a plural pronoun for the individual members.

The audience took their seats.

The audience showed *its* approval by loud applause.

Pronoun Reference

Among the most important kinds of links in sentences are those provided by the reference of certain pronouns to earlier words and phrases. When these references are clear, the sentences can be clear. When they are unclear, the sentences will be either puzzling or misleading.

As the material in Chapter 5 mentions, not all pronouns have antecedents. However, we do usually expect antecedents for certain kinds of pronouns: the third-person personal pronouns *(it, he, she, they)*, the relative pronouns in adjective clauses *(who, which, that)*, and the demonstrative pronouns *(this, that, these, those)*. Our expectations of careful reference are highest for the personal pronouns named, second highest for the relative pronouns, but significant even for the demonstrative pronouns.

Two issues are involved in the reference of these pronouns:

1. Is there a clear antecedent? If not, the sentence will be hard to understand. (See Ch. 5.)

2. Is there an acceptable type of antecedent? If not, the sentence (especially the written sentence) is poorly stated. It may also be somewhat unclear. (See Ch. 5.)

Clear Reference

In the reference of pronouns to antecedents, the absolute essential is that the reference be clear. There should be a single noun or noun-equivalent nearby that is the obvious antecedent of the pronoun.

One kind of problem is having two nearby nouns that are both possible antecedents of the pronoun used.

AMBIGUOUS　　When Mike shouted at Joe, he looked rather strange.

CLEAR　　When Mike shouted at Joe, Joe looked rather strange.
or
Mike looked rather strange when he shouted at Joe.

As these corrections show, sometimes the problem can be solved either by repeating the noun itself instead of using a pronoun or by rewording the sentence so that only the intended antecedent comes before the pronoun. At other times a more specific pronoun can be used:

> AMBIGUOUS   Diane told Martha that her friends were planning a party.
>
> CLEAR   Diane told Martha, "Your friends are planning a party."
> *or*
> Diane told Martha, "My friends are planning a party."

In this case the direct quotation makes the reference clear.

Unclear reference is also likely when the pronoun is too far from the antecedent.

> REMOTE   I have been reading the passage in Ecclesiastes 12 about the importance of serving God in our youth. In old age our senses will fail, and we will grow feeble. Finally the dust will return to the earth and "the spirit shall return unto God who gave it." *It* is poetic yet powerful.
>
> CLEAR   . . . unto God who gave it." *The passage* is poetic yet powerful.

Reference to a Noun, Not an Implied Noun

In careful speaking and especially in careful writing, it is expected that pronoun reference will be to nouns actually present in the passage.

> IMPLIED   On vacation I visited my cousin's church, and *they*
> REFERENCE   really made me feel welcome.
>
> BETTER   On vacation I visited my cousin's church, and *the people there* really made me feel welcome.

In the first version *they* stands for a noun that is never mentioned. The second version is more specific and is immediately clear. It illustrates the usual correction for implied reference: replacing the unclear pronoun with the specific noun that was implied.

Reference to a Noun That Is Not a Modifier

In following the flow of ideas through a passage, we generally expect pronouns to refer to nearby nouns that are used as subjects, direct objects, and so on. Nouns that modify (and are therefore functioning as adjectives) are less noticeable antecedents. Possessives, for instance, make poor antecedents.

REFERENCE TO A POSSESSIVE   Dave found Bob's watch, who had lost it at the track meet.

CORRECTION   Dave found the watch that Bob had lost at the track meet.
or
Dave found the watch belonging to Bob, who had lost it at the track meet.

Other modifying nouns also make poor antecedents.

REFERENCE TO A MODIFYING NOUN   They finally decided on a brick house. *That* is easier to maintain than painted siding.

CORRECTION   They finally decided on a brick house, because *brick* is easier to maintain than painted siding.
or
They finally bought a house made of brick, which is easier to maintain than painted siding.

Either the intended antecedent can be used in place of the unclear pronoun, or the sentence can be revised so that the intended antecedent is no longer a modifier.

Definite Reference of Personal Pronouns

Although indefinite pronouns such as *someone, one,* and *everybody* are intended to have indefinite reference, personal pronouns are normally expected to have antecedents and to refer to definite individuals or groups. Note the following problems.

Indefinite *They*

In written English *they* should be used only with definite reference.

INDEFINITE *THEY*   In the South they say "y'all" for the plural of *you.*
CORRECTED   In the South people say "y'all" for the plural of *you.*
MORE EXACT   Some Southerners say "y'all" for the plural of *you.*

Usually a specific noun or pronoun can be supplied in place of the indefinite *they*. "Some Southerners," for instance, tells us more than the original version did. However, at times another solution is called for.

INDEFINITE *THEY*   Last December they gave us two weeks of vacation from school.

CORRECTION   Last December we had two weeks of vacation from school.

If the specific noun is unknown or irrelevant, as perhaps in this example, the sentence can be revised to do away with the need for the indefinite *they*.

Indefinite *It*

In careful writing, *it* should not be used indefinitely in the phrase "it says." Replace *it* with the name of the source of information.

INDEFINITE *IT*   In the *Wall Street Journal* it says that interest rates are up again.

CORRECTION   The *Wall Street Journal* says that interest rates are up again.

Indefinite *You*

In conversation and informal writing, *you* is commonly used in an indefinite sense to refer to people in general.

INFORMAL   You can lead a horse to water, but you can't make him drink.

A folksy proverb of this sort would probably not be used at all in a very formal context. Some statements, however, might appear in either informal or formal writing, with appropriate adjustments.

INFORMAL   The speaker said that you have to work hard if you want to succeed.

LESS INFORMAL   . . . we must work hard if we want to succeed.
or
. . . a person must work hard if he wants to succeed.

MOST FORMAL   . . . one must work hard if he wants to succeed.
or
. . . one must work hard if one wants to succeed.

Notice that *we* can be used in a semi-indefinite sense to include the writer along with the audience. *We* is acceptable when the writer can indeed logically be included, but not otherwise. (It would be odd to read, "In the sixteenth century we had to work hard.")

The *you* in the informal examples above was an indefinite *you*, to be removed in general or formal writing. However, in all but the most formal writing, *you* can be used legitimately to refer definitely to the reader. This use is especially likely when instructions are being given.

SPOKEN AND GENERAL WRITTEN USE	Be sure the test tube is completely dry before you add the chemicals.

The imperative and the use of *you* are perfectly appropriate here. But in a very formal passage, such as a scholarly study, the second person is avoided completely.

VERY FORMAL	One must be sure that the test tube is completely dry before he adds the chemicals.
	or
	One must be sure that the test tube is completely dry before one adds the chemicals.

Academic writing, such as for research papers and reports, usually is about topics that do not allow for the use of the second person. In order to learn to do this type of writing, students may be asked to avoid all use of *you* and the imperative in some of their written compositions.

Reference to a Noun, Not a Broad Idea

The antecedent of a pronoun should be a noun, not the general idea of a preceding sentence or clause. This requirement is strongest for the personal pronouns and the relative pronouns, but it can also apply to demonstrative pronouns.

BROAD REFERENCE	Joe won the contest, and *it* surprised me.
	Joe won the contest, *which* surprised me.
	Joe won the contest, and *that* surprised me.

The first two of these sentences are faulty, and even the last one can perhaps be improved.

CORRECTION	Joe won the contest, and his victory surprised me.
	I was surprised that Joe won the contest.
	Joe's contest victory surprised me.

Part of the problem with broad pronoun reference is that it often makes the sentence less clear.

BROAD REFERENCE   I told Jack that we couldn't all fit into my car. This was a surprise to him.

CLARIFIED   I told Jack that we couldn't all fit into my car, and he was surprised that so many were going.
or
I told Jack that we couldn't all fit into my car. He was surprised to learn that I have a compact car.

Even a demonstrative pronoun should be changed when its meaning is not fully clear.

Pronoun Use

Nine kinds of personal pronouns were discussed in Chapter 1. Each of these pronoun types shows one or more of the four characteristics of pronouns: person, number, gender, and case. However, only the personal pronouns show all four characteristics. Personal pronouns are the most common and complex of the various types of pronoun; therefore, this chapter focuses mainly on the use of personal pronouns but addresses other types as needed.

Person

Every personal pronoun is classified by whether it is first, second, or third person.

FIRST PERSON   The speaker *(I)*, or the speaker and others *(we)*
SECOND PERSON   The person or persons spoken to *(you)*
THIRD PERSON   Any other person or thing *(it, he, she, they)*

Number

Personal pronouns have singular and plural number.

SINGULAR   Refers to one person or thing
PLURAL   Refers to more than one person or thing

Combining the three persons and the two numbers gives a basic six-way division for personal pronouns:

	Singular	Plural
First Person	I	we
Second Person	you	you
Third Person	it/he/she	they

Gender

Three genders differentiate the third-person singular pronouns *it, he,* and *she.*

NEUTER	Normally refers to things *(it)*
MASCULINE	Normally refers to males *(he)*
FEMININE	Normally refers to females *(she)*

As suggested by the word normally, the gender pronouns do not always follow the simple rules above. Certain animals, like pets, are usually referred to as *he* or *she,* but insects and other animals, like frogs, are usually called *it.* Also, the neuter *it* is sometimes used for infants. On the other hand, countries, ships, and certain other things can be referred to by the feminine pronoun.

Case

Case is the form of a noun or pronoun that reflects the way the noun or pronoun is used in the sentence. Although nouns have only two case forms, pronouns have three cases: subjective, objective, and possessive.

The **subjective case** is used mainly for subjects of sentences but is also used for predicate nouns. The subjective case pronouns are *I, we, you, it/he/she,* and *they.*

Objective case pronouns are used primarily for objects, that is, direct and indirect objects, and objects of prepositions. The objective case pronouns are *me, us, you, it, him, her,* and *them.*

Pronouns that are used to show possession are in the **possessive case.** There are two types of possessive pronoun: modifiers and independent possessives. Possessive case pronouns are *my/mine, our/ours, your/yours, its, his, her/hers,* and *their/theirs.*

Singular			
	Subjective	**Objective**	**Possessive**
First Person	I	me	my, mine
Second Person	you	you	your, yours
Third Person	it	it	its
	he	him	his
	she	her	her, hers

Plural			
	Subjective	**Objective**	**Possessive**
First Person	we	us	our, ours
Second Person	you	you	your, yours
Third Person	they	them	their, theirs

When a possessive noun or pronoun replaces a noun and its modifiers, it is called an **independent possessive.** Independent possessives are not adjectives because they *replace* nouns instead of *modifying* them.

> *Margaret's mittens* did not fit me.
> *Margaret's* did not fit me.

> Phil packed *his suitcase.*
> Phil packed *his.*

Correct Use of Pronoun Case

The correct case of a pronoun is determined by its use in its own clause or in the sentence. In the following list, the simplest and most important principles appear first.

You and *it* do not have different subjective and objective case forms, but the correct forms of the other personal pronouns appear in the illustrations for the first and fifth rules below.

Rule 1. Use the subjective case for subjects; use the objective case for objects.

> *We* invited *them* to the recital.
> *They* gave *him* a personal invitation.
> *You* can sit by *me.*

Rule 2. Use the same rules for case in constructions with conjunctions as in simple constructions.

> *He* and *I* invited John and *her* to the recital.
> We gave *you* and *him* personal invitations from Sam and *me.*

Rule 3. Determine the case of an appositive according to the function of the renamed word.

> The two of us, Joe and *I,* handed out programs.
>
> No one, not even *I,* expected a crowd as large as that.
>
> A prize was given to the winners, Todd and *her,* at the end.

Rule 4. Disregard an appositive noun that follows a pronoun. The case of the pronoun is not affected by the presence of an appositive.

> S App InV
>
> *We* boys worked there last Saturday. (*we* worked)

>   S   TrV DO App
>
> "Have you ever watched *us* experts?" he asked teasingly. (watched *us*)

Rule 5. In formal English, use the subjective case for a pronoun in predicate-noun position. (Informally, especially in speech, the objective case is frequently used.)

> *She* was the first speaker.
>
> The first speaker was *she.* (formal)

Remember that a linking verb is like an equal sign. In formal English it always has the same case after it as before it.

Rule 6. Use the subjective-case pronouns *who* and *whoever* for subjects.

> **INTERROGATIVE**   *Who* heard the weather report?
>
>   **RELATIVE**   I know the person [*who* heard the weather report].

All that matters in determining the correct case is the function of *who* within its own clause, not how the whole clause is used.

>   S TrV DO
>
> He found out [*who* heard it].

Rule 7. In formal English, use the objective-case pronouns *whom* and *whomever* for objects. (Informally, *who* is often used instead of *whom* at the beginning of a question.)

> **INTERROGATIVE**   *Whom* did you see?
>
>   To *whom* did you give it?
>
>   **RELATIVE**   He is the person [*whom/that* you saw].
>
>   He is the one [to *whom* you gave it].

In written English, *whom* is the proper objective-case pronoun.

Rule 8. Ignore parenthetical expressions like *do you think, I believe,* or *did they say* when you determine the function and case of *who/whom.*

S
Who [do you think] won the election?

DO
Whom [did they say] he saw?

S
He's the one [*who* {I feel} is best].

Rule 9. In a comparison, determine the correct case of the pronoun after *than* or *as* according to how the pronoun would function in the full understood clause.

	S InV
He did better than *I*.	(than *I* did)
	S TrV DO
You watched Billy more than *me*.	(than you watched *me*)
or	
	S TrV DO
You watched Billy more than *I*.	(than *I* watched Billy)
	S LV PA
Are you as tall as *he?*	(as *he* is tall)

Rule 10. Use the possessive case for the "subject" (doer) of a gerund.

S
GERUND MODIFIED *Joe's* singing has improved.
BY POSSESSIVE
DOER WORD   OP
Were you surprised by *my* cleaning the house?

Do not confuse this construction with the one in which a participle modifies a preceding noun or pronoun.

PARTICIPLE   DO
MODIFYING   Did you see *me* cleaning the house?
THE DOER

The earlier question asked whether the *cleaning* was a surprise. This one asks, "Did you see *me?*"

If the verbal with *ing* functions like a noun (S, DO, OP, etc.), it is a gerund. The doer pronoun before it, if there is one, should therefore be possessive.

Rule 11. Use the objective case for the "subject" (doer) of the infinitive. (See pp. 48-49 for "subjects" of infinitives.)

Do you want *us* to sing?

They told Joe and *me* to go ahead.

Objects of infinitives, like all other objects, are also in the objective case.

I want to see *him*.　　　　　(direct object of infinitive)

He told me to give *her* the book.　　(indirect object of infinitive)

Rule 12. Use the same case after a linking-verb infinitive as before it. That is, a pronoun in predicate-noun position after a linking-verb infinitive should have the same case as the earlier word that it renames.

- A pronoun that renames the subject of the main verb should be subjective in formal English.

  That had to be *he*.

- A pronoun that renames the subject of the infinitive should be objective.

  Everyone believed the winner to be *him*.

  They thought me to be *her*.

- Such constructions, however, may sound awkward. When they do, the sentences can be revised.

  That had to be Joe.

  Everyone thought he was the winner.

  They mistook me for her.

Problems Related to Personal Pronouns

Double Subjects

Do not use a phrase like *Joe he* as a subject. Let your pronouns replace nouns, not trail along after them.

DOUBLE SUBJECT   Joe he told me to come.

Either the pronoun or the noun should be omitted. (Usually it is the pronoun that is unnecessary.)

CORRECTION   Joe told me to come.
He told me to come.

Courtesy Order of Pronouns

Two rules of courtesy govern the order for joining personal pronouns to other pronouns or to nouns.

- Always mention yourself last. That is, always put the first-person pronoun last.

    Jackie and I will be late. (*Not:* I and Jackie will . . .)
    Between you and me I liked the original recipe better. (*Not:* Between me and you . . .)

- Unless the emphasis of your sentence suggests otherwise, put the second-person pronoun *you* before third-person pronouns or nouns. The courtesy here is the mention of your hearer before anyone else.

    You and she could take tennis lessons together. (*Not:* She and you could . . .)
    You and Bob were a good team. (*Not:* Bob and you were . . .)
    I'll go with you or Sue. (*Not:* I'll go with Sue or you.)

In summary, put yourself last, and put your hearer first.

Shifts in Person

In statements of general truths, unnamed people can appear in a number of ways. Some possible words are *people, one*, and *anyone* (all in the third person); sometimes informally *you* (second person); and *we* (first person). A problem occurs, though, when there is a shift from one person to another.

> **SHIFT** I learned that we can easily make mistakes in arithmetic, so you should always check your work when you add large numbers.

The statement of general truth begins with *we* (first person) and ends with *you* (second person). We can correct it by changing *you* to *we,* or we can revise more thoroughly for greater formality.

> **CORRECTION** I learned that because it is easy to make mistakes in arithmetic, one should always check his work when he adds large numbers.

Here is a similar problem sentence:

> **SHIFT** A *person* must work if *you* want to advance.

The sentence begins with the third person and ends with the second person. *He,* not *you,* would be the correct pronoun to carry on the person and number of the noun *person.*

> **CORRECTION** A *person* must work if *he* wants to advance.

Shifts in Number

Statements of general truths can also have problems of number. Most general statements can be made in either the singular or the plural.

> **CORRECT** The elephant is a very large animal.
> *or*
> Elephants are very large animals.

Mixing the two types of statements, though, can produce strange results.

> **SHIFT** Elephants use their trunk for many things.

This sentence seems to be talking about a number of elephants that together have just one trunk. The solution is to make the sentence either singular or plural throughout.

> **CORRECT** Elephants use their trunks for many things.
> *or*
> An elephant uses its trunk for many things.

The same kind of problem can appear in directions to a group.

> **SHIFT** Now, children, open your Bible to John 3:16.

All the children together have just one Bible? If not, make the sentence plural throughout by using *Bibles.*

Adjective and Adverb Use

Adjectives and adverbs are both types of modifiers. **Adjectives** modify nouns or pronouns by describing or limiting the noun or pronoun. **Adverbs** modify verbs, adjectives, or other adverbs.

Differences in Function

There are two important differences in the functions of adjectives and adverbs. Determining the part of speech being modified will help determine which type of modifier you need.

Adjectives	**Adverbs**
Modify nouns or pronouns	Modify verbs, adjectives, other adverbs
Can be predicate adjectives in the pattern S-LV-PA:	Can be modifiers in any pattern, including S-InV:

S	LV	PA	S	InV	(Adv)
Marissa	looks	good	Marissa	behaves	well
	(is, feels,	(sad,		(does,	(nicely,
	seems,	nice,		sings,	badly)
	became)	happy)		runs)	

Notice the difference between the two patterns given above. In the first set of sentences, we learn that *Marissa* looks good or sad or nice; the subject is described by predicate adjectives. In the second set we learn that she *behaves* or *does* or *sings* well or nicely; the verb is modified by adverbs. Adjectives are correct in the first set, and adverbs in the second.

Several more sentences illustrate the differences in the functions of adjectives and adverbs:

The salient points of the governor's speech were unappreciated by the noisy crowd.

(*Salient* modifies the noun *points;* therefore, *salient* is an adjective.)

The old man's habit of greeting all passersby with a song seemed *eccentric*.
(*Eccentric* in the predicate modifies the noun *habit;* therefore, it is a predicate adjective.)

The soldier fought *bravely* for his country.
(*Bravely* modifies the verb *fought; bravely* is an adverb.)

Having gotten only three hours rest, Mrs. Payne was *extremely* sleepy the next day.
(*Extremely* modifies the predicate adjective *sleepy* and is an adverb.)

Avoid the temptation to use an adjective in the place of an adverb following an action verb.

INCORRECT	My brother speaks *clear*.
CORRECT	My brother speaks *clearly*.

Following a linking verb, however, an adjective is correct.

INCORRECT	The syrup tasted *sweetly*.
CORRECT	The syrup tasted *sweet*.

Sometimes nouns (or nouns and their modifiers) can be used to modify verbs. They frequently have meanings of time, place, or manner.

I usually work *all day,* but *this Friday* I'm going *home* early.
I have never done it *that way* before.

Although these words meet the noun test, they modify verbs. Anything that modifies a verb is adverbial, so these are called **adverbial nouns.**
A noun and its modifiers may also modify a preceding noun.

The game *last week* was exciting.

Our vacation *this year* will be in May.

Adverbs sometimes modify nouns. When this occurs the adverb always follows the noun.

The meeting *yesterday* was more interesting than the one *now*.

Look at the picture *below.*

Differences in Form

Many adjectives and adverbs are different in form.

Adjectives	Adverbs
good (opposite of *bad*)	well (opposite of *badly*)
well (opposite of *sick*)	
bad	badly
nice	nicely
sad	sadly
terrible	terribly
eager	eagerly
(etc.)	(etc.)

When adjectives and adverbs differ in form, nearly always the adverb is made by adding *ly* to the adjective. *Well,* however, is the adverb
that matches the adjective *good*. A person may *feel* good/bad/happy/
sick/well (adjectives after a linking verb) but *sing* well/badly/happily
(adverbs after any other kind of verb).

Of course, some pairs of adjectives and adverbs have exactly the
same form. Many of these adjective/adverb pairs have no ending at all,
but others have *ly* or some other ending.

EITHER ADJECTIVES   fast, hard, far, late, straight; weekly, hourly,
     OR ADVERBS   only, early; northward

There are also adjectives (like *old*) that have no related adverb form,
and adverbs (like *often*) that have no related adjective form.

A few adverbs have forms with or without *ly,* such as *slow/slowly.*
Slow tends to be used in certain expressions ("His watch runs slow")
and in very informal or forceful speech ("Go slow around that curve").
In general, however, we use *slowly* ("He walked slowly down the
street"). Certain adverbs with *ly* have a different meaning from those
without *ly:* "He was trying *hard,*" but "I can *hardly* see that kite."

Some adjectives have forms ending in *ly* such as *friendly, manly,*
and *motherly.* Remember that an adjective plus *ly* is an adverb; a noun
plus *ly* is an adjective.

Degrees of Adjectives and Adverbs

Many adjectives and adverbs have degree forms. In the **positive degree** no comparison is made.

> The sargassum fish looks *strange*. It swims *quickly* among the seaweed.

An adjective or adverb's **comparative degree** compares two persons or things.

> The anableps fish, which has four eyes, looks *stranger* than the sargassum. It swims *more quickly* than the sargassum.

The **superlative degree** is a comparison of three or more persons or things. It indicates that something is first or last on a scale of comparison.

> The umbrella mouth gulper eel, with its gigantic dropped jaw and long tail, looks *strangest* of all. This eel probably swims *most quickly* of the three.

Often the number of things being compared is not indicated directly. A good speaker or writer considers context carefully before deciding which degree to use.

> At fifteen tons, the whale shark is the *largest* known fish.
> (The context of the sentence suggests that the whale shark is being compared to all fish, so the superlative is used.)

Avoid the temptation to use the superlative degree when comparing only two things.

> **INCORRECT** Mrs. Peters has two children. The youngest is almost two, and the oldest is four.
> (Since Mrs. Peters has only two children, the comparative degree should be used: younger and older.)
>
> **INCORRECT** Of her two hobbies, Mrs. Peters enjoys gardening most.
> (Mrs. Peters has only two hobbies; therefore, she would not enjoy one of them most.)

Regular Comparisons of Adjectives

Nearly all one-syllable adjectives are compared with *er* and *est*.

Positive	Comparative	Superlative
nice	nicer	nicest
tall	taller	tallest
big	bigger	biggest

Also, some two-syllable adjectives take *er* and *est*, especially adjectives that end in *y, ly,* and *le*.

Positive	Comparative	Superlative
busy	busier	busiest
messy	messier	messiest
early	earlier	earliest
friendly	friendlier	friendliest
noble	nobler	noblest
simple	simpler	simplest

Otherwise, you can expect an adjective to be compared with *more* and *most*.

Positive	Comparative	Superlative
careful	more careful	most careful
famous	more famous	most famous
beautiful	more beautiful	most beautiful

Absolute Comparative and Superlative of Adjectives

The comparative and the superlative are sometimes used in an "absolute" sense—that is, without any intention of specific comparison to other things.

ABSOLUTE COMPARATIVE (MOSTLY A FEW SET PHRASES)	My cousin, who teaches college English, has always been involved in *higher education.* (There is no phrase "high education" for the level just before college.)
ABSOLUTE SUPERLATIVE FOR EMPHASIS	He gave me the *strangest* look. (No comparison intended, just the meaning "a very strange look.")

Although the absolute superlative is perfectly legitimate, when written it is likely to be misunderstood for normal comparison with something unnamed. For that reason it should be used in written material only with caution. And in a sentence like "She wore the most beautiful dress yesterday," the emphasis of the absolute superlative can easily become a gushy overemphasis.

Regular Comparisons of Adverbs

Some adverbs have no change in form at all, but others have the same changes for comparison that adjectives have. Most dictionaries give you help as to whether to use *er/est* or *more/most*. One reliable rule is that adverbs made from adjectives by the addition of *ly* always take *more* and *most,* never *er* or *est.*

He walked . . .

Positive	Comparative	Superlative
soon	sooner	(the) soonest
fast	faster	(the) fastest
often	more often	(the) most often
carefully	more carefully	(the) most carefully
happily	more happily	(the) most happily

Irregular Comparisons of Adjectives and Adverbs

There are some exceptions to the rules for comparing adjectives and adverbs. A few adjectives, such as *red* and *common,* can use either *er/est* or *more/most.*

After applying the dye, Angela thought her dress looked *more red* than she had intended.

Reggie's face had never been *redder* than when he fell off his bike in the church parking lot.

Fried chicken is arguably the *most common* picnic food.

Ants are often the *commonest* guests at an outdoor event.

Some adjectives are irregular. When in doubt, check a dictionary.

little	less	least
ill	worse	worst
good	better	best
bad	worse	worst

The forms for the most common irregular adverb are *well, better,* and *best.*

> Carter sews *well.*
>
> His mother sews *better* than he does.
>
> Grandma Lewis sews the *best* in that family.

Use only one negative word to make a sentence convey negative meaning. Using another negative word along with the adverb *not* is called a **double negative.** To correct a double negative, eliminate one of the negative words.

> INCORRECT   We did*n't* bring *nothing* to change into.
>
> CORRECT   We brought nothing to change into.
> We didn't bring anything to change into.

Placement of Modifiers

Misplaced Modifiers

If the position of the modifier makes it seem to modify the wrong word in the sentence, it is **misplaced** and should be moved closer to the word it modifies. A modifier needs to be reasonably close to the word it modifies.

> ADVERB   I asked him what he meant, but he *only* laughed.
>
> ADJECTIVE   *Only* the red berries are any good.
> He picked *only* the red ones.

In the second and third sentences *only* is an adjective that limits the meaning of *berries* or *ones.*

In sentences like the third example, there is a very strong tendency (especially in spoken English) to move this limiting adjective to the adverbial position before the verb:

> SPOKEN STYLE   He only picked the red ones.

In spoken English this construction is usually perfectly clear because the speaker can add his own emphasis (usually to the word *red*). However, in writing there may be a problem, since the reader must guess at the author's emphasis. A reader may wonder: Is it that he only *picked* them (but never *ate* them or *baked with* them, etc.)?

In writing, a word like *only* that appears in the adverb position is considered a **misplaced modifier.** It should be moved next to the word or phrase it is intended to modify.

These are the main words to watch:

almost	just
especially	merely
even	nearly
exactly	only
hardly	simply

Although *not* is more freely movable, it too can cause problems.

PROBLEMATIC	All of them were *not* late.
BETTER	*Not* all of them were late.

Phrases and clauses too should be near what they modify. If they are not, confusion or unintended humor may be the result.

MISPLACED MODIFIER	*Living an average of twenty years,* the park guide explained that some grizzly bears prefer to return to the same den each year for hibernation.
CORRECTION	The park guide explained that some grizzly bears, *living an average of twenty years,* prefer to return to the same den each year for hibernation.

An adjectival phrase that comes before the subject is usually assumed to modify the subject. Move the misplaced modifying phrase next to the word it should modify.

Misplaced modifying phrases may occur elsewhere in the sentence also.

MISPLACED MODIFIER	The best-of-breed winner was the French poodle *standing in front of the judge* with a ribbon around his neck.
CORRECTION	The best-of-breed winner was the French poodle with a ribbon around his neck, *the one standing in front of the judge.*

Furthermore, clauses too may be misplaced.

MISPLACED MODIFIER	Yesterday we saw a hot-air balloon above the lake *that was carrying two women.*
CORRECTION	Yesterday we saw a hot-air balloon *that was carrying two women* above the lake.

Two-way Modifiers

A **two-way modifier** is unclear because it stands between two sentence elements that it might modify. We cannot tell which of the two it modifies, so we cannot be sure what meaning was intended.

TWO-WAY MODIFIER   Our teacher said *in the fall* we could observe the migration of birds.

Did she say it in the fall? Or can the observation be done in the fall? The sentence can be corrected to express either meaning.

CORRECTED FOR   *In the fall* our teacher said that we
ONE MEANING   could observe the migration of birds.

CORRECTED FOR   Our teacher said that *in the fall* we could observe the
OTHER MEANING   migration of birds.

Dangling Modifiers

Picture dangling modifiers as dangling in space, having nothing to modify. A dangling modifier cannot be corrected simply by moving it, for the word that it should modify is not in the sentence.

DANGLING   *Coming down the street,* the Wrigley Building appeared
MODIFIER   on our left.

DANGLING   *While in the South,* "Swanee River" became one of my
MODIFIER   favorite songs.

Who or what was coming down the street? Surely not the Wrigley Building. The modifier is "dangling" because the implied subject of *coming* is not the same as the actual subject of the sentence. *While in the South* is a dangling modifier because it should describe *I* but instead seems to describe *"Swanee River."*

One way to correct a dangling modifier is to change the modifier into a complete clause that includes the missing element:

CORRECTION   *As we were* coming down the street, the Wrigley
Building appeared on our left.

CORRECTION   *While I was living in the South,* "Swanee River" became one of my favorite songs.

Another way is to change the rest of the sentence so that the missing element is supplied right next to the modifier:

CORRECTION	Coming down the street, we saw the Wrigley Building on our left.
CORRECTION	While in the South, I acquired a new favorite song, "Swanee River."

Modifiers That Split Infinitives

Sometimes a modifier comes between the *to* of an infinitive and the next verb word. The resulting construction is called a **split infinitive.** Split infinitives are not ungrammatical in English, but they may be awkward—especially if the modifier is several words long.

AWKWARD SPLIT INFINITIVE	She began *to* with faltering steps *walk* toward the front.
IMPROVED SENTENCE	With faltering steps, she began *to walk* toward the front.

Some people disapprove of all split infinitives, but it is worth noticing that the proposed alternatives are themselves sometimes awkward.

ACCEPTABLE SPLIT INFINITIVE	*To* really *understand* his problem, you should hear what happened yesterday.
AWKWARD WORDING	Really *to understand* his problem, you should hear what happened yesterday.

Often, though, you can improve a sentence by eliminating a split infinitive.

Verb Use

Principal Parts

All the forms of nearly every English verb can be made from just three basic forms, or **principal parts,** of the verb. That is, if you know the three principal parts of a verb and how to use them, you can make any form of that verb. (*Principal* here means "main.")

Regular Verbs

Grammarians differentiate between regular and irregular verbs. **Regular verbs** form their second and third principal parts by adding *d* or *ed* to the first principal part; therefore, the second and third principal parts are identical.

carry	carried	carried
kick	kicked	kicked
want	wanted	wanted

Notice that the second and third principal parts of *carry, kick,* and *want* are made by adding *ed* to the first principal part. Notice that *carry* is considered a regular verb despite the spelling change. A few otherwise regular verbs substitute *t* for *d* or *ed*. (See Ch. 12 for additional spelling hints.)

bend	bent	bent
build	built	built

Irregular Verbs

Irregular verbs form their second and third principal parts in various ways. Some irregular verbs show a pattern of vowel changes in each principal part.

begin	began	begun
drink	drank	drunk
break	broke	broken
grow	grew	grown

Many have two principal parts that are the same.

flee	fled	fled
win	won	won

And for a few verbs all three principal parts are the same.

cost	cost	cost
quit	quit	quit

A good dictionary will help you find the three principal parts of any words with which you are unfamiliar.

Uses of the Principal Parts Active Voice			
Principal parts:	break (present)	broke (past)	broken (past participle)
	PRESENT	**PAST**	**FUTURE**
SIMPLE	break/breaks	broke	will break
PROGRESSIVE	am/are/ is breaking	was/were breaking	will be breaking
PERFECT	have/has broken	had broken	will have broken
PERFECT PROGRESSIVE	have/has been breaking	had been breaking	will have been breaking

NOTE: For passive voice all tenses use *broken*.

Troublesome Verbs

Present	Past	Past Participle
begin	began	begun
bite	bit	bitten
blow	blew	blown
break	broke	broken
bring	brought	brought
burst	burst	burst
buy	bought	bought
catch	caught	caught
choose	chose	chosen
climb	climbed	climbed

cling	clung	clung
come	came	come
dig	dug	dug
dive	dived (or dove)	dived
do	did	done
drag	dragged	dragged
draw	drew	drawn
drink	drank	drunk
drive	drove	driven
drown	drowned	drowned
eat	ate	eaten
fall	fell	fallen
fly	flew	flown
forget	forgot	forgotten or forgot
freeze	froze	frozen
get	got	gotten or got
give	gave	given
go	went	gone
grow	grew	grown
hang (by the neck)	hanged	hanged
hang (other meanings)	hung	hung
hide	hid	hidden
kneel	knelt (or kneeled)	knelt or kneeled
know	knew	known
lay "place"	laid	laid
lead	led	led
lie "recline"	lay	lain
light	lighted (or lit)	lighted or lit
lose "mislay"	lost	lost
raise "lift up"	raised	raised
ride	rode	ridden
ring	rang	rung
rise "go up"	rose	risen
run	ran	run
see	saw	seen
set	set	set
shake	shook	shaken
shine "polish"	shined	shined
shine "beam, polish"	shone (or shined)	shone or shined
show	showed	shown or showed
shrink	shrank (or shrunk)	shrunk
sing	sang	sung
sink	sank (or sunk)	sunk
sit	sat	sat

sneak	sneaked	sneaked
speak	spoke	spoken
spring	sprang (or sprung)	sprung
steal	stole	stolen
swim	swam	swum
swing	swung	swung
throw	threw	thrown
weep	wept	wept
wring	wrung	wrung
write	wrote	written

Verb Tenses

English tenses are sufficiently complicated that whole books have been written on some of them, but below is a systematic summary of the basic tense meanings. These meanings have to do mainly with time.

Verbs express action or state of being. (State-of-being verbs are used to describe a state or condition. They are not necessarily linking verbs.) The difference between action verbs and state-of-being verbs turns out to be important for some tenses. For example, present time is expressed by the plain present tense for state-of-being verbs.

I *like* band music.

I *have* a new coat.

For action verbs, though, we must use the present progressive to express present time.

He *is walking* to school (right now).

If we try to use the plain present tense with action verbs, we get instead a statement of what normally happens.

He *walks* to school (every day).

Notice that we do not use the present progressive for state-of-being verbs.

UNGRAMMATICAL   I *am liking* band music (today).

I *am having* a new coat (this year).

The point is that tense forms sometimes depend on which kind of verb is used.

Certain verbs can be used either as action verbs or as state-of-being verbs. We have used *have* as a state-of-being verb meaning "to possess."

Have can also be used as an action verb, and in that sense it can take the present progressive.

> She *is having* a party tonight.

In other words, whether a verb expresses an action or a state of being may depend on the rest of the sentence.

Simple Tenses

The difference between action and state-of-being verbs is particularly important in understanding the uses and meanings of the present tense.

The **present tense** expresses present time for state-of-being verbs.

> Our school *has* two soccer teams.
> I *like* band music.

For action verbs, the present tense expresses habitual action, telling what normally happens.

> He *walks* to school every day, but he *rides* the bus home.
> The sun *rises* in the east.

The **past tense** expresses past time—either an action that was done in an earlier time period or a state that existed in an earlier time period.

> It *rained* a lot last year.
> He *studied* all day yesterday.
> We *had* two soccer teams.

The **future tense** expresses future time, for either an action or a state.

> Maybe it *will rain* this afternoon.
> I *will study* it again before the test.
> Next year we *will have* two soccer teams.

Perfect Tenses

The perfect has to do mainly with actions or states of being that are completed ("perfected"). The perfect tenses always use some form of the auxiliary *have*.

Strictly speaking, tense has to do only with time (past, present, and future), and the added meanings of perfect and progressive are **aspects,** having to do with the *kind* of action a verb expresses. The perfect aspect refers basically to *completed* actions and the progressive aspect to *continuing* actions in the past, present, or future. However, for convenience we do often refer to the "present perfect tense," for example.

109

The **present perfect** expresses an action or state completed during the present time period or one that has continued up to the present moment. This tense uses the auxiliary *have* or *has*.

It *has rained* a lot this year.
He *has studied* all evening.
I *have done* my homework.
I *have* always *liked* band music.

The **past perfect** expresses an action that was completed (or a state that existed) before a certain time in the past. Past perfect tenses use the auxiliary verb *had*. Past perfect should be used only when two past actions are being discussed, one of which occurred before the other one.

When the sun rose, we *had been* awake for an hour already.
(Both the sun's rising and the being awake happened in the past; the being awake occurred before the sun's rising.)

We learned that it *had rained* during the night.
(Two past actions, one occurring before the other.)

The **future perfect** expresses an action that will be completed (or a state that will exist) by or before a certain time in the future. The future perfect tense uses *will have* or *shall have*.

Don't worry—by test time I *will have studied* it two more times.
By this time tomorrow she *will have taken* that medicine for a whole week.
In early October we *will have had* our first soccer team just one month.

Progressive Tenses

The progressive expresses continuing action (action in progress). The progressive is made by adding some form of the auxiliary *be,* and by putting an *ing* suffix on the next word in the complete verb.

The **present progressive** expresses present time for verbs that show action.

He *is walking* to school right now.
The sun *is rising.*

The **past progressive** expresses a continuing action in past time. It is used especially to show that the action was in progress at the time of another event.

It *was raining* when I left the house.

I *was sleeping* when the sun rose.

At seven o'clock we *were doing* our homework.

The **future progressive** expresses continuing action in the future.

Do you think it *will* still *be raining* at four o'clock?

We *will be writing* letters when Marcy walks in.

Perfect Progressive Tenses

The **present perfect progressive** expresses a continuing action that was done during the present time period. It emphasizes that the action has continued over a period of time.

He *has been studying* all evening.

It *has been raining* all day.

Have you *been listening* to the radio?

The **past perfect progressive** expresses a continuing action that was completed before a certain time in the past. It emphasizes that the action was a continuing one.

When the sun rose, we *had been working* for an hour already.

We learned that it *had been raining* all night.

The **future perfect progressive** expresses a continuing action that will be completed by or before a certain time in the future.

When you get back from the store, I *will* probably *have been working* on the car for quite a while.

In another ten minutes it *will have been raining* for an hour.

Consistency and Sequence of Tenses

Correct tenses are especially important for clarity so that the reader will know the time and order of the events being described.

Consistency of Tenses

The present tense is often used to tell about the events in someone's story or other literary work. This fictional present time is sometimes called the "literary present." In a present-tense passage, the present perfect tense is used for earlier events.

LITERARY PRESENT   After he *has been* on the island for a while, Crusoe *sees* footprints on the beach. (present perfect, present)

The past (and past perfect) can also be used to tell a story.

NORMAL PAST   After he *had been* on the island for a while, Crusoe *saw* footprints on the beach. (past perfect, past)

Either system of tenses is correct, but the two should not be mixed.

MIXED TENSES   Crusoe *has been* on the island for a while. Then one day he *saw* footprints on the beach.

Crusoe *had been* on the island for a while. Then one day he *sees* footprints on the beach.

Mixed tense systems make writing seem carelessly done.

In conversation an ordinary series of past events may be expressed in the present tense to make it seem more vivid.

ORAL   "So then the manager *comes* into the room and *asks* us what we *want*."

In writing, however, the past tense is usually expected.

WRITTEN   Then the manager *came* into the room and *asked* us what we *wanted*.

Again, it is important not to mix the two.

MIXED (INCORRECT)   Then the manager *comes* into the room and *asked* us what we *want*.

Sequence of Tenses

The concern with "sequence of tenses" has to do with how the tenses of two clauses work together to relate the times of two events.

Especially in written English, the past perfect is the proper tense to use for an action that precedes another action in the past. Do not use the plain past tense for both of them.

IMPRECISE   After he *spent* some time there, he left.
BETTER   After he *had spent* some time there, he *left*.

Notice the tenses in Acts 18:22-23.

> "And when he *had landed* at Caesarea . . . he *went* down to Antioch.
> And after he *had spent* some time there, he *departed,* and *went* over all the
> country of Galatia and Phrygia. . . ."

In both sentences, the first clause uses the past perfect tense for an action already completed before the past event of the second clause.
Sometimes the second clause portrays the earlier action.

> He *misplaced* the book that he *had read.*

Of course, two verbs in the plain past tense properly describe two things that happened (or were true) at the same time.

> He *misplaced* the book that he liked the best.

An Exception: Present Tense for a Universal Truth

If two things took place or were true at the same time in the past, usually we express both of them in the past tense.

> Columbus *showed* that the world *was* round.

However, when one of them is an enduring truth—something still true today—we normally use the present tense for the universal truth.

> Columbus *showed* that the world *is* round.

Auxiliaries for Modal Expressions

Modal auxiliaries express certain things about the speaker's attitude toward the action or state he is talking about. These auxiliaries show such things as whether the speaker thinks the action or state is possible, doubtful, likely, permitted, or necessary.

> I *may learn* a great deal this year.
> That man *might be* a dentist.

The common modal auxiliaries are as follows: *can, could, may, might, should, would, must, ought (to).* These auxiliaries always come first in the complete verb, and in standard English only one is used at a time.

An Auxiliary for Emphasis and Other Uses

In the active voice the simple present and the past tenses have no auxiliary. However, there are a number of situations in which an auxiliary is needed—to show emphasis, to help make a sentence negative, to form many kinds of questions, and so on. In those situations, if there is not already an auxiliary, one of the simple forms of *do* is added to the verb: *do, does,* or *did.*

One obvious use of the auxiliary *do* is for emphasis. Notice these two examples:

"I will take out the trash later."

"No, you won't—you'll forget."

"Oh yes, I *will* take it out. I'll remember."

"Jeff likes the blue plaid best."

"Oh? I'm sure he'd choose the green, as always."

"No, he *does* like the blue best; he told me so."

In the first example, where the auxiliary *will* already appears in the statement, greater stress on the *will* emphasizes the whole statement. In the second example, the verb *likes* has no auxiliary, so it is changed to *does like* and heavy stress is put on the *does* for emphasis.

The auxiliary *do* can perform several functions in addition to showing emphasis. In all these functions it is used only when some other auxiliary is not already present. Notice the parallel between the uses of *did* and *will* in the situations below. The basic sentences are "He finished" and "He will finish."

NEGATIVE	He did not finish.
	He will not finish.
QUESTION	Did he finish?
INVERSION	Will he finish?
TAG QUESTION	He finished, didn't he?
	He'll finish, won't he?
OMISSION OF	He finished, and I did too.
MAIN VERB	He'll finish, and I will too.

Voice

Just as each verb has a tense, all verbs have voice. **Voice** is the verb-form difference that signals the role of the subject in relation to the verb. English has two voices, the **active** and the **passive.**

Defining Active and Passive

In most sentences the subject does something or is something.

The twins slept.

Your uncle is an effective preacher.

My new friend chose a good story today.

In sentences like these, when the subject either "is" or *acts,* the verb is **active,** and the sentence is active. As a matter of fact, all the basic sentence patterns are for active sentences. Some sentences, though, can be restated in such a way that something is done *to* the subject.

A good story was chosen.

or

A good story was chosen by my new friend.

When the subject is *acted upon,* as in these sentences, the verb is **passive.** Only transitive verbs—those that have direct objects—can be made passive.

All passive voice sentences use a form of the auxiliary *be* just before the main verb.

	Active	**Passive**
PRESENT	breaks	*is* broken
PRESENT PROGRESSIVE	are breaking	are *being* broken
PAST PERFECT	had broken	had *been* broken
PRESENT WITH MODAL AUXILIARY	might break	might *be* broken

Making Active and Passive Sentences

To make a passive sentence, we start with an active sentence that has a transitive verb and a direct object.

     S   TrV-A   DO

My new friend chose a good story today.

The label TrV-A shows that this is the normal, active form of the transitive verb. (TrV-P will stand for the passive form.) First, move the direct object to the subject position.

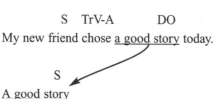

```
        S   TrV-A        DO
My new friend chose a good story today.


            S
A good story
```

Then change the verb from active to passive, keeping the same tense. Here the past active verb *chose* becomes the past passive verb *was chosen*.

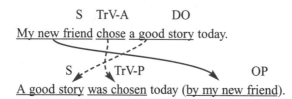

```
        S   TrV-A        DO
My new friend chose a good story today.


        S        TrV-P
A good story was chosen
```

If the doer is mentioned, it becomes the object of the preposition *by*. Here we will put the *by* phrase inside parentheses to show that it could be omitted. Adverbial modifiers like *today* stay in the same general part of the sentence.

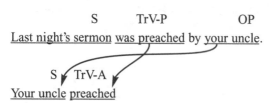

```
        S   TrV-A        DO
My new friend chose a good story today.


        S        TrV-P                OP
A good story was chosen today (by my new friend).
```

The resulting sentence, as well as the complete verb, can be called passive. The sentence is passive because the subject is not the doer, but the receiver of action. That is, it is *acted upon*.

You can also start with a passive sentence and change it to active. In that case, do all the steps in reverse. Take the object of the preposition *by* and make it the subject (leaving out the *by*), and change the verb back to active voice.

```
        S        TrV-P                OP
Last night's sermon was preached by your uncle.


        S   TrV-A
Your uncle preached
```

Then take the passive subject and make it the direct object.

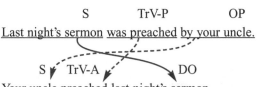

Last night's sermon was preached by your uncle.

Your uncle preached last night's sermon.

Notice that the active sentence here seems more "active" and interesting.

If you ever want to make an active sentence out of a passive sentence that does not mention the doer, you either have to figure out who the doer is or use an indefinite word like *someone*.

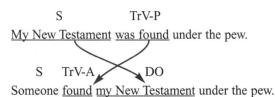

My New Testament was found under the pew.

Someone found my New Testament under the pew.

It is usually best not to use *they* as an indefinite subject.

POOR	They teach piano at this school.

IMPROVED	Piano is taught at this school.
	We take piano at this school.
	Miss Solberg teaches piano here after school.

Remember that the passive-voice tenses are made up of the regular tense forms of *be* added to the past participle (the third principal part) of the verb in question.

Using Active and Passive Sentences

Sometimes what you have written can be improved by changing an active sentence to a passive, or a passive to an active.

Advantages of Active Sentences

Although the passive can be useful, the best general advice is this: do not overuse the passive. Your writing will be more lively and strong if you normally mention the doer first, then the action, and then the receiver of the action. An occasional passive sentence is fine, but too many of them hang weights on your writing. Notice the difference:

TOO MANY PASSIVES	He was first discouraged by the thought of all that work. Then he was reminded that he would be helped by God, and he was cheered up.

BETTER At first the thought of all that work discouraged him. Then he remembered that God would help him, and he cheered up.

Besides being more direct and vivid, the second version is also shorter. Shortness and directness often go together.

Advantages of Passive Sentences

Although the active voice is usually preferred, sometimes the passive is useful. Clearly, the passive is a handy way to avoid mentioning the doer of an action. For instance, the doer may be unimportant or unknown.

GOOD USE OF The money was kept in the store's safe overnight.
PASSIVES The doors to the Sunday school rooms are opened before 9:00 A.M. on Sunday.

You may also use the passive to keep your subjects the same for several verbs in a row. Doing so may help your sentences flow more smoothly.

ACCEPTABLE When *parents* ask children to help in the home, *the children* learn responsibility. If *parents* expect children to do their share, *these children* will also be more thoughtful when they grow up.

BETTER When *children* are asked to help in the home, *they* learn
(CONSISTENT responsibility. If *they* are expected to do their share as
SUBJECTS) children, *they* will also be more thoughtful as adults.

Again, the better version also turns out to be shorter.

Finally, the passive lets us move certain kinds of things from the subject position to the end of the sentence. For example, it is often awkward to have a long phrase as a subject.

AWKWARDLY LONG *Parents, brothers and sisters, other relatives,* and *even*
SUBJECT *friends* teach the young child.

BETTER *The young child* is taught by parents, brothers and sisters, other relatives, and even friends.

The end of the sentence is a naturally strong position. Therefore, it is usually better to save the new or more important information for the end of the sentence, putting the old information at the beginning.

PASSIVE USED TO Emphasis can be obtained by *several methods.*
MOVE A PHRASE
TO THE END

Retained Objects in Passive Sentences

Some transitive sentences in the active voice have both direct and indirect objects (complements). When an active sentence is made passive, one of the two complements becomes the subject of the new sentence, and the other remains as a complement. This complement is called a **retained object.**

		S TrV-A IO DO
ACTIVE		Tom gave Joan a party.

		S TrV-P RO
PASSIVE		Joan was given a party (by Tom).

Subjective Complements in Passive Sentences

When a sentence with the pattern S-TrV-DO-OC is made passive, the objective complement is made a **subjective complement** because it now renames or describes the subject.

	S TrV-A DO OC
ACTIVE	Yesterday the boss called Stan a hard worker.

	S TrV-P SC
PASSIVE	Yesterday Stan was called a hard worker.

Consistency of Voice

We have much more freedom in varying between active and passive voice than we have in changing from one tense to another. However, a shift in voice can create an awkward, unfocused sentence.

Try not to shift from one voice to another within the same sentence, especially if that shift prevents the subjects of the verbs from being the same.

POOR SHIFT IN VOICE In that way our work *could be completed,* and we *could go* shopping sooner.

The first verb is passive, and the second is active. Notice the improvement when both are made active.

BETTER In that way we *could complete* our work, and we *could go* shopping sooner.

BETTER YET In that way we *could complete* our work and *go* shopping sooner.

The final version combines the two clauses into one.

Mood

The three moods (or "modes") of English verbs have no simple overall meaning, but they have to do with the speaker's attitude toward what he is saying.

INDICATIVE MOOD   Factual, real, or probable
IMPERATIVE MOOD   Commanded
SUBJUNCTIVE MOOD   Nonfactual or doubtful

However, the moods are recognized more by their form than by their meaning.

Indicative Mood

The indicative mood is the "normal" mood, the one most used. We need the term only to differentiate the normal forms from those of the imperative and subjunctive moods.

I *played* two songs.

Marta *enjoys* missionary biographies.

Imperative Mood

The imperative mood is used to give direct commands. The verb is in its simple present form, with no auxiliary; and the subject *you* is usually omitted except for clarity or special emphasis.

IMPERATIVE   *Clean* up your plate first.
                 You *sit* here, and Jack can sit there.

Other, less direct ways of giving commands or making requests are in the indicative mood.

INDICATIVE   You *will* please *bring* your own paper.
               You *must bring* your own paper.

Subjunctive Mood

The subjunctive mood, used much less today than in former centuries, consists of a set of common verb forms that are used in special ways. In general, the subjunctive expresses the idea that a thing is untrue though perhaps desired. It may also express a wish, a necessity, or an obligation.

Forms of the Subjunctive

The subjunctive-mood verb forms themselves all look familiar, but they are used differently from the indicative forms. Specifically, they are subjunctive because their time reference differs from what it would be in the normal indicative mood.

The verb *come* is used below as typical of all verbs other than *be*.

Subjunctive Form	Time	Example
were	present or future	1. If he were here now, he would tell us. 2. If he were here tomorrow at 3:00, we might be able to use his help.
had been	simple past	3. If he had been here last night, he would have told us.
came	present or future	4. If he came now, it might help. 5. If he came tomorrow, it would be too late.
had come	simple past	6. If he had come, he would have brought his neighbors.
be	timeless	7. She insisted that he be on time.
come (no *s*)	timeless	8. It was (is, will be) necessary that he come too.

The two forms marked "timeless" might be considered as unlimited by time (always true), or they may be understood in relation to the time of the main verb.

Notice that the top part of the table contains forms that look like past verbs, and notice that all these are used in clauses with *if*. The last two forms in the table are the same as those used in infinitives (to *be*, to *come*).

Uses of the Subjunctive

The three main uses of the subjunctive are all illustrated in the table above.

Conditions contrary to fact are expressed by subjunctive forms in educated general usage. These are clauses that begin with *if* (condition clauses) and that speak of something known to be untrue (contrary to

121

fact). In the table above, the first, third, and sixth examples are conditions contrary to fact. By contrast, when we do not know whether a condition is true or not, we use an indicative verb.

> If he *is* here now, he *will* tell us.
>
> If he *was* here last night, he probably *enjoyed* the meeting.

However, it is not correct to use the indicative in conditions that are contrary to fact; here only the subjunctive is acceptable in standard English. Remember, "I say 'if I *were* you' because I am *not* you."

Doubtful future conditions may also use the subjunctive, as in sentences 2 and 5 in the table. These, however, may instead be expressed by the auxiliary *would.*

> If he would be here tomorrow . . .
>
> If he would come tomorrow . . .

The sentences with the subjunctives show perhaps more doubt than the ones with *would,* but either form is correct.

Clauses after expressions of obligation and recommendation use the subjunctive mood. As sentences 7 and 8 in the table show, these expressions may be verbs *(insisted)* or adjectives *(necessary).* Sometimes the expression of obligation or recommendation may even be a noun, such as the noun *suggestion.*

> She made the suggestion that he *be* on time.

Here are some additional examples:

> I move that the meeting *be adjourned.*
>
> The letter demands (asks, suggests) that she *keep* her dog quiet at night.
>
> It is recommended (imperative) that some babies *be given* fluoride.

Without the subjunctive, the idea of obligation would disappear:

> The letter suggests that she keeps her dog quiet at night.

Now the letter suggests merely what the fact is, not what she should do.

Even though the plain indicative cannot substitute for the subjunctive in such sentences, sometimes the sentence can be acceptably reworded with an auxiliary like *should.* (This substitution would work with *suggests,* but not with *demands,* for instance.)

Finally, certain **set expressions** use the subjunctive. Notice that several of these express desire.

God be with you.	So be it.
God be praised.	Thy will be done.
Thy kingdom come.	Be that as it may,
Heaven forbid.	Come what may,
Long live the King!	Suffice it to say,

Idiomatic Use of Verbs

Some verbs can have direct objects and others cannot. Sometimes it also makes a difference what kind of direct object follows the verb.

Transitive and Intransitive Verbs

Certain verbs, normally intransitive, sound odd when they are used transitively, that is, with an object.

UNIDIOMATIC TRANSITIVE   The programmer *vanished* the numbers from the screen.

CORRECTION   The programmer *made the numbers vanish* from the screen.
The programmer *deleted* the numbers from the screen.

There are also verbs that are always transitive; these sound odd in an intransitive construction.

UNIDIOMATIC INTRANSITIVE   That explanation just *confuses.*

CORRECTION   That explanation just confuses *me.*

UNIDIOMATIC INTRANSITIVE   He tried not to *embarrass.*

CORRECTION   He tried not to embarrass *his friend.*

Desk dictionaries label verbs as transitive or intransitive or both. (Transitive verbs can have objects and be made passive; in a dictionary, intransitive verbs are all the others.) If a particular verb can be either transitive or intransitive, the meanings will be clearly grouped into the two categories. Use this information to correct the kinds of problems illustrated above.

Verbs That Require Personal Objects

Certain verbs require personal objects. That is, either the direct or the indirect object must refer to a person in some way.

UNIDIOMATIC   "It won't be hard to use," he *reassured.*

CORRECTION   "It won't be hard to use," he reassured *them.*
"It won't be hard to use," he *said.*

Here is another example:

UNIDIOMATIC   The computer will *enable* better inventory control.

CORRECTION   The computer will enable *us* to control our inventory better.
The computer will *make possible* better inventory control.

As is illustrated here, corrections can be made by supplying the personal object or by replacing the verb.

Verbs That Require Nouns, Not Clauses, as Direct Objects

There are a few verbs that can be followed by nouns or pronouns, but not directly by an object clause.

UNIDIOMATIC   The chairman likes *that we will all help.*
CORRECTION   The chairman likes the *idea* that we will all help.

In the second version *idea* is the direct object, and the noun clause is the appositive to *idea.*

UNIDIOMATIC   She could not accept *that he would do that.*

CORRECTION   She could not accept the *idea/fact* that he would do that.
She could not *believe* that he would do that.

Solve this kind of problem by supplying a noun to be the direct object or by changing the verb.

Verbs That Allow Gerunds, Infinitives, or Clauses as Direct Objects

Relatively few verbs can have gerunds, infinitives, or noun clauses as direct objects. *Prefer* is unusual in allowing all three.

GERUND PHRASE	She prefers *driving alone.*
AS OBJECT	She prefers *our following her.*
INFINITIVE PHRASE	She prefers *to drive alone.*
AS OBJECT	She prefers *us to follow her.*
NOUN CLAUSE	She prefers *that she would go first.*
AS OBJECT	She prefers *that we (would) follow her.*

Other verbs are less flexible. For instance, *like, love,* and *hate* can be followed by gerunds or infinitives, but not clauses beginning with *that.* *Ask* can be followed by infinitives and clauses but not gerunds. *Want* takes infinitives but not gerunds or clauses. And *declare* and *read* take clauses but not verbals.

Normally these special uses give us no problem; we learned them easily as children. Breaking one of these restrictions, though, would produce an unidiomatic sentence. The remedy is to change either the verb or the following construction.

UNIDIOMATIC	Parker likes *that he paints.*
CORRECTION	Parker likes *painting.*
	Parker likes *to paint.*
UNIDIOMATIC	She invited *that we would ride back with her.*
CORRECTION	She *suggested that we ride back with her.*
	She invited us *to ride back with her.*

Marks of Punctuation

Try to imagine having to write without any kind of punctuation marks. You would have no way to signal the end of your sentences; and without commas, your ideas would all run together. Punctuation gives writing a better "sound": it slows down your sentences, gives pauses, and creates emphasis. Correct use of punctuation will give your writing more credibility and increase its effectiveness. As you study the following rules, remember the primary purpose of punctuation: to keep the meaning clear.

End Marks

Sentences end with periods, question marks, and exclamation points. These end-punctuation marks are associated with specific types of sentences: declarative, imperative, interrogative, and exclamatory.

Period

Most sentences end with a period. A period signals the end of all declarative sentences and most imperative sentences.

The ship sailed safely through the dangerous enemy territory.

Use the phone at the end of the hall.

Question Mark

A question mark comes at the end of a direct question.

At what time did you deposit the money?

Indirect questions do not end with a question mark.

He asked if he could help carry these heavy boxes.

A request courteously stated like a question does not end with a question mark.

Would you please set those packages by the door.

A question mark follows interrogatives that end a sentence.

> He looked at his to-do list and asked himself, what should I do first?

A question mark follows each question in a sentence with elliptical questions.

> When you paint the two new rooms, will you need a bucket? paint? a brush?

Exclamation Point

An exclamation point shows strong feeling. It ends brief exclamations, exclamatory sentences, and some imperative sentences. It also follows some interjections.

> Wait! Don't move!
> There's a fire in the building!

The exclamation point should be used mainly in quoting spoken exclamations and should be used sparingly. The overuse of exclamation points usually seems overly emotional and may weaken the effectiveness of writing.

Other Uses of the Period

Initials and Abbreviations

Periods follow most abbreviations and initials.

Names and titles	Dr. Timothy Moore Sr.
	Anna Hall, M.D.
Periods may be omitted after most abbreviations of the names of government agencies and international organizations, including well-known businesses.	NASA (National Aerobatics and Space Administration)
	AT&T (American Telephone and Telegraph)
Terms in addresses	Redwood Ave.
	P.O. Box 50017
	New Brighton, MN 55112
Periods do not follow state or province postal abbreviations.	DE (Delaware)
	PEI (Prince Edward Island)

Times and dates	5:00 A.M.
	500 B.C.
Measurements	5 ft. 2 in.
	185 lb.
Periods should not be used with metric measurements.	8 km
	100 g

Outlines and Lists

A period follows each number or letter that shows a division of an outline.

I. Building dams
  A. Design
  B. Construction
II. Purposes for dams
  A. Water storage
    1. Land irrigation
    2. Electric power
  B. Flood control

A period follows each number or letter that precedes an item in a vertical list.

1. Choose party theme
2. Plan games
3. Purchase refreshments
4. Send invitations

For a list within a sentence, however, use parentheses and no periods.

In preparing for the party, we need to (1) choose the theme, (2) plan the games, (3) purchase the refreshments, and (4) send the invitations.

Commas

The comma is probably the most important mark of punctuation used inside the sentence. It is certainly the one used most often.

Commas in a Series

Although commas are used most often to set off certain elements from the rest of the sentence, they do have other customary uses.

In a Series of Equal Elements

A series of three or more words or groups of words of the same type, joined with a conjunction, should be punctuated as follows:

First item, second item, conjunction *third item*

First item, second item, third item, conjunction *fourth item*

The items joined might be single words or groups of words.

Marble, quartzite, and *slate* are metamorphic rocks.

Marble is used *for statuary and monuments, for fireproof floors and walls,* and *for the decoration of buildings.*

In some informal writing, the comma before the conjunction is omitted. However, you would be wise to make a habit of always using that comma; it is often needed and is never wrong.

With Coordinate Adjectives in a Series

Groups of adjectives can modify nouns in two different ways. One adjective may build on another:

a big red balloon   his new gray sweater

Here *big* tells us what kind of red balloon it is, and *new* tells us which gray sweater is meant. This is the usual situation, which does not call for any commas.

However, sometimes two adjectives have a similar meaning, so that both would not really be necessary to identify the thing described. These adjectives, called **coordinate adjectives,** modify the noun separately; we put a comma between them.

In the lobby of an office building, marble walls can give an *elegant, rich* appearance.

Participles can be coordinate in the same way.

That store has a *shining, glistening* appearance.

There is a test that can help you identify coordinate adjectives: coordinate adjectives can usually have *and* put between them and still sound correct.

an elegant **and** rich appearance = an elegant, rich appearance

(but not "his new and gray sweater")

In a Series of Independent Clauses

A comma is used to separate the first independent clause from the conjunction in a compound sentence. (Do not use a comma before a conjunction that joins the parts of a compound predicate.)

> Joe likes Mexican dishes, but Mark prefers Greek cuisine.
>
> (*But:* She walked down the street to the doctor's office but rode the bus to the mall.)

When two independent clauses are very short, the comma may be omitted before the conjunction.

> The air is warm and the water is calm.

If a compound sentence contains three or more independent clauses, a comma is used after all except the last.

> The air is warm, the sky is clear, and the water is calm.

See page 139 for the occasional use of a semicolon before the coordinating conjunction in a compound sentence.

Commas after Introductory Elements

Use a comma to set off certain kinds of elements when they come first in the sentence.

Introductory Participial Phrases

An introductory participle or participial phrase should be set off by a comma.

> *Knowing your ability,* I think you can do better.

Long Introductory Prepositional Phrases

A long prepositional phrase or multiple prepositional phrases at the beginning of a sentence should be set off by a comma.

> *In comparison with a month,* a week does not seem long.

There is no definite rule for "how long is long." Often, as here, a phrase of five or more words seems long enough to merit a comma.

Introductory Numbering Words

Commas are often used after numbering words like *first, second, next, finally,* and *last.*

> *First,* you should revise your story.

Introductory Adverb Clauses

An introductory adverb clause always requires a comma.

If you will work on it, that story can be really good.

Other Introductory Elements

Other introductory elements that may require commas include modifiers of the sentence as a whole.

To see it with fresh eyes, read it again after a week.

When the introductory phrase contains a verbal, a comma is often needed.

After rereading your story, you will probably see some ways to improve it.

Commas to Set Off Certain Sentence Elements

Commas often set off a word or a group of words from the rest of the sentence. The number of commas needed depends on where the word or word group is—at the beginning, in the middle, or at the end of the sentence.

However, I'd like you to wait awhile.
I'd like you, however, to wait awhile.
I'd like you to wait awhile, however.

At the beginning and at the end, just one comma is needed. In the middle, two commas are needed—regardless of whether or not you can "hear" them both. The following sentence elements are set off by commas wherever they come in the sentence.

Appositives

Most appositives are set off by commas.

Miss Campbell, *our English teacher,* would advise the same thing.

The exception is that no comma is used with a "close appositive"—a short appositive that is more specific than the noun before it.

Even the famous poet *John Keats* did much rewriting.

Adjectives After a Noun

Adjectives or participles joined by a conjunction often come after the noun. The modifying phrase is then set off by commas.

The hunters, *weary and dirty,* came in late.

An adjective modified by an adverb may come before or after the noun it modifies. Commas set off the adjective phrase if it follows the noun.

> Adv   Adj
> The *unusually lively* children kept the playground supervisor busy.

> Adv   Adj
> The children, *unusually lively,* kept him busy all hour.

Interjections

Most interjections are set off from the rest of the sentence by commas.

> *Yes,* I know the contest closes in three weeks.
> *Well,* wouldn't you rather send a better story?

Nouns of Direct Address

Sometimes we call a person by his name or courtesy title when we speak to him. That name or title, called a **noun of direct address,** should be set off by commas.

> *Jon,* you are the best writer in the class.
> Thank you very much, *sir,* for your encouragement.

Conjunctive Adverbs

Conjunctive adverbs like *however* and *though* are often said in such a way that there seems to be a pause before and after them. As long as the word does not come between two independent clauses, we indicate those two pauses with a pair of commas.

> Your story won't be good, *however,* if you hurry.

See pages 138-39 for conjunctive adverbs in compound sentences with semicolons.

Parenthetical Expressions

We use commas to set off a phrase that could be left out of the sentence.

> Haste, *as the saying goes,* does make waste.
> *As the saying goes,* haste does make waste.
> Haste does make waste, *as the saying goes.*

Tag Questions

Each sample sentence below was made into an interrogative sentence by the addition of a tag question. The tag question is separated from the rest of the sentence by a comma.

You did see my suggestions, *didn't you?*

John has not read the story yet, *has he?*

Phrases That Show Contrast

A phrase that shows contrast should be set off by commas, particularly when the phrase begins with a negative word like *not* or *never.*

Short stories, *not novels,* are his specialty.

He produces his first drafts at the keyboard, *never with pencil and paper.*

Restrictive and Nonrestrictive Elements

A **restrictive** modifier is one that is necessary to identify (restrict the possibilities to) the particular thing that is meant. Restrictive modifiers use no commas.

A **nonrestrictive** modifier gives extra information but is *not* necessary for identification of the thing modified. Nonrestrictive modifiers are set off by commas.

The examples below include nonrestrictive and restrictive modifiers of various types. Since appositives follow the same punctuation rule, they are included as well.

NONRESTRICTIVE ADJECTIVE CLAUSE	White-water rafting, *which we all enjoy greatly,* is done with inflatable rubber rafts.
RESTRICTIVE ADJECTIVE CLAUSE	The kind of white-water rafting *that we like most* uses six-person rubber rafts.
NONRESTRICTIVE PHRASE	Our first guide, *with enough experience to make up for our total lack of it,* taught us what we needed to know about rafting.
RESTRICTIVE PHRASE	A guide *with enough experience and skill* can help novices have an exciting yet safe trip.
NONRESTRICTIVE APPOSITIVES	Inexperienced rafters, *people like us,* usually go on the easier section of the river, section 3.

RESTRICTIVE APPOSITIVE ("CLOSE APPOSITIVE")	The magazine *Whitewater* did a feature story on the challenging rapids of section 2.
NONRESTRICTIVE ADVERB CLAUSE	A blue sky and the wild forest made a beautiful setting, *although the rushing water was what we watched most.*
RESTRICTIVE ADVERB CLAUSE	Sometimes we would just float along *after we had come out of a set of rapids.*

Commas with Quotations, Dates, and Addresses; and Commas in Letters

With Direct Quotations

A "quotation tag" *(John said, said she,* and so on) is joined to the quoted sentence with one or two commas. One comma is used if the quotation tag comes at the beginning or at the end, and two are used if it comes in the middle of the quoted sentence.

Young Susan asked, "What is Michelangelo famous for?"

"Well, Susan," *answered her father,* "the great artist Michelangelo is best known for his powerful marble statues."

"Many of his statues can still be seen in Italy today," *he added.*

No comma is used at the end of a quotation if a question mark or an exclamation point is needed there instead.

"When did Michelangelo live?" *she asked.*

Commas always go *before* quotation marks.

"Well, Susan," answered her father. . . .

". . . in Italy today," he added.

See page 139 for special uses of quotations when commas should not be used.

With the Parts of a Date

When using the normal order of month-day-year, put a comma between the day and the year.

Michelangelo was born on March 6, 1475.

If the date does not end the sentence, put a comma also after the year.

On February 18, 1564, he died in Rome.

With the Parts of an Address

Use a comma between the parts of an address. Also use a comma after the last word in the address if the sentence is not yet finished.

He was born in the village of Caprese, Tuscany, Italy, to a family from Florence, Italy.

Do not use a comma between the state and the ZIP code.

Our new address is 15 Gray Green Road, Taylors, South Carolina 29687.

After Certain Parts of a Letter

A comma is used after the salutation in a friendly letter.

Dear Dad,   Dear Pastor Davis,

In either a business letter or a friendly letter, a comma is used after the complimentary closing.

Love,   Sincerely yours,
Susan   Susan Miller

Commas with Transposed Words and Phrases

A comma can signal that words or phrases are out of the normal order. For instance, a direct object might be put first in a sentence for special emphasis.

Mark didn't particularly care for some of the food at the party. *The quesadillas with fresh guacamole,* he really liked.

This is similar to the comma that signals that a person's last name is given first.

Stapleton, Albert C.

Commas in Place of Omitted Words

A comma can show the omission of what would otherwise be a repeated word in a parallel construction.

Brent collects stamps and old postcards; his brother, autographs of famous preachers.

Commas with Certain Additions to Names

Use a comma between a personal name and a following abbreviated degree. Do not use a comma before numerals that follow any kind of name.

Janice Jaeggli, M.A.	*Pioneer 10*
Harold Jackson III	Psalm 100
Arthur Lane IV, Ph.D.	Chapter 23

Do not use a comma before the abbreviations *Jr.* and *Sr.* when they follow a name, *Harold B. Jackson Jr.*

Incorrect Commas

Commas in the wrong places can be distracting and even confusing.

Before a Conjunction That Joins Only Two Elements

No comma should be used when only two words, phrases, or dependent clauses are joined by a conjunction.

> **WRONG** Tammy, and her sister are in the yard.
> **RIGHT** Tammy and her sister are in the yard.

Between a Subject and a Verb

Do not put a comma between a subject and a verb.

> **WRONG** Anyone, really should know better than that.
> **RIGHT** Anyone really should know better than that.

However, a *pair* of commas (not just one) may set off an item between the subject and the verb.

> **RIGHT** Absolutely anyone, it seems, should know better than that.

Do not try to use a comma to salvage a sentence that has an awkwardly long subject. Revise the sentence instead.

> **AWKWARD** Checking with the Sunday school superintendent before you moved the tables was wise.

> **BETTER** It was wise of you to check with the Sunday school superintendent before you moved the tables.

After a Conjunction

A comma should not ordinarily follow a conjunction.

> **WRONG** We wanted to do the right thing, and, we thought we
> knew how to do it.

> **RIGHT** We wanted to do the right thing, and we thought we
> knew how to do it.

Of course, a *pair* of commas may set off an item after a conjunction as
well as anywhere else.

> **RIGHT** We wanted to do the right thing; and, surprisingly, we
> thought we knew how to do it.

Here the comma before *and* has become a semicolon because other
commas are used in this compound sentence.

With Quotations Used in Certain Ways

When a quotation functions as either the subject or the predicate
noun of the sentence, it should not be set off by commas.

> **SUBJECT** "Trust God and work hard" was his motto.
> **PREDICATE NOUN** His motto was "Trust God and work hard."

Like other restrictive appositives, a quoted restrictive appositive is not
set off by commas. (See pp. 134-35 for restrictive appositives.)

> **RESTRICTIVE** His motto "Trust God and work hard" carried him
> **APPOSITIVE** through the hard times successfully.

Semicolons

The semicolon signals a more important break in the sentence than
does the comma. Though the semicolon has several uses, it always joins
equal elements. Because it is a fairly strong mark of punctuation, the
semicolon should not be overused.

Between Two Independent Clauses

A semicolon may connect two closely related independent clauses.
Often the second independent clause reinforces the first, and there may
or may not be a transitional word, or conjunctive adverb, within the second independent clause.

> Africa is the second largest continent in the world; it contains about a fifth
> of the world's land area.

Africa is rich in natural resources; however, many of those resources are as yet undeveloped.

Notice that the conjunctive adverb *however* is part of the second clause. The conjunctive adverb is usually set off by commas, depending on where it comes in the clause.

Africa is rich in natural resources; many of those resources, however, are as yet undeveloped.

Before the Conjunction in a Long Compound Sentence

Usually a compound sentence has a comma before the coordinating conjunction. However, a semicolon is often substituted for that comma when the sentence contains other commas.

Nearly everyone knows that Spanish, French, and Italian are Romance languages; but not many know that Romanian is also a Romance language.

Between Word Groups Containing Commas

Because it is a stronger mark of punctuation than the comma, the semicolon is used to separate word groups in a series when any of the word groups contain internal commas. However, the series must be at the end of the sentence.

Sitting on the platform were the new mayor, Robert D. Workman; the chairman of City Council, David Eaves; and the three new members of City Council.

Even if a list does not have internal commas, it may still have semicolons if (1) the whole list is introduced by a colon and (2) the items in the list are somewhat long:

On the platform were the following officials: Mayor Robert D. Workman; City Council Chairman David Eaves; and the three new members of City Council.

Semicolons also separate Bible references when any of the references contain commas or other punctuation.

Genesis 10:5, 18, 25; 11:1-9

Because of the colon (other punctuation) in Bible references, a semicolon is generally used whenever a new chapter is mentioned (Psalm 4:5; 47:6; 40:6; 51:17).

Colons

The colon is a strong mark of punctuation, separating elements almost as definitely as the period. The colon often points up what follows it, marking the following item as being important, explanatory, or more specific.

In Bible References and Expressions of Time

An unspaced colon separates the chapter and the verse in Bible references.

I Corinthians 10:13   Joshua 1:8-9

An unspaced colon also separates the hour and the minute in expressions of time.

7:30 A.M.

After the Salutation of a Business Letter

A colon follows the salutation of a business letter.

Dear Sir or Madam: Dear Senator Smith:

Before a Series at the End of a Sentence

A colon can introduce a series that comes at the end of a sentence. Often *the following* or *as follows* appears somewhere before the colon, as in the second example below.

There are three main types of rocks: igneous, sedimentary, and metamorphic.

Crystals can easily be seen in the following igneous rocks: granite, gabbro, and syenite.

A colon can introduce such a series *only* if the series is not part of the basic structure of the sentence. That is, we do not put a colon before a direct object, an object of a preposition, a predicate adjective, or a predicate noun.

WRONG   Crystals can be seen in/ granite, gabbro, and syenite.

                          OP   OP   OP
RIGHT   Crystals can be seen in granite, gabbro, and syenite.

OP

> Crystals can be seen in certain igneous rocks: granite, gabbro, and syenite.

The phrases *such as* or *including* do not need to be followed by a colon.

For emphasis, a colon can also introduce a single appositive at the end of a sentence.

> He has one dominant trait: honesty.

Before a Long or Formal Direct Quotation

A colon is often used before a long or formal direct quotation, especially if the introduction to it is rather formal.

> Assistant Secretary of War Charles A. Dana made the following personal observation of President Lincoln: "He was calm, equable, uncomplaining. In the discussion of important questions, whatever he said showed the profoundest thought, even when he was joking. He seemed to see every side of every question."

The quotation after the colon must be last in the sentence, as it is in the example.

Between the Title and the Subtitle of a Book

A book's subtitle appears on the title page below the title; usually it is unpunctuated. However, when you refer to the book by both its title and its subtitle, you should supply a colon between the two parts.

> He bought a copy of Joseph M. Williams' book, *Style: Ten Lessons in Clarity and Grace.*

The colon is also used for this purpose in reference notes and in bibliographies.

In Certain Compound Sentences

A colon can be used between two independent clauses when the second explains, expands, or illustrates the point made in the first.

> Charles Dana said that President Lincoln was a calm person: Lincoln never seemed impatient or hurried, and "he never tried to hurry anybody else."

Quotation Marks

Quotation marks have two main uses: to enclose direct quotations and to indicate the titles of shorter works. Quotation marks are always used in pairs. The correct use or omission of commas with quoted material is covered on page 135.

Direct Quotations

Quotation marks indicate that the exact words of a writer or speaker are being reported.

> In the report Dr. Pennington argues that "the therapy was never intended to be, nor should it be used as a substitute for medical treatment."

> "There will be a penalty for any late papers," warned Mr. Smallwood.

Sometimes the quotation tag (such as *he said*) comes in the middle of the quoted sentence. In that case commas surround the quotation tag, and both halves of the divided quotation are enclosed in quotation marks.

> "If you just got them," Dale replied, "I probably haven't seen them yet."

(In American usage, commas and periods always come before quotation marks.)

> There are two common exceptions to the usual need for quotation marks around someone's exact words.
>
> (1) Quotation marks are not used within a play for the speeches of the dramatic characters.
>
> (2) They are often not used for well-known proverbs (including certain biblical sayings): *She remembered too late that a stitch in time saves nine.*

Dialogue

When reporting dialogue, a new paragraph should begin whenever there is a change in speaker.

> Delaine shouted, "It looks like rain!"
>
> "It hasn't rained in two months," said Karl. "There's not a cloud for miles."

In this example, a period is used after the quotation tag because the preceding quotation is a complete sentence.

Indirect Quotations

An indirect quotation gives the idea but not the exact words of the speaker or writer. Indirect quotations should not have quotation marks.

> **DIRECT QUOTATION**   Mark said, "**I** paid a quarter apiece for the used books."

> **INDIRECT QUOTATION**   Mark said **that he** paid a quarter apiece for the used books.

Titles of Short Works

Titles of short works are normally enclosed in quotation marks. A piece of writing is considered a short work if it is part of a larger work or is too short to be a book by itself. Short works include articles, chapters of a book, short stories, essays, songs, and most poems. Quotation marks are also usually used for the titles of radio or television programs that are part of a continuing series.

> Chapter 5 of *Changed into His Image,* "Mortifying Your Flesh," explains the power and danger of our sinful natures.

> I was able to use information from the chapter for my essay, "Freedom in Christ."

> We listen to "Daily Disciplines" on the radio each morning while we are driving to school.

An exception is that we use only capitalization—no quotation marks—with the major subdivisions of the Bible:

> For his devotions that day, he read the Twenty-fourth Psalm from the Old Testament and the sixth chapter of Ephesians from the New Testament.

Another exception is that no quotation marks are used with a title when it stands as the heading of the work itself.

Words Used in a Special Sense

Quotation marks can be used occasionally to signal a special sense of a word. For instance, a word may be used ironically to mean its opposite. In most cases, it is better to revise the sentence to clarify the meaning.

> **ACCEPTABLE**   Loud music, talking, and laughing could usually be heard each evening coming from the "study room."

> BETTER   Loud music, talking, and laughing could usually be heard each evening coming from the so-called study room.

Quotation marks may also set off a word that belongs to a noticeably different level of usage from the rest of the passage. For example, there could possibly be reason to use an exceptional slang word in a general or formal passage.

> The teens at the youth group would occasionally visit the ice-cream shop to "hang out."

However, it is generally better to avoid slang expressions entirely.

Single Quotation Marks

Single quotation marks should be used whenever quotation marks are needed within quotation marks.

> The teacher asked, "Has anyone ever read the poem 'The Return' by Ezra Pound?"

> Senator Robert Kenny challenged his opponent's integrity in his campaign speech: "The Governor promised, 'I will decrease crime in our state,' but theft and violence have never been more prevalent."

Quotation Marks and Other Punctuation

In American usage, commas and periods always go before adjacent quotation marks, regardless of what may seem logical.

> In the Declaration of Independence, Thomas Jefferson stated that "all men are created equal," and he believed that freedom is a natural right of all men.

Colons and semicolons always go after closing quotation marks. (Because the colon or semicolon is punctuation for the whole sentence, it stays outside the quoted item.)

> According to the Declaration, "governments are instituted among men, deriving their just powers from the consent of the governed"; therefore, the people have the right to amend or throw off any government that abuses its power.

Question marks and exclamation marks go inside the quotation marks unless the entire sentence is meant to be exclamatory or interrogative.

> The people cried, "England cannot tax the colonies without representation in Parliament!"

> Do you know that the signers of the Declaration of Independence agreed to risk "[their] lives, [their] fortunes, and [their] sacred honour"?

The concluding period of a sentence is omitted if the sentence ends with an interrogative or exclamatory quotation.

> The students asked, "What persuasive techniques did Jefferson use in the Declaration of Independence?"

Ellipses

Ellipses (or "ellipsis marks") are three spaced dots that most often indicate the omission of something in quoted matter. The dots look like periods, but there should be a space before and after each one.

Omission of Words in a Quotation

Whenever words are omitted within a sentence, a set of three spaced dots should appear where the word or words would have been.

> ORIGINAL   Unfortunately, we often do not understand the treachery that lies in our heart. We sometimes think we are pretty good people who "mess up" once in a while. The biblical picture is just the opposite: we are all pretty bad people who do right only by the grace of God. (Jim Berg, *Changed into His Image*)

> WITH OMISSIONS   We often do not have a correct view of our sinful hearts: the Bible teaches that "we . . . do right only by the grace of God."

Of course, honesty requires that the omissions not distort the meaning of the original. Also, the quoted passage must remain readable and grammatically correct.

Within a quoted passage of two or more sentences, use a period followed by three spaced dots to show the omission of (1) the end of the preceding sentence or (2) the beginning of the following sentence. What precedes the four dots must be a grammatically complete sentence and what follows them must be too.

> "Unfortunately, we often do not understand the treachery that lies in our heart. . . . [W]e are all pretty bad people who do right only by the grace of God."

In addition, a full line of spaced dots may be used to indicate the omission of one or more lines of poetry.

Ellipses are not needed at the beginning or end of a quoted passage.

> The book explains that "we often do not understand the treachery that lies in our heart."

Halting or Unfinished Speech

Ellipses may be used to indicate hesitant pauses in speech, and they may also show that a sentence has just slowly trailed off before completion. Inside a sentence three spaced dots are used, but at the end of the sentence a period precedes the three spaced dots.

> Mike shuffled his feet while speaking to the principal. "I wasn't sure if . . . well, I didn't know. . . ."

Brackets

Brackets are not used very often, but they are necessary for an insertion into quoted material. Parentheses are not a substitute for brackets.

For Insertions or Replacements in Quoted Material

It is important that your reader be able to tell the difference between your own words and those of the person being quoted. Therefore brackets are used for your words, whether they add to, replace, or correct something in the quoted material.

> ORIGINAL   Americans are losing their love and appreciation for national literature. Dr. Brook Harcourt's interviews conducted at ten large high schools verified what many educators have feared. Very few students had read more than one of the great America classics. While some could name a few contemporary writers, they knew

next to nothing about the great writers who created a national literature that was distinctly American.

AN ADDITION AND A CORRECTION "Dr. Brook Harcourt's interviews conducted at ten large [public] high schools verified what many educators have feared. Very few students had read more than one of the great America[n] classics."

An alternative to correcting an obvious error (or changing what might look like an error) is to add the word *sic* in brackets. *Sic* is Latin for "thus," and it means that you have reproduced the original faithfully even though it may look strange. Because *sic* is a foreign word, you should underline it to indicate italics. (See p. 149.)

ERROR NOTED AS FROM THE ORIGINAL Very few students had read more than one of the great America [*sic*] classics.

Sometimes a quotation will need to be changed in order to fit the structure of the new sentence. A change such as person, pronoun, or verb tense needs to be indicated by brackets.

Most educators consider the classics to be important but "very few students had read more than one of [them]."

For Parentheses Inside Parentheses

On rare occasions brackets should be used as parentheses inside other parentheses.

The governor defended his earlier statements (his decision to fund "exceptional [more advanced] schools for gifted students") with assurances that the general public schools would not be neglected.

Although the division of the sentence into subject and predicate is basic and widely recognized (for instance, see Randolph Quirk, et al. *A Grammar of Contemporary English* [London: Longman, 1972], p. 34), Chauncey's curriculum guide ignores the subject entirely.

However, it is best to avoid such a situation when possible. Often the sentence can be rewritten or the information given in a footnote or endnote.

Underlining for Italics

Italic print is used mainly to indicate titles of books and other long works. In handwritten papers, underlining is used instead of italics.

HANDWRITTEN VERSION — John Bunyan's <u>Pilgrim's Progress</u> is an all-time bestseller.

WORD PROCESSED OR PUBLISHED VERSION — John Bunyan's *Pilgrim's Progress* is an all-time best-seller.

Titles of Long Works

Italicize or underline the title of any work that is long enough to be published by itself.

BOOKS — *Great Expectations,* by Charles Dickens
Exception: the Bible

PERIODICALS — *National Geographic*
English Journal

NEWSPAPERS — *San Francisco Chronicle*

EPIC POEMS — Milton's *Paradise Lost*

MUSICAL COMPOSITIONS — Tchaikovsky's *The Nutcracker Suite*

PLAYS — *Hamlet,* by William Shakespeare

Italicize or underline the names of works of art.

MOTION PICTURES — *It's a Wonderful Life*

WORKS OF VISUAL ART — da Vinci's *The Last Supper*
Michelangelo's *David*

Large Transport Vehicles

Italicize the names of specific ships, aircraft, trains, and spacecraft.

SHIPS — USS *Floater*
AIRCRAFT — *Spirit of St. Louis*
TRAINS — *Empire*
SPACECRAFT — *Atlantis*

Words, Letters, and Numerals Being Discussed

Italicize words, letters, and numerals that are referred to as words.

In American spelling the word *Savior* has no *u* in it.

There are two *p*'s in the word *opportunity*.

Johnny needs more practice multiplying by *7*s and *9*s.

Notice that the plural *s* is not italicized in the last sentence.

Foreign Words and Phrases

Foreign words and phrases used in a sentence should be italicized. Some dictionaries mark foreign words and phrases in a special way, but others give no guidance. In general, if a word or phrase is in fairly common use in English, do not italicize it.

ITALICS NOT NEEDED	Although she had practiced for the driving test, Marla still had a considerable amount of angst as she got behind the wheel.
	The picnickers were so laden with blankets, bug spray, sunscreen, umbrellas, radios, et cetera, that they forgot the picnic basket in the van.
ITALICS NEEDED	Karl's father is a *Blumenhändler* in Berlin—a florist, that is.
	Your claim of *je ne sais pas* is not very convincing when you have been given the information.

If a whole sentence in a foreign language is quoted, the sentence should be in quotation marks rather than in italics.

Even though we thought he knew the answers, Michel kept answering, "Je ne sais pas."

Emphasis

Occasionally italics can be used to indicate special emphasis. Normally, however, it is better to obtain the emphasis by placing the important word at the end of the sentence or clause.

ITALICS FOR EMPHASIS	You may attend two performances without extra charge, but only according to *our* choice of times.
EMPHASIS ACHIEVED BY PLACEMENT	You may attend two performances without extra charge, but the choice of times will be ours.

Apostrophes

Apostrophes were once used in English only to indicate that one or more letters had been omitted from a word. Today they are used mainly with contractions and possessives.

Omission of Letters and Numbers

In a contraction, an apostrophe indicates that a letter or letters have been omitted. It appears at the spot where the missing letter or letters would have been.

can't	let's
I'm	ma'am
don't	he'll

Any noun or pronoun subject can form a contraction with an appropriate form of *be, have, will,* or *would.*

Tom**'s** coming in, and someone**'s** apparently told him.

It**'s** Casey who**'ll** have the best answer.

The contraction *it's* (for *it is* or *it has*) should not be confused with the possessive *its.*

In informal writing, an apostrophe may be used to replace the first two figures for a year.

the class of '05

the '00 election

Special Plurals

Regular nouns do not use apostrophes to create plurals; however, some special plural forms of letters and words do need apostrophes. An apostrophe is used to form the plurals of letters or words being discussed. An apostrophe is not necessary to form the plurals of numbers, symbols, and dates.

Good descriptive writing relies on nouns and verbs. Be careful not to use too many *really*'s or *very*'s to emphasize your adjectives.

Some people's capital *N*'s look like *W*'s.

For some reason, the computer did not print any of the 5s in Jesse's audit sheet.

To make her pamphlet more eye-catching, Lauren changed the *and*'s to &s.

The 1990s saw a return to the bright neon colors of the 1970s.

Possessives

Nouns and many indefinite pronouns can be made possessive by the addition of *'s* or sometimes just the apostrophe.

For most singular nouns or indefinite pronouns, add *'s* for the possessive.

Matt's briefcase

her father-in-law's car

anyone's guess

the boss's desk

The *s* after the apostrophe may be omitted if the possessive suffix would not be pronounced as a separate syllable.

Jesus' disciples

W. B. Yeats' poetry

If a regular plural noun ending in *s* is made possessive, add only an apostrophe.

the ladies' meeting

the counselors' lounge

If a plural noun does not end with an *s,* add *'s* to form the possessive.

children's toys

the men's department

Individual or Joint Ownership

When two or more persons possess something together, the possession is expressed just once, at the end of the series.

Jessica and Jeanine's birthday party will be in December.

When the possession is separate, each noun or pronoun should be possessive.

Jessica's and Jeanine's guest lists are similar.

Hyphens

The hyphen, about half as long as the dash, is used to join the parts of words, or sometimes to join separate words together.

Omission of Connecting Word

A hyphen can be used in place of a single connecting word, especially between figures.

Romans 12:1-2   June 5-9   the Rome-Paris Express

A hyphen can replace a single connecting word, but it cannot be used when there is a *pair* of connecting words, such as *from* and *to* or *between* and *and*.

He traveled from Rome to Paris between June 5 and June 9.

Word Division at the End of a Line

When necessary, use a hyphen to divide a word at the end of a line. The hyphen, of course, goes at the end of a line, not at the beginning of the next line.

A word to be divided must contain at least two actual (pronounced) syllables, but the accepted places for dividing the written word may not exactly follow the division between pronounced syllables. Consult a dictionary to see the places where any specific word can be divided. You may divide the word at any of those spots as long as the following two rules are not violated: (1) At least two letters and the hyphen must remain on the first line. (2) At least three letters must appear on the second line.

If you cannot satisfy these requirements, do not divide the word. For example, *ocean* (**o • cean**) should be carried entirely to the next line.

Numbers and Fractions

When you spell out the multiword numbers from twenty-one through ninety-nine, use a hyphen between the parts. Also hyphenate these numbers when they are part of larger numbers spelled out, as on a check.

   One hundred twenty-nine and no/100   dollars

Use a hyphen between the numerator and the denominator of a spelled-out fraction, unless either of these already contains a hyphen.

two-thirds   four and one-half   forty-two hundredths

Prefixes

Some prefixes require hyphens when added to a word. The following prefixes are always hyphenated: *all-, ex-* (meaning "former"), *half-,* and *self-.*

The all-consuming love of Christ draws the sinner to salvation.

Lila is an ex-waitress who landed the job of president of the company.

"We hold these truths to be self-evident: that all men are created equal."

Certain other prefixes, like *non-* and *anti-,* are hyphenated by some publishers but not by others. Both styles are permissible, but the trend is toward writing these words solid rather than with a hyphen.

Other prefixes are generally not hyphenated but may be when the prefix comes before a number, a proper adjective, or a proper noun.

All of Jenny's post-2000 yearbooks were damaged by water; the others were salvaged.

The pre-Christmas shopping rush made the cashier lines very long.

Sometimes a prefixed word needs a hyphen to distinguish it from a word spelled similarly.

re-creation	recreation
re-collect	recollect
un-ionized	unionized

Sometimes a hyphen is used after a prefix in order to separate identical vowels: *co-owner, anti-inflationary.* In keeping with the general trend away from hyphens, some words of this type can be written either way. Other words are now regularly written without hyphens: *cooperate, coordination.* Follow a reliable recent dictionary. (If the word is not listed, follow the analogy of similar words there.)

Compounds

Hyphens are used to create some compound words.

father-in-law

two-year-old

Multiword Modifiers

When two or more words function as a single unit to modify a following noun, this "temporary compound" should be hyphenated.

Multiword Modifier of Following Noun	Other Uses
the first-grade room	He is in first grade.
a know-it-all attitude	Do you know it all?
a thank-you note	Thank you for the help.
a spelled-out number	The number is spelled out.

Common Elements

If two or more hyphenated words have the same final element, that element may be omitted from all but the last word. In that case, you should hyphenate and space the words as follows:

the first-, second-, and third-grade rooms

in pre- or post-Revolutionary days

Dashes

The dash—a rather informal mark—is used mainly for interrupting elements, for emphasis, and for abrupt changes in thought. It should be used sparingly. In appearance a dash is about twice as long as a hyphen.

Interrupting Phrase and Clause

An interrupting phrase or clause is commonly set off by a pair of dashes.

John Derham was one of the many Black Americans—and, indeed, there were many—who made positive contributions to our society.

However, interrupting elements of this type should not be overused. See page 157 for the different uses of commas, dashes, and parentheses for setting off material within the sentence.

Emphasis

A dash can be used occasionally to give special emphasis to a phrase or a clause. Often this phrase or clause appears at the end of the sentence.

NORMAL PUNCTUATION	Derham was an American slave in the eighteenth century, a century of increasing slavery.
EMPHATIC	Derham was an American slave in the eighteenth century—a century of increasing slavery.

Such emphasis can be very effective if it is not attempted too often.

Elements within the sentence may also be emphasized by the use of dashes. Notice that the interrupting element given in the earlier section (*—and, indeed, there were many—*) was somewhat emphasized by the dashes around it.

Interrupted Speech

The dash is used to show various kinds of interruption in speech.

FALTERING SPEECH	"But he—he wasn't the one who told me."
	"Then I went to get the—uh—capacitor at the parts department."
ABRUPT BREAKING OFF OF A SENTENCE	"But I thought—" Sandra interrupted.
ABRUPT CHANGE IN THOUGHT	"Well, you see, he first—oh, I can't explain it."

Internal Appositive Series

Normally an appositive is set off by commas, as discussed on page 132. Sometimes, however, the appositive is a series of items. Because commas are required within a series of three or more items, something stronger than commas is needed to set off the whole appositive clearly. In that case, a pair of dashes is used.

I need to cut up three more fruits—peaches, green grapes, and bananas—before I can finish the salad.

Summarizing Statement After an Introductory List

If a sentence begins with a list and then continues with a grammatically complete summary statement, a dash is used to connect the two parts.

Peaches, green grapes, and bananas—these were all I needed to complete the salad.

Parentheses

Parentheses, as well as commas and dashes, are used to enclose extra information within the rest of the sentence. Parentheses (singular, *parenthesis*) are always used in pairs, regardless of whether the extra information comes in the middle or at the end of the sentence.

Supplementary Elements

Parentheses are most often used to enclose words, phrases, or clauses that give additional, often explanatory information.

Our next meeting (the annual election of officers) will be held on March 19.

Next month's meeting has been postponed for one week (schedule enclosed).

Sometimes an entire sentence appears within parentheses.

Next month's meeting has been postponed for one week. (The enclosed schedule gives the dates of our next six meetings.)

Placement of Other Punctuation with Parentheses

Notice the examples just above. When an entire sentence is enclosed in parentheses, the end punctuation comes before the final parenthesis. Otherwise, sentence punctuation goes outside the parentheses.

The only partial exception is that a question mark or an exclamation mark would go inside if the parenthetical material itself is a question or an exclamation.

Terry, I hear that our next meeting (can you come?) will be on March 19.

Because a parenthesized Bible reference in a paragraph is considered part of the sentence to which it refers, it follows the general rule.

The passage begins by commanding, "Let every soul be subject unto the higher powers" (Romans 13:1).

The appropriate sentence punctuation goes after the final parenthesis, not at the end of the quotation. Of course, if the quotation is itself a question or an exclamation, it is punctuated appropriately.

Jesus asked John's two disciples, "What seek ye?" (John 1:38).

Numbers or Letters That Identify Divisions Within a Sentence

Parentheses enclose numbers or letters used as in the following sentences:

> In order to participate, you will need to bring (1) a pen or a pencil, (2) several sheets of notebook paper, and (3) the ten-dollar fee in cash.

> The writing contest included three categories: (a) short story; (b) personal essay, editorial, or letter to the editor; and (c) short poetry.

Comparison of Parentheses with Pairs of Commas and Dashes

Pairs of commas, dashes, and parentheses can all be used to set off extra information in the sentence:

1. **Commas** are the normal, neutral punctuation for setting off short phrases and clauses.

   > The first step toward clear writing, as I told you yesterday, is clear thinking.

2. **Dashes** make the enclosed material appear important. They also tend to be less formal.

   > The first step toward clear writing—as I told you yesterday—is clear thinking.

3. **Parentheses** indicate that the enclosed material is rather unimportant.

   > The first step toward clear writing (as I told you yesterday) is clear thinking.

Capitalization

This chapter is about capitalizing words correctly. Capitals indicate beginnings and distinguish proper nouns from common nouns. Most words that need capitalization are proper nouns, important words in titles of works, or the first words of certain units like sentences and parts of an outline.

The recent trend is toward not capitalizing many words that have been capitalized in the past. This chapter attempts to present a balance between traditional rules and those changes that are becoming widely accepted. Where useful, some of these changes are reflected in the charts below. As always, you should check with your instructor or a reputable dictionary or style manual when making decisions about which rules you should follow.

Proper Nouns and Adjectives: Personal Names, Religions, Nationalities

Capitalize proper nouns and adjectives, that is, specific names for particular persons or specific descriptive words. (See p. 5 for an explanation of common and proper nouns.)

Names and initials	Jared **Z.** Caldwell Kirsten **L.** Martin
Titles used with a name	**Dr.** Marshall Siddens Roxanne **P.** Gray, **M.D.** **President** Reagan **Duke** Ferdinand
Do not capitalize titles used in place of a person's name.	The senator called for volunteers to attend the meeting.
Family words used as proper nouns	Have you seen **Grandpa's** new car?

If a word for a family relationship is modified by an adjective, it is not being used as a proper noun.	My **grandpa** tapped maple trees for syrup when he was a boy.
Terms used as descriptive substitutes for proper nouns	the **G**reat **E**mancipator (Abraham Lincoln) **A**ngel of the **B**attlefield (Clara Barton) **P**rince of **P**reachers (Charles Haddon Spurgeon)
Personifications	Open-ey'd **C**onspiracy His time doth take. (Shakespeare, *The Tempest*) With these celestial **W**isdom calms the mind, And makes the happiness she does not find. (Samuel Johnson, *The Vanity of Human Wishes*)
Names of religions	**C**atholicism **I**slam
All nouns and personal pronouns referring to the one true God	The **B**ible teaches that **J**esus **C**hrist came to earth, and **H**e died to save us from our sins.
Do not capitalize common nouns or pronouns referring to mythological gods.	The early Greeks prayed to Zeus, who was considered the father of the other gods.
The words *Holy Bible* or *Bible* and the parts of the Bible as well as the names of sacred writings of other religions	**S**eptuagint **R**evelation **K**oran
Nationalities Races Languages	**I**rish, **W**elsh **A**sian, **H**ispanic **P**idgin, **L**atin
Proper adjectives	**B**ritish colonies **C**hristian fellowship **A**merican freedoms

Do not capitalize a word modified by a proper adjective unless the two together form a proper name.	Dad enjoys his German automobile, a 1971 Volkswagen.

Proper Nouns: Place Names, Conveyances, Astronomical Terms

Countries	Tunisia
Continents	Africa

Flags	**Old Glory**
	French Royal Banner
	Canadian Red Ensign

Cities	**South Roxana**
States	**Illinois**

Sections of a country or the world	**New England**
	Upper Peninsula
	Far East
Do not capitalize compass words when they indicate direction.	a northwest wind
	a southbound flight

Geographic features and recreational areas	Stonehenge
	Carlsbad Caverns
	Oak Canyon National Park
Streets and roads	**Marshall Avenue, Blue Ridge Parkway**
Bodies of water	**Gulf of Mexico, the Black Sea, the Pacific Ocean**
Do not capitalize a geographical noun unless it is part of a proper noun.	We investigated a cavern near our campsite.
	My family lives on a street near the church.
	We crossed the river in a skiff.

Aircraft	*Grey Goose*
Spacecraft	*Challenger*
Ships	*Titanic*
Trains	*Super Chief*

Planets	Saturn
Stars	Polaris
Other heavenly bodies	the Milky Way, the Big Dipper
Capitalize the words earth, sun, *and* moon *only when they are listed with another specific heavenly body.*	The rocket was launched from Earth and orbited Jupiter.
Never capitalize earth *when it is preceded by* the.	The earth is an oblate ellipsoid.

Proper Nouns: Businesses and Organizations, Cultural and Historical Terms

Businesses	North Street Map Shop
	Campbell Soup Company
Do not capitalize the common noun for a business.	Lee and Ann often visit area antique shops on Saturdays.
Brand names of business products	Firestone
	Crest
	Ford
Do not capitalize the product name unless it is part of the brand name.	Firestone tires
	Crest toothpaste
	Ford car (*But:* Ford Mustang)
Government departments	Department of Commerce
	Federal Bureau of Investigation (FBI)
Programs	Head Start
Political parties	Whig Party
Organizations	North Ridge Spartans Booster Club
	Girl Scouts of America
Do not capitalize the common noun for a team or club.	Many parents join the school's booster club in order to support the team.

Members of most organizations	a **Republican** a **Boy Scout**
Schools	**Eastside High School** **Rose-Hulman Institute** of **Technology** **University** of **Connecticut**
Do not capitalize the common name for a school.	Marie attended a two-year business college before transferring to Bob Jones University.
Buildings Structures Monuments	**Flatiron Building** **Osaka Port Bridge** (Japan) **Lincoln Memorial**
Months Days	**March, July** **Sunday, Wednesday**
Do not capitalize the names of the seasons unless personified.	summer, winter *But:* The **Night** is mother of the **Day**, 　　The **Winter** of the **Spring**. (Whittier)
Holidays	**Boxing Day** (Great Britain) **Passover** **Easter**
Abbreviations B.C. and A.D.	The **Hittite Empire** was powerful in **Asia Minor** from circa 1600 to circa 1200 B.C.
Notice that B.C. *("before Christ") is correctly placed after the year and that* A.D. *(anno Domini, "in the year of the Lord") is correctly placed before the year.*	Martin Luther nailed his ninety-five theses to the door of the cathedral in Wittenberg in A.D. 1517.
The abbreviations A.M. and P.M. may be either capitalized or not. (Whichever you choose, be consistent in your writing.)	6:00 A.M., 10:00 P.M. 6:00 **a.m.,** 10:00 **p.m.**
Historical events and periods	**Battle** of **Milvian Bridge** **Stone Age** **Fabulous Forties**

Historical documents and awards	Treaty of Trianon Magna Carta Pulitzer Prize
Special events	Apple Butter Festival Montreal World's Fair

Proper Nouns: Titles, First Words, and Single Letters

Capitalize the first and last words in a title, as well as all other important words. Do not capitalize articles, coordinating conjunctions, the *to* of the infinitive, or prepositions of fewer than five letters.

Newspapers and magazines *Do not capitalize the word* the *when referring to a newspaper.*	*Los Angeles Free Press* *U.S. News and World Report* the *New York Times*
Literary compositions (including books, essays, poems, and plays)	*The Life of Hudson Taylor* "Upon a Spider Catching a Fly" "The Philosophy of Composition" *Love's Labour's Lost*
Sections of a book or play *Some authorities do not capitalize the parts of a book or play unless they appear as a title.*	Chapter 10 Appendix Act II Foreword The students performed part of act 3 from *Hamlet*.
Musical compositions (including songs, operas, and instrumental music)	"Away in a Manger" *Barber of Seville* *Well-Tempered Clavier*
Works of art	Degas' *At the Milliner's* Bartholdi's *Liberty Enlightening the World* (the Statue of Liberty)

Television and radio programs	**Antiques R**oadshow **All T**hings **C**onsidered
Specific courses of study	**Basic C**hemistry **H**istory of the **R**oman **E**mpire **G**eometry II
Do not capitalize the common noun for a course.	Don't forget your geometry book today—the quiz is open book!
First word in a sentence	**W**e listen to books on tape in the car.
Do not capitalize the first word of a sentence that is in parentheses within another sentence.	The desire to rule the world (this is an age-old dream) can cause powerful men to commit horrible crimes.
First word in a line of dialogue	Joe asked, "**D**o you like this poem?"
Do not capitalize the second part of a divided quotation unless the second part is the beginning of a new sentence.	"Yes, I like the poem," Mara replied. "**I** enjoy the vivid descriptions." "And the other reason," she continued, "**i**s that the author has always been one of my favorites."
First word in a line of poetry	**J**esus, I am resting, resting **I**n the joy of what Thou art. **I** am finding out the greatness **O**f Thy loving heart.

First word (and any proper nouns or proper adjectives) in each item of a formal outline	I. **T**he first campaign
	   A. **B**attle for the delta
	   B. **C**onquest of the seas

First word of a statement after a colon	The novel has a familiar theme: **M**an's faith in himself is a hopeless faith.
You may capitalize or not capitalize the first word of a formal or explanatory statement following a colon, as long as you are consistent.	The novel has a familiar theme: **m**an's faith in himself is a hopeless faith.

First word and all nouns in the greeting of a letter	Dear Patrick and Family, My dear Friends, Dear Sir:
First word in the closing of a letter	Sincerely yours, Respectfully,
Personal pronoun *I*	What if **I** come early?
Archaic address-form *O*	We trust, **O** Lord, in Thee.
Single letters used as words (including academic grades, vitamins, musical notes, and major keys)	Josey maintained a **B** average during first semester. Green, leafy vegetables are a good source of vitamin **B**. The eager toddler repeatedly pounded middle **C** on the neighbor's piano.
Letters used to clarify a following word	Mark's **V**-neck vest was too dark for the photograph. The foreman realized that the crew was short three **I**-beams to complete the project. The building was **L**-shaped.

Spelling

For at least two hundred years people have been judging education and intelligence by the quality of other people's spelling. Those judgments may not be fair, but still people make them. A further problem with poor spelling is that readers often find it distracting, even confusing.

That's the bad news. The good news is that with a reasonable amount of the right kind of effort, you can conquer most—perhaps all— of your remaining problems with spelling.

Ways to Improve Spelling

Spell by syllables.

Dividing a word into its individual syllables and mentally sounding it out will help you spell a problem word correctly. Think about prefixes, suffixes, and other word parts as you spell words by syllables.

Mis+spell	Misspell
Un+necessary	Unnecessary
Dis+courage	Discourage
Under+rate	Underrate
Thank+ful+ly	Thankfully

Look up the spelling of doubtful words.

Use your dictionary to look up the spelling of any word you are not sure how to spell. Even if you do not know the exact spelling, you should be able to make a reasonable guess. The guide words at the top of the pages will help you find the word in the dictionary.

Keep a list of words that are problems for you.

When you realize that you have misspelled a particular word repeatedly, add the word to a list that you can refer to frequently. Practice writing those words correctly and be conscious of their spelling when you see or hear them.

Look for possible groupings among your problem words.

If you find a group of similar words, try either to figure out or to find a rule for that group. For instance, if you have problems with *ie* and *ei,* study the rule on page 171.

Compare related words.

Often the sound of a related word can be a clue to the spelling of an unclear vowel.

Unclear Vowel	Clue Word	Unclear Vowel	Clue Word
president	presidential	grammar	grammatical
occupant	occupation	heresy	heretical
specify	specific	similar	similarity
exhibit	exhibition	rapid	rapidity
transitive	transition	repetition	repetitive

However, some related words are spelled differently. Correct pro-nunciation helps with the spelling of many of these.

pronounce	pronunciation
similar	simulate
example	exemplify
proclaim	proclamation
space	spatial

Study your list of problem words systematically.

Begin by writing a word several times, concentrating on its appearance and sound. Repeat this procedure on three or four different days within the next week. Then ask someone to quiz you on that word. If you can write the word correctly without hesitation, transfer it to your "learned" list. If the problem remains, keep working on that word.

Spelling Singular Present-Tense Verbs and Plural Nouns

If the word ends in *ch, sh, s, x, or z,* add *es.*

parch	parches
ax	axes
push	pushes
fizz	fizzes
mass	masses

If the word ends in *y* preceded by a consonant, change the final *y* to *i* and add *es*.

try	tries
lily	lilies
folly	follies
deny	denies
pony	ponies

If the word ends in *y* preceded by a vowel, add *s*.

buy	buys
pray	prays
chimney	chimneys
key	keys
joy	joys

If the word ends in *f* or *fe*, consult your dictionary. For most of these words, add *s;* for others, change the *f* to *v* and add *s* or *es*.

chief	chiefs
quaff	quaffs
safe	safes
elf	elves
life	lives

If the word ends in *o*, consult your dictionary. For most of these words, add *es;* for others, add *s*. Musical terms are likely to require *s* rather than *es*.

go	goes
potato	potatoes
Oreo	Oreos
gazebo	gazebos
portfolio	portfolios
solo	solos

Add *s* to most other words.

cook	cooks
jump	jumps
menu	menus
plug	plugs
ski	skis

Some nouns have irregular forms. Consult your dictionary for nouns with irregular plurals.

alumnus	alumni
crisis	crises
deer	deer
mouse	mice
species	species

The plurals of proper nouns are made by adding *s* or *es* according to the preceding rules, but without any other spelling changes. Never use an apostrophe in making the plural of a proper name.

two Toms	three Marcys	the Joneses	the Hubbards

Some of the plurals of personal titles are irregular.

General or Formal	*General or Informal*
Messrs. Smith and White	Mr. Smith and Mr. White
Mmes. Davis and Ryan	Mrs. Davis and Mrs. Ryan
Misses Diane Black	Miss Diane Black and
and Susan Dill	Miss Susan Dill
Drs. Poll and Truman	Dr. Poll and Dr. Truman

A plural title can be used also when the same title applies to two or more persons with the same name.

Formal	*General*
the Messrs. Smith	the Mr. Smiths
the Drs. Jervey	the Dr. Jerveys

Attach the *s* or *es* to the end of most compounds.

Nouns	*Verbs*
cease-fires	babysits
cupfuls	brainwashes
five-year-olds	freeze-dries
standbys	sidesteps
baseballs	water-skis

Pluralize the first element of certain compound nouns—those in which the first element is felt to be the most important part of the compound. When in doubt, consult your dictionary.

sisters-in-law	passersby
commanders-in-chief	poets laureate

Spelling with *ie* or *ei*

When the sound is "long *e*," put *i* before *e* except after *c*.

i *before* e	*except after* c
believe	ceiling
yield	perceive
grief	receipt
shield	deceive
niece	conceit

Exceptions: *caffeine, leisure, protein, seize, weird, financier. Either* and *neither,* in their American pronunciation, are also exceptions to this rule.

When the sound is "long *a*," put *e* before *i*.

vein	eight
freight	beige
sleigh	neighbor

When the two vowels are pronounced separately, spell according to the pronunciation of the first vowel.

atheist	variety
quiet	deist
science	proprietor

Adding Suffixes

Doubling a final consonant

If a one-syllable word ends with a single consonant preceded by a single vowel, double the final consonant before adding a suffix.

hop	hop**ped**
wrap	wrap**ped**
run	run**ning**
spin	spin**ner**
snob	snob**bish**

If a multisyllable word with its main accent on the final syllable ends with a single consonant preceded by a single vowel, double the final consonant before adding a suffix.

begin	begin**ning**
admit	admit**ted**
confer	confer**ring**
occur	occur**ring**

If a word ends with a single consonant preceded by two vowels, do not double the final consonant before adding a suffix.

droop	drooping
pair	paired
fool	foolish
heat	heating
lead	leading

Exceptions:
The consonant does not double when the suffix causes the main accent to shift away from the final syllable: *conference* vs. *conferring*.
The final *l* sometimes doubles regardless of the location of the main accent, especially in British usage: *counselor* or (mainly British) *counsellor*. Consult your dictionary.

Changing the final *y* to *i*

If a word ends with a consonant followed by *y*, change the final *y* to *i* before adding a suffix.

fry	fried
apply	applied
mercy	merciful
likely	likelihood
plenty	plentiful

However, if the suffix itself begins with *i*, do not change the final *y* to *i*.

fry	frying
fortify	fortifying

Exceptions:
Some words keep the *y: babyhood, shyness.*
In a few established spellings, the *y* has become *i* in spite of the preceding vowel: *daily, paid.*

Dropping the final silent e

Drop the final silent *e* preceded by a consonant before adding a suffix beginning with a vowel.

live	li**ving**
achieve	achie**ving**
tune	tu**ning**
name	na**ming**

Keep the final silent *e* before adding a suffix beginning with a consonant.

live	lively
achieve	achievement
tune	tuneful
name	nameless

Exceptions:
The *e* is kept to signal the "soft" pronunciation of *c* or *g* before a suffix beginning with *a* or *o*: *noticeable, courageous.*
A word ending in *ue* normally drops the *e* even when the suffix begins with a consonant: *truly, argument.*
Words ending in *dge* lose their *e* (in American English) before *–ment*: *judgment, acknowledgment.*
A few other words are exceptions, some of them to distinguish homonyms: *dyeing* (vs. *dying*), *singeing* (vs. *singing*).

Numbers

There are several special rules for writing numbers, but the main question is when to spell them out and when to use figures. In technical writing usually all numbers are expressed in figures, but in other situations certain numbers are spelled out.

Numbers Spelled Out

In general, numbers that can be expressed briefly are spelled out. The following are examples of such numbers:

Exact numbers under one hundred

Spelling out numbers under one hundred is a safe rule to follow, although other rules do exist for various purposes. (Newspapers, for example, generally spell out only the numbers below ten.)

So far there are still **forty-five** vacancies for Friday night.

Round numbers and any numbers that can be expressed as even hundreds, thousands, or millions

Spell out approximate numbers and any numbers that can be expressed as even hundreds, thousands, or millions.

Twelve thousand people attended the rally.

The football game drew **thirty-five hundred** spectators.

Numbers that begin sentences

Any number that begins a sentence must be spelled out. Sometimes it may be worthwhile to avoid the problem by rewording the sentence.

Nineteen seventy-six was a year of bicentennial observances.

During **1976** many bicentennial observances were held.

Numbers Expressed in Figures

Regardless of the size of the number, all of the following types of numbers should be expressed in figures.

Years and usually days

Dates may be expressed in the following ways:

July 4, 1776   4 July 1776 (no comma if day is first)
July 4   the Fourth of July (established holiday)

An exception to the use of figures is found in the extremely formal language of a wedding invitation.

Pages and other parts of a book

Use figures for locations in a book.

Chapters 2-3   page 11   footnote 2 on page 37

Numbers in lists and outlines

A vertical list or an outline requires figures. (See p. 185 for outline form.)

1. The executive branch
2. The legislative branch
3. The judicial branch

Numbers used for identification and location

Use figures for such things as house numbers and other parts of an address (except possibly for low-numbered street names), telephone numbers, and various identification numbers.

Apartment 3B, 1411 Sixth Avenue   Delta Airlines flight 466
130 W. 104th Street   Visa card 4123 4567 8901 2345

Numbers used with abbreviations and symbols

Use figures with abbreviations and symbols. (Most of the abbreviations and symbols themselves are more likely to be used in writing that is either technical or informal, or both.)

Technical or informal	*Other*
3 mi.	three miles
78°F	seventy-eight degrees Fahrenheit
60 mph	sixty miles per hour
4' by 8'	four by eight feet

Exact time and amounts of money normally require figures and symbols: 9:15 P.M., $3.75.

Mixed numbers, decimal fractions, and percentages

Use figures for any kind of mixed number or percentage.

3 1/2 minutes	27% (technical writing)
an average of 2.2 miles	27 percent (other writing)

Numbers associated with other numbers expressed in figures

In a paragraph, be consistent in writing numbers that deal with the same topic. If one of the numbers in some category must be written in figures, all should be.

Roman Numerals

Roman numerals appear with the major points of most outlines. In lowercase form (for example *iii* for three), they enumerate the preliminary pages of a book. They are sometimes used for chapters and larger parts of books, for acts and scenes of plays, and for volumes in a set or series. They are also used for dates on public buildings.

1 I	14 XIV	70 LXX	1000 M
2 II	15 XV	80 LXXX	1004 MIV
3 III	19 XIX	90 XC	1100 MC
4 IV	20 XX	100 C	1200 MCC
5 V	21 XXI	112 CXII	1300 MCCC
6 VI	24 XXIV	200 CC	1400 MCD
7 VII	25 XXV	300 CCC	1500 MD
8 VIII	29 XXIX	400 CD	1600 MDC
9 IX	30 XXX	500 D	1700 MDCC
10 X	31 XXXI	600 DC	1800 MDCCC
11 XI	40 XL	700 DCC	1900 MCM
12 XII	50 L	800 DCCC	1965 MCMLXV
13 XIII	60 LX	900 CM	2000 MM

Abbreviations

Abbreviations are convenient, but they should be used appropriately. The following rules may be supplemented by dictionary entries for certain individual abbreviations.

Abbreviations Always Used

Certain abbreviations are correctly used in any type of writing.

Expressions of time

7:15 P.M.	8:45 EST (Eastern Standard Time)	
1:00 A.M.	A.D. 1066	2500 B.C.

Personal titles

Mr. Roberts	Dr. J. J. Roberts
Mrs. Roberts	Ms. Mary Roberts

Likewise, abbreviate *Junior, Senior,* and academic degrees.

John J. Roberts Jr.   Mary Roberts, Ph.D.

Other personal titles are abbreviated only when they precede the *full* name of the person.

Sen. David Patterson   Senator Patterson

Miss, of course, is not an abbreviation.

Abbreviations in company names

Abbreviations and symbols that are part of the official name of a company or other organization should be used as they stand.

Pleasantburg Pets & Grooming Inc.   Ironside Computer Corp.

When to Use Other Abbreviations

Additional abbreviations and symbols are often used in technical writing and in informal writing. However, in most writing it is best to avoid abbreviations not mentioned above.

Spacing with Abbreviations

Do not put a space within most abbreviations.

M.Ed.	R.S.V.P.	CBS
e.g.	D.C.	FBI

However, the initials of a person's name require spaces, as do most abbreviations consisting of more than single initials.

R. C. Barbe   Lt. Gov. Rilkie

Abbreviations for the States

The two-letter postal abbreviations for the states should be written as two capital letters with no space in between. Check your dictionary if you are unsure of the correct abbreviation for a state.

PART THREE

Composition Tools

Writing Process Overview

Good writing will just flow out if you wait for the perfect inspiration to strike—right? Wrong! Easy writing makes hard reading. Following the right process, though, can make writing a pleasure, especially as the results become better and better.

Planning

What you do before you begin to write (that is, the planning stage) can be just as important as the actual writing. Without proper planning, your attempts at writing will prove frustrating for both you and your audience. Taking extra time and care in the planning stage will pay off later as you draft and revise your work.

Choosing a Topic

For your writing projects, you will either be assigned a writing topic or be given a list of topics from which to choose. Choose one that you are familiar with or that you would enjoy researching. Personal life experiences often make the best choices for topics; however, you may also enjoy the challenge of researching and learning about something new. The following strategies will help you find a topic that will work for you.

Making a list

Write down memories, experiences, or important events from your past that you could write about. Jog your memory by reading journal entries, looking at scrapbooks and photograph albums, and observing everyday surroundings and routines.

Asking questions

Ask yourself questions to get started. The following questions may help you think of other or related topics:

- What are my favorite hobbies or pastimes? Why?
- What books have I enjoyed reading? Why?

- What is my best (or most difficult) subject? Why?
- What is the funniest thing that ever happened to me?
- Whom do I admire? Why?
- What would I like to do when I get older?

Brainstorming

Start with one topic. Then list everything about that topic that you can remember. Write down every idea that you think about. When you have finished, you will have many topic possibilities, both general and specific.

Clustering

Similar to brainstorming, clustering goes into more detail. Instead of a list, clustering yields a diagram that shows relationships between ideas. Clustering will help to generate topic ideas and suggest ways of organizing your information. Write the general topic and circle it. Then write down related ideas and circle them. Next, draw lines connecting ideas to one another and to the main topic.

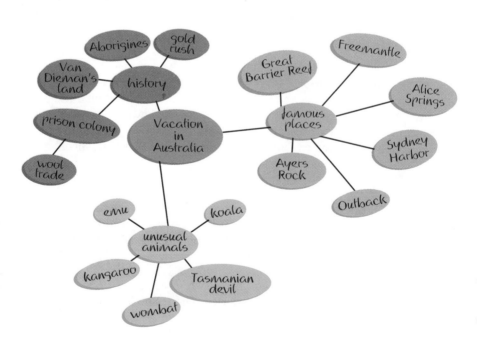

Freewriting

Choose a general topic. Then set a time limit (five minutes, for example) and write about the topic for the entire time without stopping. After you have finished, look for ideas that you can explore further.

Interviewing

If you have an idea about a topic and know someone who might be of help to you, interview the person. Prior to the interview, make a list of helpful and directive questions that you can ask. The answers may give you ideas of topics to write about.

Narrowing Your Topic

Many students are easily frightened by the length requirement of various writing assignments. Students often feel that they need a broad, general topic. It is better to say more about less than to say less about more. In other words, a better writer will cover a narrow topic thoroughly and completely. Ask yourself these questions: *How long will my paper be? Is my topic too broad to be adequately covered in the assigned pages?* If the answer to the second question is yes, try focusing on one aspect of your topic. For example, the topic *Shakespeare's Influence on World Literature* would be too large for a paper of almost any length. (Indeed, that topic would fill several volumes.) Narrowing the topic to *Reflections of* Romeo and Juliet: *Shakespeare's Tragic Lovers as Seen in Twentieth-Century Literature* would be a step in the right direction. The topic *A Rose by Any Other Name: Quotations from* Romeo and Juliet *in 1990s Advertising* could possibly be covered in a five- to seven-page paper.

Considering Audience

People use language in different ways, depending on the situation. Part of maturing in your use of English is observing some of these differences and then learning to make them for yourself. Doing so will keep you from sounding stiff when you write to close friends, and it will keep you from sounding uninformed when you write an academic essay. Good writers consider their audience by asking *How large is my audience—one person, several, or many? In general, how much do the readers know about my topic? What is their relationship to me? What areas of my topic will interest my audience?* These factors affect the formality of a piece of writing. A history textbook, for example, is more formal than a newspaper. A legal document or a debate resolution would be more formal than a textbook.

Determining Purpose

It is important to decide early what the purpose of your writing will be. Is it to inform? to entertain? to persuade? to describe? The reason for a personal letter to your grandmother may be *to entertain* her with the story of your performance in the school play, whereas the purpose for an economics paper may be *to describe* the effect of the value of the American dollar on European currency. Include in your writing only information that will achieve your purpose.

Gathering Information

Once you have decided on a topic, whether for an assignment or for some other reason, your next step should be to jot down what you already know about the general subject area. You may already have done some of this in the initial stage of choosing your topic. After you have written down some of your ideas, look for additional information. Besides encyclopedias and books, remember magazines and electronic media. If you cannot find enough information on your topic, then you may have to change your idea. If you find too much information for one paper, you will need to either drop that idea or narrow the topic.

Outlining the Paper

You should always outline a paper before you begin to write it, using at least a tentative outline. The outline will help you remember to cover the important ideas, and it will help you cover them in a logical order.

A Tentative Outline

A tentative outline is always helpful. Simply jot down the ideas you will include in your paper. After you have the ideas written down, you can rearrange them in the best order for the paper.

The following tentative outline was done after some research on the senses of snakes.

A snake's vision
—stimulated by movement
—can't close eyes (?)
Sense of smell
—tongue
—Jacobson's organs

Hearing
—airborne sounds maybe
—vibrations

Outline Forms

A well-organized outline can be a real help in writing a paper. Sometimes you will be asked to hand in an outline along with a paper. Any outline that others will see should follow one of the two forms given below.

A **topic outline** uses phrases only—no sentences and no verbs except verbals. Points numbered or lettered in the same series should have the same grammatical form (nouns or adjectives or prepositional phrases or participles, for instance).

Introduction: snakes' strange abilities

   I. A snake's sense of hearing
      A. Airborne sounds
      B. Sound waves
  II. A snake's sense of vision
      A. Eyes always open
      B. Movement
      C. Supplemented by heat sensitivity
         1. In pit vipers only
         2. Even at night
 III. A snake's sense of smell

Conclusion: senses as aids to survival

A **sentence outline** includes more information than a topic outline does because every point in it is a complete sentence.

Introduction: Although snakes are fearful to many, their senses are fascinating.

   I. The snake's sense of hearing is somewhat poor.
      A. Snakes cannot hear most airborne sounds.
      B. They can "hear" ground vibrations.
  II. The snake's sense of vision is unusual.
      A. Snakes cannot close their eyes.
      B. They cannot see still objects.
      C. Some can "see" night victims.
 III. The snake's sense of smell is incomparable.

Conclusion: These senses are important to the snake's survival.

Drafting

Once you have planned your paper, you are ready to write your rough draft. The rough draft is simply your first try at writing the paper. You will have a chance to improve it later, so you need not spend much time trying to find exactly the right word for something. It is usually better to write the whole paper fairly quickly, and then go back to improve it later.

Paragraphs

Writing Introductory Paragraphs

Some writers like to write the whole rough draft straight through, beginning with the introduction. (Often they thoroughly rewrite the introduction later.) Others prefer to write the introduction after they have finished the rest of the paper.

A good introduction accomplishes three purposes: it catches the reader's interest, introduces the topic, and draws attention to the main idea in the topic sentence. You may want to begin with an interesting story, a compelling question, or a problem to solve. Sometimes a key quotation makes a good introduction. Whatever you do, keep the introduction short and interesting. An introduction functions like a funnel: it is wide at the beginning where it introduces the broad topic, and it narrows to the specific topic sentence at the end.

Usually the best plan is to begin the paragraph with the arouser of interest and then tie it to the subject of your paper. Do not say, "In this paper I will tell you about such-and-such"; instead simply mention the "such-and-such" in the very last sentence of the introductory paragraph.

Below are three sample introductions, any one of which could introduce the paper about the unusual senses of snakes.

Example 1

The field mouse froze in terror, suddenly aware of an enemy that could not yet be seen. There was a different movement in the wavering of the tall grass, a subtle but deadly slithering that chilled the heart. Suddenly, panic took over, and the mouse scurried for safety. That was the fatal mistake. Quickly and efficiently, the black snake struck. Like most snakes, it rarely missed. But without the snake's unusual senses, perhaps none of this would have happened.

Example 2

Snake—the word itself makes some of us feel a chill up our spine. The poet Emily Dickinson called him "a narrow fellow in the grass" that leaves us with "a tighter breathing, and zero at the bone." Our initial fear, though, should not keep us from recognizing that God has given snakes special senses to help them find food.

Example 3

Jesus instructed His disciples to be "wise as serpents." Why did he call the snakes "wise"? What special traits has God given snakes? Certainly their senses are unusual.

Building Good Paragraphs

The body (main part) of your paper should consist of thoroughly-developed paragraphs, each one dealing with a single division of the subject you have chosen. These divisions, of course, come from your outline. You may want to begin by marking the paragraph divisions on a copy of your outline.

Writing Topic Sentences

Not all good paragraphs contain topic sentences, but many paragraphs in informational or persuasive writing do. A **topic sentence** embodies the main idea of the paragraph. Usually the topic sentence begins the paragraph, and then everything else in the paragraph relates to the subject matter of that topic sentence.

If you used just a tentative outline or a topic outline to organize your paper, you will need to compose topic sentences as you write each paragraph. On the other hand, if you used a sentence outline, you may be able to use the main points of the outline as the topic sentences. (Of course, any prewritten topic sentences are likely to need some modification as you write the paper.)

For the paper outlined above, you might come up with these three topic sentences:

- There is some question about whether snakes can hear at all.
- A snake's vision is unusual in several ways.
- Believe it or not, a snake's best "smeller" is its tongue.

Developing Supporting Sentences

Once you have your main idea in a paragraph, you need to develop that idea with sentences that support your topic. Your supporting sentences use the information that you gathered in the planning stage. Keep in mind your audience and purpose as you provide evidence to support your topic.

Paragraphs may be developed in several ways. One obvious way is to back up the topic sentence with facts, examples, details, or reasons. Another way is to explain the topic further, perhaps even defining a key term. You may also compare or contrast two things or ideas. Often you will not adhere strictly to one method of development.

FACT	A statement presented as real or demonstrable
EXAMPLE	A fact or an occurrence that illustrates a point
STATISTIC	A fact expressed in numbers
INCIDENT/ ANECDOTE	A personal event that relates to the subject
SENSORY DETAILS	The use of sense words—taste, touch, smell, etc.
COMPARISON/ CONTRAST	Similarities and differences between two things

Organize your supporting sentences logically so that your reader can follow your writing from beginning to end. Keeping your audience and purpose in mind, choose an organizational method that will best suit your needs and meet your goals.

CHRONOLOGICAL	A presentation of events in order of their occurrence	Use in stories, biographies, news reports, and process or historical writing
SPATIAL	A description according to how something is arranged in physical layout	Use in descriptive writing—especially descriptions of places or objects
ORDER OF IMPORTANCE	A move from least important to most important or vice versa	Use in persuasive or descriptive writing

Writing Concluding Paragraphs

The purpose of the ending—usually a final paragraph—is to clinch the main idea and to give a sense of completeness. Therefore, you need to restate or at least refer to the main idea. Then go on to draw some logical conclusion from the main idea or to show the reader why that idea is important. Occasionally a short quotation may help end your paper strongly.

The sense of completeness can be obtained simply by your echo of the idea stated at the end of the introductory paragraph. If you began the paper with an attention-getting incident, you might even be able to tie the ends together by some further reference to the incident. Whatever method you use, though, keep the ending short. Below are three sample conclusions for the paper on snakes.

Example 1

The field mouse probably would have survived unseen a bit longer if it had not moved. However, the snake still could have used its tongue to follow the scent of the mouse. Such abilities make the snake a deadly enemy indeed. What other animal can smell with its tongue and "hear" with its whole body?

Example 2

Now, the next time you are being chased by a snake, there are several evasive maneuvers you need to consider. First, to counteract its sense of hearing, try flying or swinging on a vine. Just don't risk touching the ground! Next, to confuse its sense of sight, sit perfectly still. Don't move at all! Finally, to escape its sense of smell—oh well, you can't win them all. Do you feel that chill up your spine again?

Example 3

A snake's God-given senses are indeed unusual. Yet those senses are perfectly suited to the reptile's life. Its senses of hearing, sight, and smell all help the snake avoid danger and catch its prey.

Revising

Revision of the first draft should always be *re-vision*—seeing the material again. That is, you look at the rough draft again after a day or so to see whether you have said what you wanted to say and to see how you can improve the saying of it. The lapse of time helps you see it more objectively, as other people will see it.

No experienced writer skips the process of revision, nor should you. Revision is the way you improve whatever you are writing at the time, and it will gradually help you turn out better first drafts too. There are three main areas for revision: ideas, style, and correctness.

Revising for Ideas

Clarity of Purpose

Check your composition to see whether you have fulfilled your purpose in writing it. Have you clearly informed, or perhaps persuaded, your readers as you intended to? A paper that has not zeroed in on its purpose probably also lacks unity and clear organization.

Interest

If a paper is not interesting, it will not do its job well. But how can you tell whether it is interesting? Even the most lively piece of writing may seem dull after you have worked on it for a while. One solution is to let one or more friends read it for you and tell you their reactions. You can also try writing an alternate introduction or conclusion and ask a friend to help you decide which one is more interesting and effective.

Unity of Ideas

Ideas within a paragraph should relate to the topic of that paragraph. Leave out any unrelated or indirectly related ideas. (The same principle applies to the paper as a whole: every paragraph should relate to the main idea or thesis of the entire paper.) All illustrations and examples also need to relate directly to the main idea. Think of every example and anecdote, sentence and paragraph as working together to achieve a goal.

Coherence

Coherence requires that all of the parts of a paper cohere (stick together) well; that is, the relationship among ideas, sentences, and paragraphs is obvious and logical. In a cohesive paper, clear links move the reader naturally from each sentence or paragraph to the next. One way to achieve coherence is to use transitional expressions. Transitional words, phrases, or paragraphs act as links to keep the various parts of a paper together. Look at the following sample transitional expressions.

Type of transition	Examples of transitional expressions	
TIME	after	next
	during	first
	before	then
	always	meanwhile
	finally	again
	while	second
SPACE	behind	below
	here	in front of
	over	in the center
	on the left of	around
	on top of	
DEGREE	first	more important
	second	less important
	mainly	least important
COMPARISON	as	in the same way
	either . . . or	than
	likewise	neither . . . nor
	similarly	also

CONTRAST	yet	unlike
	on the contrary	but
	in contrast	on the other hand
	however	instead
CAUSE AND EFFECT	because	consequently
	although	therefore
	as a result	for this reason
	since	so that
	if . . . , then	
INTRODUCTORY	as	like
	that is	for example
	such as	namely
	for instance	to illustrate
	in particular	
EMPHASIS	indeed	in fact
	in other words	
FURTHER INFORMATION	in addition	moreover
	similarly	besides
	also	furthermore
	as well as	
EXPLANATION	for example	in other words
	that is	

Revising for Style

Emphasis

Good writers use emphasis to make important ideas stand out. Varying sentence type, length, and structure; using parallelism; planning comparisons and contrasts; and paying attention to sentence rhythm all produce writing that is interesting and effective. Another tool for attaining emphasis is positioning the most important idea of a paragraph at the end or at the beginning of the paragraph.

Precise Words

As you revise, correct the inaccurate or imprecise words. Precise, specific words help you to get your message across to your reader clearly. Use precise nouns and verbs. Some words may be general (like *city* or *said*), and some words may be specific (like *London* or *shouted*). Use specific, precise words whenever applicable. A thesaurus may help you find the specific word you need.

Conciseness

Elimination of Obvious Redundancy

All writing contains a certain amount of redundancy, but you should get rid of any that is noticeable. When it is clear that fewer words will do the job, then fewer words should be used.

Reduction of Clauses

You can often help a problem sentence by reducing a dependent clause to a shorter, simpler element. (See Ch. 14.) Often the reduced clause is not only more concise but also more flexible in sentence position. Many times clauses can be reduced to the various types of phrases.

Smoothness

Everyone wants his writing to read smoothly. Some people can "listen" for problems as they read silently, but others find this difficult to do. A good way to judge the flow of your writing is to read the paper aloud. You can ask someone to read it aloud while you listen. Then revise any phrase or sentence that sounds awkward. The following are seven reasons that a sentence might be awkward.

(1) The language is not fully natural. (See information on idiomatic use of prepositions and verbs, pp. 24-25 and 123-25.)

(2) The subject is too long.

(3) There is a long interruption between the subject and verb.

> AWKWARD   Musicians, *it has always seemed to me though I am no expert,* should begin performing early in life.

> IMPROVED   It seems reasonable that musicians should begin performing early in life.

(4) There is an interruption between a verb and its object.

> AWKWARD   My brother played *at age nine* his first violin solo.
> IMPROVED   My brother played his first violin solo at age nine.

(5) There is a string of modifying nouns in the sentence.

> AWKWARD   Mr. Martin did research on college students' *pre-college music performance experience.*

> IMPROVED   Mr. Martin studied college students' earlier experience in performing music.

(6) The sentence is excessively complex.

AWKWARD Mrs. Fields practiced a scientific procedure when she observed that people in front of large audiences tend to lose their composure and then devised a plan using that observation.

IMPROVED Mrs. Fields practiced a scientific procedure based on observation. After noticing that people in front of large audiences often lose their composure, she devised a plan using that observation.

(7) The same structure appears more than once in the sentence, apart from intentional parallelism.

AWKWARD *In* the first place, *in* a good performance there is variety.

IMPROVED First, in a good performance there is variety.

Fresh Words

Overused words or phrases can drain vitality from a paper. Find a fresh replacement for a word that is repeated too often in your paper. A thesaurus may help you find suitable synonyms. A similar problem is a cliché, a worn-out phrase that has lost its effectiveness. Substitute simpler expressions or new comparisons for clichés like *cool as a cucumber, stick out like a sore thumb, pride and joy, first and foremost,* and *to the bitter end.*

Revising for Correctness: Proofreading

The final step in revising your paper is to proofread for correctness. If the working copy of your paper is so full of editing marks and changes that the draft is difficult to read, then type or write a new copy for final proofreading. The fresh copy will enable you to read the paper smoothly and give you a better chance of catching errors.

Sentence Structure and Grammatical Forms

Be sure that you correct fragments, comma splices, or fused sentences. Also be sure that the grammatical forms in the paper are correct.

Usage

Be sure that your subjects and verbs agree and that your pronouns and antecedents agree. Check such areas as pronoun case.

Spelling and Other Conventions

Check your final draft carefully for spelling; do not wait until you have made the clean copy to hand in. Look up every word you are not completely sure of. Use all tools at your disposal. However, always read carefully yourself because those tools cannot possibly catch every error. For example, a computer word processor's spell checker will catch only nonwords like *thier,* not substitute words like *there.* Also check for punctuation and capitalization errors, repeated or omitted words, and in-correct division of a word at the end of a line.

Good proofreading takes practice, but you can learn to do it well. Unless you are already an expert proofreader, the most important princi-ple is this: do not expect to find every error (or every kind of error) in a single reading. Read in different ways to find different things.

First, read your paper slowly and carefully, thinking about the mean-ing as you go. This reading will help you catch errors like the substitu-tion of *threw* for *through;* both are spelled correctly, but one cannot replace the other. Then examine the paper even more slowly, looking de-liberately at each word to see whether it is spelled correctly. This kind of proofreading is not easy because we normally take in whole phrases at a time when we read. Some people make themselves slow down by using a blank card to cover what has not yet been examined. Others read the paper aloud. Still others look at the words in reverse order, as if they were reading backwards.

Finally, you may want to read the paper through more quickly a few times, looking each time for some particular problem area that has been difficult for you in the past. For instance, it is fairly easy to spot comma problems when you read looking only for commas.

Careful proofreading does take some time. It is only a little more time, however, in comparison with what you have already invested in your project. And it can make an important difference in people's im-pressions of your work.

Publishing

Once you have revised and carefully checked your paper, you are ready to make a neat copy of the final draft, the copy to turn in. Publishing your paper simply means that you are sharing it with others.

Title

Before you publish, you need to choose a title for your work. Choosing a title is important. The title tells the reader what he is about to read. The title should generally be short, usually no more than five or six words. If possible, it should be interesting, inviting the audience to read more. Finally, a title should be specific. Rather than just the general subject area, it should suggest the subject and perhaps the approach of that particular paper.

TOO GENERAL	Snakes
	Unusual Characteristics of Animals
GOOD	How the Snake Locates the Mouse
POSSIBILITIES	Unusual Senses of Snakes
	"Wise as Serpents"
	A Snake's Senses

Neat Copy

Be sure that if you publish for a class, you know what form the teacher expects and follow that form carefully.

Handwritten papers usually must be written on $8^1/_2$-by-11-inch lined notebook paper, on one side only, in blue or black ink. The teacher may prefer that you use the standard wide-lined paper or that you write on every other line of the narrow-lined paper. Leave even margins on the right and left sides, and leave the last two lines blank.

Word-processed papers should be printed in black ink on standard-sized paper one side only and should use the font style and size that your teacher dictates. Double-space your paper, leaving at least one-inch margins on all four sides.

Follow your teacher's instructions about the placement of your name, the date, and the name of the class.

Other Ideas for Publishing

- Send it to your local newspaper.
- Put together a class collection.
- Use your work for programs.
- Share it with your English class.
- Read your work to someone at home.
- Mail it to a friend or relative.

After you finish your final draft, you may want to put it in a folder or notebook where you keep your writing. By the end of the year, you could have a complete collection of your work. You and your teacher may find these folders helpful because the folder allows you, your parents, and your teacher to see your progress over the weeks, semesters, or year. The folder also can help you see mistakes that you have made in the past so that you will not make them again in your future papers.

Essays

An essay is a composition consisting of several paragraphs developed around one main idea. Most essays have three main parts: introduction, body, and conclusion. In a three-paragraph essay, each of these elements consists of one paragraph. In a five-paragraph essay, the introduction and conclusion are each one paragraph, and the body of the essay consists of the other three paragraphs. In an in-class essay, the entire essay may be only one paragraph, with the thesis and the concluding statement each a single sentence.

Writing a Thesis Statement

The main idea of the entire essay is stated in the **thesis statement,** which usually appears at the end of the introduction. It is similar to the topic sentence in a paragraph. A good thesis statement tells your audience your topic and what you will say about that topic.

> **POOR**   Snakes are unusual animals.
> **GOOD**   A snake's sense of smell is highly developed.

Writing Introductory and Concluding Sentences

In the in-class essay, there is no introductory paragraph; rather, the thesis statement serves to introduce the topic and plunge the reader directly into the topic at hand. Sentence two is the first supporting sentence (point *I* of the outline). Begin a new paragraph for each major point in your outline and place the supporting sentence first in the paragraph. Likewise, there is no conclusion—only a **restatement** of the thesis. Below is an example of an in-class essay about snakes. The sentences in bold are the thesis statement and restatement; the sentences in italics are the three supporting sentences.

> **The snake has a remarkable set of senses.** *Although they hear poorly, some types of snake use a unique set of heat-sensitive organs to find their prey.* These *pit organs* allow the snake to locate exactly another animal using the body heat the animal emits. Even in the dark, a snake can strike accurately and quickly.
>
> *The snake's sense of vision is also unusual.* Its beady eyes cannot close and seem always to be locked in a steely stare. Located on either side of its head, the eyes allow for wide peripheral vision. Surprisingly, a snake cannot see an object that remains still. However, most animals are forced to move eventually, and the snake watches every move.

Snakes have an incomparable sense of smell. Their long, forked tongues serve as sensors for the slightest scent of friend or foe. A scent organ located in the snake's mouth receives odors from the ever-flicking tongue. Using these special organs, a snake can even track another animal. **Indeed, the snake is well equipped with extraordinary sense organs.**

Writing Strategies

Knowing how to follow the basic writing process, knowing the basic grammar rules, and getting the punctuation correct makes you a good writer, right? Not exactly. Many writing strategies exist that can help you polish and smooth out your writing. These strategies can help you state ideas more clearly and in a more interesting fashion. This chapter focuses on different writing strategies that you can follow to create an even better composition.

Sentence Variety and Emphasis in the Paragraph

You have chosen an interesting topic and have considered your audience. However, the writing itself needs to maintain the reader's interest. An important key is found in this simple formula:

> Variety + Emphasis = Interest

First consider how the formula would apply to a style of speaking. A boring voice is one that is always the same. It has the same tone, the same speed, the same loudness—the same everything. Nothing seems more important than anything else, and soon to our sleepy ears nothing at all seems important.

In writing, too, variety and emphasis help to create and maintain interest. An effective writer uses a variety of sentence types, making good use of the choices open to him as he builds his sentences. At the same time, he uses those choices to give emphasis to whatever is most important. Good sentence-construction choices with variety and emphasis result in clear, interesting sentences.

Using Variety to Achieve Emphasis

Four general principles will enable you to draw attention to important ideas in your sentences. The list is ordered from the least to the most powerful principle.

First, a fuller expression is often more noticeable, or more emphatic, than a brief one.

ADEQUATE	A good writer uses good choices *to emphasize* whatever is most important.
MORE EMPHASIS	A good writer uses good choices *to give emphasis to* whatever is most important.

Second, certain kinds of words are stronger than others.

WEAK	The sin of spiritual apathy is difficult to *get rid of.*
STRONGER	The sin of spiritual apathy is difficult to *overcome.*

The verb *overcome* is much stronger than the preposition *of.* Verbs are nearly always stronger than prepositions. A well-chosen noun can be stronger than an adjective or adverb.

Third, a short sentence before or after a series of longer ones can be emphatic because of contrast. Unusual types of sentences can serve the same purpose. (See pp. 204-5.)

No one will care if I take another helping. It looks so delicious just sitting there all alone in the middle of the pan. Won't its feelings be hurt if it's the only piece not taken? "Pie, please." A paragon of self-control I am not.

Finally, putting the important word or phrase at the end of the sentence achieves natural emphasis, for these words are the last the reader will see. A similar result comes from putting the important item before other kinds of pauses in the sentence, such as at the end of a clause or before an interrupting word. (Moving an element to the beginning of the sentence can also give a certain amount of emphasis.)

EMPHASIS ON GOING TO WAR	In William Jennings Bryan's opinion, a public vote should be taken before the nation could go to war.
EMPHASIS ON TAKING A VOTE	In William Jennings Bryan's opinion, before the nation could go to war a public vote should be taken.

These principles, of course, are helpful only if they are not overused. It is important to emphasize only what needs pointing out, what is truly important.

Varying the Length and Complexity of Sentences

A skillful writer avoids both a series of short sentences and a series of extremely long sentences. The ideal is a comfortable mix of short, medium, and longer sentences. Typically, some of these sentences would be simple, others would be compound, and still others would be complex or compound-complex.

Here is a paragraph that needs improvement.

> Genghis Khan was the leader of the Mongols. His name means "universal ruler." He established a vast empire. It stretched from eastern Europe to the Sea of Japan. It included parts of China and Russia. The empire's greatest accomplishment was reopening the Silk Road. Renewed trade led to an East-West cultural exchange. Marco Polo's visit was an eventual result of such action. *(eight simple sentences)*

The style above is choppy; all ideas are treated as if they were equally important. Revised, the paragraph reads better:

> Genghis Khan, whose name means "universal ruler," was the leader of the Mongols. He established a vast empire that stretched from eastern Europe to the Sea of Japan, including parts of China and Russia. The empire's greatest accomplishment was reopening the Silk Road. Renewed trade led to an East-West cultural exchange, and that exchange resulted eventually in the visits of men like Marco Polo. *(four sentences: compound, complex, simple, compound)*

Varying Sentence Patterns

Good writing seems naturally to include a variety of basic sentence patterns. Most of the time we need not think about this aspect of writing. Sometimes in the process of revision, though, we may realize that we have overused one or two of the sentence patterns. Then it is time to work consciously for variety.

Notice the following poor example, which uses a high proportion of intransitive verbs.

> Seventeen-year-old Marco Polo traveled from Venice, Italy, to China (S-InV). He went there with his father and his uncle (S-InV). Kublai Khan was desirous of one hundred Catholic missionaries from the Pope to convert the Khan's people (S-LV-PA). However, only two friars were willing to go and serve (S-LV-PA). Both deserted long before the end of the journey (S-InV), but the Polo family continued on (S-InV). Their journey lasted over three years (S-InV). Marco then served in the Khan's court for seventeen years (S-InV). He became fluent in four languages (S-LV-PA). He

ruled over a major city (S-InV), and he went on many important missions for the Khan (S-InV).

Revision produces much greater variety.

> Seventeen-year-old Marco Polo traveled from Venice, Italy, to China with his father and his uncle (S-InV). Kublai Khan had asked the Pope for one hundred Catholic missionaries to convert the Khan's people (S-TrV-DO). Only two friars, however, offered the Pope their services (S-TrV-IO-DO), and they deserted the Polo family long before the end of the three-year journey (S-TrV-DO). Marco then served in the Khan's court for seventeen years (S-InV). He became fluent in four languages (S-LV-PA). He ruled a major city (S-TrV-DO), and the Khan sent him on many important missions (S-TrV-DO).

Varying the Sentence Beginnings

A style becomes dull quickly when every sentence begins with a subject and verb. To achieve variety, you can move phrases, modifiers, or clauses to the beginnings of sentences. Keeping in mind that overuse of any one type of beginning is monotonous, consider beginning sentences with the following: adverb, adjective, participle, participial phrase, infinitive, infinitive phrase, prepositional phrase, or dependent clause. Look at a few examples of varied sentence beginnings.

REGULAR SUBJECT AND VERB	An intruder entered our home last evening and then ran away.
ADJECTIVE	Tall and bald, the intruder was easily identified.
PARTICIPIAL PHRASE	Yelling at the policeman, the intruder was subdued.
DEPENDENT CLAUSE	When I returned home from the police station, I took a long nap.

Choosing Wisely for Variety and Emphasis

In expressing our thoughts we routinely choose between certain constructions. These choices are usually automatic, but at times we may wish to think about them in order to improve a piece of writing. The kind of choices mentioned below can be used for both variety and emphasis.

Active vs. Passive

Chapter 9 defines active and passive voice and gives a number of suggestions about good use of active and passive voice. Note two simple principles:

1. Although an occasional passive may be useful for variety or for some other purpose, it is best not to overuse the passive.
2. Using the passive voice instead of the active allows a writer to position something at the end of the sentence for emphasis.

Indirect Object vs. Prepositional Phrase

Any sentence with an indirect object can instead be worded with a prepositional phrase.

WITH INDIRECT OBJECT   Brad also brought his mother a dozen yellow roses.

WITH PREPOSITIONAL PHRASE   Brad also brought a dozen yellow roses to his mother.

The first sentence focuses on the roses, suggesting perhaps that he had already brought her something else. The second sentence draws more attention to his mother; possibly Brad had already given roses to someone else. Obviously, then, the interchange of these two constructions allows us to bring either noun phrase to the place of focus, the end of the sentence.

Coordination and Subordination

A pleasing paragraph normally uses both coordination and subordination, resulting in a variety of sentence structures. Of course, the main purpose of coordination and subordination is to show the relations between the ideas being expressed.

In any paragraph, some ideas are more important than others. Ideas of equal importance can be left in separate sentences, or they can be joined on an equal basis, often by a coordinating conjunction.

ORIGINAL SENTENCES   Alexander Hamilton came to the American colonies in 1772. From 1773 to 1774 he studied at King's College, now Columbia University.

COORDINATED SENTENCES   Alexander Hamilton came to the American colonies in 1772, and then he studied briefly at King's College, now Columbia University.

COORDINATED PREDICATE	Alexander Hamilton came to the American colonies in 1772 and studied briefly at King's College, now Columbia University.

Ideas of unequal importance in the paragraph can be joined on an unequal basis.

ORIGINAL SENTENCES	By 1776 he had written several articles and pamphlets. These writings effectively supported the colonial cause.
SUBORDINATED (DEPENDENT CLAUSES)	By 1776 he had written several articles *that effectively supported the colonial cause.*
SUBORDINATED (PARTICIPIAL PHRASE)	By 1776 he had written several articles and pamphlets *effectively supporting the colonial cause.*

The choice, then, between coordination and subordination normally depends on the relative importance of the ideas.

Using Unusual Types of Sentences to Provide Emphasis

Certain unusual types of sentences can be used sparingly for effect. They obviously contribute to sentence variety, but their primary function is to provide emphasis.

The Periodic Sentence

A periodic sentence is a fairly long sentence whose main idea is not complete until the end of the sentence. All the less important elements come earlier in the sentence. (A sentence in which some less important ideas trail after the main idea is called a *loose sentence.*)

PERIODIC SENTENCE	There is reason to believe that in 1685 London had been, during about half a century, the most populous capital in Europe.—*Thomas Macaulay*
LOOSE SENTENCE	There is reason to believe that London was the most populous capital in Europe during the half century before 1685.

The Rhetorical Question

A rhetorical question is asked simply for effect, with no answer expected. The rhetorical question can be a means of special emphasis, as long as it is not overused.

NORMAL SENTENCES	No one else should care whether we get green or gold candles for the banquet. Either color will look good.
RHETORICAL QUESTION	Why should anyone care whether we get green or gold candles for the banquet? Either color will look good.

The Inverted Sentence

Special emphasis can come from an occasional inversion of a sentence. Most common is to put the complement at the beginning of the sentence.

A genius he is not. (PN-S-LV)

Another possibility is to bring the main verb to the front of the sentence or clause, leaving the auxiliary behind.

Trotting? That horse may have been cantering or galloping, but trotting he was not.

The effect of all such inversions is to emphasize both what is brought to the front and what comes last.

The Short Fragment

Usually we avoid fragments, but a rare, skillfully written short fragment can be used for emphasis. It can also express an ironic afterthought.

EMPHASIS	A ski-jump champion needs nerve and skill. Todd is short on skill, but nerve he has. Hence the broken leg.
IRONIC AFTERTHOUGHT	A ski-jump champion needs nerve and skill. Todd is short on skill, but nerve he has. Or had.

Even for these purposes, sentence fragments are less successful for formal and impersonal writing. If you doubt the wisdom of such a fragment, either avoid it or, on a school paper, write "intentional fragment" by it in the margin. At least then the teacher will know that the fragment was not a careless error.

Sentence Energy

How nice it would be if all of our writing were not only correct but also interesting. Here we look at how to make a sentence come alive.

Verbs That Act

Action verbs are more interesting than state-of-being verbs. (Remember that not all state-of-being verbs are linking verbs.) The most colorless state-of-being verb, the verb *be,* can often be replaced by a verb with more color and life.

STATE-OF-BEING VERBS	The weather *had been* wet for two days. The cold, heavy rain *would* probably *last* another day at least. The storm drains *were* nearly full, and pedestrians *were* at the mercy of water splashing from passing cars.
ACTION VERBS	It *had* already *rained* for two days. The cold, heavy rain *would* probably *fall* for at least another day. Water *poured* down the storm drains, and passing cars *splashed* pedestrians mercilessly.

Do not feel that you must replace every state-of-being verb with an action verb, but do look critically at them. A sentence is often more lively with a verb that acts.

Details

Lively sentences give the reader the details he needs in order to imagine the situation.

FEW DETAILS	Janet waited for the bus at a drugstore. The rain let up, and she got on the bus. Her feet were cold and wet.
MORE DETAILS ADDED	Janet took momentary shelter in the entrance to Plumb's drugstore as she waited for a bus. The rain let up just as the bus approached, but the bus stopped too far from the curb. As she stepped down into the running water, Janet wished she had not worn open-toed shoes.

The secret to giving details is to visualize the scene or the situation completely. Then give the reader the important details that will help him visualize it too.

Accuracy

Lively writing is accurate writing—using just the right words in the right way.

Accurate Words

Be su~ ~' at the words you choose have the meaning you intend. If in doubt 't your dictionary.

WRONG WORD	The British took Australia from *descendants* of today's aborigines.

CORRECTION	The British took Australia from the *ancestors* of today's aborigines.

Accurate Phrasing

Sometimes a sentence misses the mark because a whole phrase is misused or misstated. Correct the phrasing and the sentence directly hits the target.

INACCURATE PHRASING	Mr. Johnson *will open us* in prayer.

CORRECTION	Mr. Johnson will *open our meeting* in prayer.

Appropriate Connotation

Connotation, the emotional coloring of a word, can at times be as important as denotation (the word's actual meaning). For example, the phrase *my male parent* has the same meaning as *my father,* but not the same connotation. It is important to recognize differences in connotation and to use them to create the effect you want.

NEUTRAL	I received a birthday card from *the preacher at my church.*

MORE FAVORABLE	I received a birthday card from *my pastor.*

Specific, Concrete Words

A colorless sentence may become more vivid when a specific word is substituted for a general one.

GENERAL	As he thought about the hunt to come, Jay finished his *food* quickly.

SPECIFIC	As he thought about the hunt to come, Jay finished his *bacon and scrambled eggs* quickly.

Even a statement that presents a generalization may become more interesting when specific words are used to suggest the whole category.

GENERAL	Our treasure is in heaven, yet we all are in danger of caring too much about *material possessions.*

MORE SPECIFIC	Our treasure is in heaven, yet we all are in danger of caring too much about *stylish clothing, a late-model car, or a fine home.*

Simple, concrete words are more interesting than abstract ones.

ABSTRACT	Mr. Owings usually had good ideas, but he disliked *opposition.*
MORE CONCRETE	Mr. Owings usually had good ideas, but he disliked *arguments or even questions about his ideas.*

Pauses for Breath

A long, strung-out sentence leaves the reader gasping for air—and perhaps wondering what the main point was. A stringy sentence should usually be broken into two or more sentences.

STRINGY	It is a good idea to be neat, and I like neatness as much as anyone, but it is just hard to remember to put things away as soon as I have finished with them, and not leave them lying around in a handy position.
SPLIT INTO THREE SENTENCES	It is a good idea to be neat, and I like neatness as much as anyone. However, I have a hard time remembering to put things away as soon as I have finished with them. Too often I fall for the temptation to leave things lying around in a handy position.

Figurative Language

Clarity and vividness often increase when we describe one thing in terms of another. The general term for all such comparisons is **metaphor.** In the narrow sense, metaphors are stated or implied comparisons like the following:

STATED COMPARISONS	"The Lord is my *rock,* and my *fortress,* and my deliverer; my God, my strength, in whom I will trust; my *buckler,* and the *horn* of my salvation, and my high tower" (Ps. 18:2).
IMPLIED COMPARISON	"The heathen are sunk down in the pit that they made: in the net which they hid is their own foot taken" (Ps. 9:15).

Implied in the second example is a comparison of the heathen enemy to a hunter who tries to catch his prey in a pit or a net. Other comparisons, technically called **similes,** are made in statements with *like* or *as:*

> "But the wicked are *like the troubled sea,* when it cannot rest, whose waters cast up mire and dirt. There is no peace, saith my God, to the wicked" (Isa. 57:20-21).

Such comparisons show metaphor to be a valuable tool. However, this tool can easily slip in our hands.

Mixed Metaphors

The most obvious problem to avoid is the metaphor that points in two directions at once. For instance, here is a poor version of the preceding sentence:

> **MIXED**   The most obvious trap to avoid is a comparison that
> **METAPHORS** swims both upstream and down.

Are we talking about a trap or a fish? (A trap that swims?) The next example is even more ludicrous.

> **MIXED**   When Mr. Smith was put out to pasture, he had to
> **METAPHORS** tighten his belt and pinch pennies.

> **POSSIBLE**   When Mr. Smith was retired, he had to tighten his belt
> **IMPROVEMENTS** a notch or two.
> When Mr. Smith was retired, he had to be more careful with his money.

Stretched Metaphors

Another problem is the overly elaborate metaphor. A metaphor that tries too hard is more of a hindrance than a help.

> **STRETCHED**   The acid of bitterness can eat deep into the soul. It
> **METAPHOR** never etches an agreeable image on its container, but instead pits and mars it. Without the neutralizing effect of forgiveness, it only becomes more and more potent with the passage of time.

The basic comparison here is fitting, but the way it is presented turns our attention away from the subject (bitterness) and to the comparison (acid). Furthermore, the metaphor breaks down in some of its details. (Acid is used in etching, but not when it is in "its container." And forgiveness would *replace* bitterness, not just make it weaker.)

SIMPLIFIED, IMPROVED METAPHOR	Bitterness always destroys its own container. The only remedy for bitterness is a forgiving spirit.

A metaphor can be developed at greater length, but care is needed: extended metaphors are hard to write well. In a good example, such as Psalm 23, the metaphor illuminates without getting in the way.

Misused Dead Metaphors

Many of our common expressions originated as metaphors. For instance, we can *grasp* an idea, *pick up* new ideas, *hold* them in mind, and even *tear* them apart. We may *tear into* or *wade into* a problem without ever thinking of the picture that these words once called to mind. The metaphor, we say, is now dead. Dead metaphors are usually harmless, but sometimes they suddenly come to life and make trouble.

The most frequent problem is an unthinking use of two dead metaphors that clash. The clash often revives the original meaning, creating the mixed-metaphor problem.

DEAD METAPHORS	He waded into the problem and tackled it at the source. (making a tackle against something that can be waded into?)
MIXED CORRECTED	He attacked the problem at its source.

DEAD METAPHORS	He got to the root of the problem right off the bat. (finding the root of a plant that has just been batted?)
MIXED CORRECTED	He found the root of the problem right away.

Dead metaphors may also come to life disconcertingly when something in the context makes us think of their literal meaning.

INAPPROPRIATE DEAD METAPHOR	Before he presented his report on caterpillars, Tommy had butterflies in his stomach.

Here it would be better to say that Tommy was nervous.

So far, dead metaphors sound like a problem, but they need not be. They can be used appropriately and even turned to advantage.

Sentence Expansion and Reduction

What if every English sentence were a bare-bones simple sentence? We would need to read many more sentences than we do. And we would likely be bored in the process. As you know, we can join thoughts in a number of ways. We can join them on an equal basis, making compound sentences. We can also join them on an unequal basis, pointing up certain ideas as more important. The ideas that are less important to us we subordinate in a variety of ways.

Combining Thoughts Using Dependent Clauses

Sometimes you can make a sentence interesting by adding another thought to it in the form of a dependent clause. A dependent clause is like a simple sentence in having a subject and a predicate, but its form has been adjusted enough to make it usable as part of another sentence.

There are three kinds of dependent clauses, based on how the clause is used in the larger sentence. Refer to Chapter 3 for a complete explanation of clauses.

ADJECTIVE CLAUSE   Modifies a noun or pronoun

James Fenimore Cooper was probably the first American *who made a living by writing novels.*

ADVERB CLAUSE   Usually modifies a verb

If you have read any of the Leatherstocking Saga, you know about Natty Bumppo.

NOUN CLAUSE   Functions as a noun: subject, direct object, and so on

Critics feel *that Cooper romanticized the pioneers too much.*

Often we combine clauses within a sentence in order to make the sentence more interesting and to show the connections between certain ideas. Sometimes, though, we find that the resulting sentence is too complicated, or too heavy, for its setting. Then it is helpful to know some ways of reducing clauses to simpler expressions.

Reducing Combined Independent Clauses

Compound Sentence to Simple Sentence with a Compound Part

In certain constructions, we almost always eliminate possible repetition. In fact, with this first group we often perform the process automatically as we originally make the sentence. However, looking at these examples will perhaps make it easier to understand some that may not be quite so obvious.

Sam *let us out at the entrance* and (~~Sam~~) *then went to park the car.*

We may *visit the zoo* or (~~we may~~) *spend the afternoon in the park.*

We drove *by City Hall* and (~~we drove~~) *near the library.*

I like to watch *the lions* and (~~I like to watch~~) *the tigers.*

Each of these pairs of ideas can be expressed in a compound sentence. However, as shown by the cross-outs in parentheses, the repeated word or words can be left out. (The process of leaving out of a sentence something that will still be understood is called **ellipsis.**) What remains in each example is a simple sentence that contains some compound part. The italic print shows which parts are joined by the conjunction in the simple sentences.

Ellipsis in a Compound Sentence

Sometimes when we leave out repeated words in a compound sentence, we do not end up with a simple sentence containing a compound part. Instead we still have a compound sentence, but now one in which some of the words are understood rather than expressed.

The lion sometimes roars, but I doubt that it will (~~roar~~) today.

The monkeys do tricks in the morning, and the seals (~~do tricks~~) in the afternoon.

Foxes are canines, but goats are not (~~canines~~).

The omission of these words can be called **ellipsis,** and the result is an "elliptical independent clause" in a compound sentence. This kind of ellipsis can be a useful way to eliminate extra words.

Reducing Adjective Clauses

By using an adjective clause we can add significant information to one of the nouns in a sentence. At times, though, we may want to express the information in fewer words.

If the subject of an adjective clause is a relative pronoun, we can usually reduce the clause to just a phrase or even just a word. The usual first step—and often the only step—is to drop both the relative-pronoun subject and either the auxiliary *be* or the verb *be*. What is left of the former adjective clause depends mainly on what was there in the first place.

Adjective Clause to Participle

An adjective clause can often be reduced either to a simple participle or to a participial phrase.

People [~~who are~~ having problems] should seek biblical advice.

Here we simply leave out *who are:* "People *having problems* should seek biblical advice." All that is left of the former clause is a participial phrase modifying the noun.

Advice [~~which is~~ based on God's Word] is worth following.

Back in the first sample sentence, the adjective clause with an active verb produced a present participle. Here the adjective clause with a passive verb produces a past participle. (The past participle is more accurately called a "passive participle.")

So far we have produced participial phrases, and the phrases stayed after the nouns modified. Notice, though, what usually happens when all that remains of the clause is a simple participle:

Everyone appreciates a face [~~that is~~ smiling].

We normally move a simple participle to a position before the noun, as if it were a regular adjective.

Everyone appreciates a smiling face.

We could not have done so with the participial phrases—for instance, we would never say "*Having problems* people should seek biblical advice." However, a participle modified only by a preceding adverb can usually be moved.

Everyone appreciates a face [~~that is~~ honestly smiling.] → Everyone appreciates an honestly smiling face.

So far it has appeared that the clause must have a form of *be* in it already. Actually, though, many clauses without *be* could be reworded with *be* and then reduced.

people who have problems (= people who are having problems) ➔ people
   having problems

a face that smiles (= a face that is smiling) ➔ a smiling face

the cup that he broke (= the cup that was broken) ➔ the broken cup

anyone who laughed ➔ anyone laughing

anyone who laughs ➔ anyone laughing

The last two examples show that specific tense reference is missing with participles. They also show that simple participles do not move to a position before indefinite pronouns.

Adjective Clause to Appositive

If the adjective clause contains a predicate noun after a form of *be,* the clause can be reduced to an appositive.

Our pastor, [~~who is~~ a biblical counselor], does not believe or use the ideas of Freud, Rogers, or Skinner.

Our pastor, a biblical counselor, does not believe or use the ideas of Freud, Rogers, or Skinner.

Notice that the commas around the nonrestrictive adjective clause remain around the nonrestrictive appositive. A restrictive adjective clause would produce a restrictive appositive.

The apostle [~~who is~~ Paul] tells us to finish the course.

The apostle *Paul* tells us to finish the course.

Adjective Clause to Prepositional Phrase

An adjective clause with a prepositional phrase after a form of *be* can be reduced to just the prepositional phrase.

First the Scriptures teach us of salvation through faith [~~which is~~ in Christ Jesus].

First the Scriptures teach us of salvation through faith *in Christ Jesus.*

Sometimes an adjective clause that has no prepositional phrase in it can nevertheless be converted into a prepositional phrase. The most obvious example is a clause containing the verb *have.*

People [who have problems] should seek biblical advice.

People *with problems* should seek biblical advice.

A clause with *have* can usually be converted into a *with* phrase. The preposition *of* is also useful.

> The principle [that is found in Philippians 4:8] is the way to control your thoughts.
> The principle *of Philippians 4:8* is the way to control your thoughts.

Adjective Clause to Adjective

If an adjective clause contains a predicate adjective after the linking verb *be,* it can be reduced to just the adjective.

> A heart [~~that is~~ godly] has God's peace.
> A godly heart has God's peace.

Just as with a simple participle, a simple adjective nearly always moves to a position before the noun. A qualifying adverb would move with the adjective.

> The Christian life is the life [~~that is~~ really joyful].
> The Christian life is the really joyful life.

However, if the adjective should happen to be modified by a phrase, the adjective and its phrase would not move.

> He has a spirit [~~that is~~ always joyful in the Lord].
> He has a spirit always joyful in the Lord.

Adjective Clause to Adjectival Adverb

Occasionally, an adjective clause containing an adverb is reduced in such a way that only the adverb remains to modify the noun.

> The lesson [~~that was taught~~ today] was on Philippians 4:6-9.
> One principle [~~which is seen~~ here] is that right feelings follow right actions.

Adverbs, unlike adjectives, do not move to a position before the nouns.

> The lesson today was on Philippians 4:6-9.
> One principle here is that right feelings follow right actions.

Usually adverbs used in this way have a meaning of place or time.

Reducing Adverb Clauses

The information given in an adverb clause can sometimes be expressed more briefly. Though certain clauses should be spelled out fully, it is often useful to be able to reduce a clause to a simpler structure.

Adverb Clause to Infinitive

If an adverb clause expressing purpose has the same subject as the main clause, the purpose clause can usually be converted to an infinitive phrase.

to

We chose this neighborhood [so that we would be close to the church and the school].

We chose this neighborhood to be close to the church and the school.

When the "purpose" meaning of the infinitive is not fully clear, *in order to* can make it clear.

We chose this neighborhood *in order to* be close to the church and the school.

The purpose infinitive, like the purpose clause, is adverbial and can come at the beginning of the sentence.

In order to be close to the church and the school, we chose this neighborhood.

Adverb Clause to Participle

If an adverb clause has the same subject as the main clause, and if it expresses a meaning of time, cause, or condition, it may be reducible to a phrase based on a participle. (If an adverb clause with a different subject is reduced to a participle, the result is a dangling modifier, a serious error: *Arriving here, the house pleased us.*)

Arriving

[As/When we arrived here], we met one of our new neighbors.

Arriving here, we met one of our new neighbors.

In reducing a time clause, we use a present participle to indicate the same time as in the main clause. To express prior time, we use a perfect participle.

Having arrived
[~~After we arrived~~ here], we tried to meet our other neighbors.

Having arrived here, we tried to meet our other neighbors.

Clauses of cause are reduced in the same way:

Being
[~~Because you are~~ creative], you can surely find a way to use our old curtains in this room, can't you?

Being creative, you can surely find a way to use our old curtains in this room, can't you?

In every case, the participial phrase has a less explicit meaning than the full adverb clause, mainly because the subordinating conjunction is omitted. This reduction in information may be desirable or not, depending on how much you want to say. Usually, of course, the context will allow the reader to figure out the omitted subordinating conjunction (*when, after, because,* etc.). Sometimes a small difference in the main clause signals a significant difference in the implied adverb clause:

Cleaned up, this house will be attractive.
Cleaned up, this house would be attractive.

The first participle comes from a time clause ("When this house is cleaned up"), but the second from a clause of condition ("If this house were cleaned up").

Even though the adverbial meaning can usually be figured out, it is no longer expressly stated. Therefore the participial phrases are generally considered to be adjectival, modifying the subject of the main clause. That is, a participle is considered to modify whatever noun (or pronoun) it tells something about.

Adverb Clause to Prepositional Phrase

Certain kinds of adverb clauses can be reduced to prepositional phrases.

[Because ~~there was~~ a decrease in humidity], the heat was not oppressive.
Because of a decrease in humidity, the heat was not oppressive.

When the clause contains no noun that can become the object of the preposition, sometimes a noun can be made from another part of speech.

[After it rains in the desert], plants seem to appear by magic.

After a desert rainfall, plants seem to appear by magic.

Adverb Clause to Absolute Phrase

If the subject of the adverb clause is different from that of the main clause, we may be able to turn the adverb clause into an absolute phrase. Usually the adverb clause expresses some sort of associated circumstance, which might be stated as time or cause.

having been
[~~Because~~ his gym bag ~~was~~ lost], Hal had to use his old running shoes.
His gym bag having been lost, Hal had to use his old running shoes.

We reduce a clause to an absolute phrase by dropping the subordinating conjunction and changing the verb to a participle. What remains is a typical absolute phrase (See Ch. 3).

In the example above, the present perfect participle *having been* indicates about the same time as in the main clause. The reduction could be carried one step further, to a prepositional phrase: "With his gym bag lost."

Adverb Clause to Elliptical Adverb Clause

When we reduce an adverb clause either to a verbal or to an absolute phrase, we drop the subordinating conjunction. However, another way to reduce an adverb clause is to keep the subordinating conjunction and simply drop one or more other words—words that will be clearly understood from the context.

[While (~~he was~~) in school], he did best in his math courses.

Because the subordinating conjunction remains, the word group's origin as an adverb clause is still clear and we call it an "elliptical clause." (*Elliptical* means that some words have been left out.) An elliptical clause has the same function in the sentence as a full adverb clause.

In the example above, the rest of the sentence makes plain that *While in school* is short for *While he was in school.* Notice the difference in this one:

While in school, you must learn all you can.

This time the elliptical clause is short for *While you are in school.* The writer can always expand a correctly used elliptical clause in this way. (Note: Do not reduce an adverb clause whose subject is different

218

from that of the main clause. The result would be a dangling modifier: *While in school,* math was his favorite subject.)

Some additional examples follow. Notice the kinds of things that can be left out and the various meanings of the clauses.

[Though (~~he is~~) not very tall], he is a good basketball player.

[When (~~they are~~) given a chance], the new players do well.

[While (~~I was~~) climbing the stairs], I stumbled.

I'll go [if you will (~~go~~)].

[Because Mom couldn't (~~do it~~)], Cindy is doing the shopping.

[Although (~~he was~~) sad], he was not grief-stricken.

The second and third examples above show that elliptical adverb clauses can include participles, reduced from verbs.

We often use elliptical clauses of comparison.

Jack is taller [than Joe is (~~tall~~)].

You made more baskets [than I made (~~baskets~~)].

In both of these examples, though, further ellipsis is possible.

Jack is taller [than Joe (~~is tall~~)].

You made more baskets [than I (~~made baskets~~)].

Some short clauses of comparison are fine either with or without ellipsis.

He is less discouraged now [than (~~he was~~) before].

I tried to do as well [as he (~~did~~)].

Here too, the reader can expand correctly formed elliptical clauses.

Reducing Noun Clauses

Many noun clauses cannot be reduced to any simpler construction. When a noun clause is reduced, however, the sentence usually becomes noticeably more trim.

Noun Clause to Gerund or Infinitive

Sometimes a noun clause could be reduced to either a gerund or an infinitive.

My preference is [that I would stay with you].

My preference is *staying with you.* (gerund)

My preference is *to stay with you.* (infinitive)

In this particular set of examples, the infinitive may be preferable, since the gerund could possibly be misread as part of a progressive verb ("is staying"). These sentences, though, can be made even more direct.

> I prefer *staying with you.*
> I prefer *to stay with you.*

In the original sentence above, the subject of the noun clause was the same as the implied actor of the main clause *(I prefer, I stay).* When the two subjects or actors are different, the subject of the noun clause cannot just be dropped. With a gerund, the pronoun "subject" appears as a possessive modifier:

> DO
> I know [that he lived in Spain for a while].

> I know about *his* living in Spain for a while. (gerund OP)

With an infinitive, the former subject of the noun clause appears as an objective-case pronoun.

> PN
> The plan is [that we would arrive first and claim the tables].

> The plan is for *us* to arrive first and claim the tables. (infinitive PN)

The "subject" of the infinitive is always introduced by *for,* unless the infinitive phrase is used as a direct object after certain verbs.

> S
> It's unbelievable [that the roof would just collapse].

> It's unbelievable for the roof just to collapse. (infinitive S)

> DO
> They requested [that he conduct a full investigation].

> They requested him to conduct a full investigation. (infinitive DO)

Noun Clause to Noun Phrase

At times a noun clause can be reduced to a simple noun phrase. Usually this can happen only if a noun exists that is related in meaning to the verb of the noun clause.

DO

I know [that he *lived* in Spain for a while].

I know about his *residence* in Spain. (noun OP)

Less information is given by this noun phrase than by the noun clause, but in some contexts no more would be needed. As with the gerund phrase, *about* is added after *know,* and the former subject of the clause becomes the possessive modifier *his*. Here are two more examples.

S   OP

[How he will *do*] depends on [how hard he *works*].

His *success* depends on his *diligence.*

DO

I want to see [*whoever* is in charge].

I want to see the *person* in charge.

Conversions from noun clause to noun phrase often do a great deal to streamline the sentence.

Reducing Certain Complex Sentences to Simple Sentences with Adverbs

Some complex sentences with predicate adjectives can be reduced to simple sentences that contain adverbs as sentence modifiers.

It is fortunate [that no one else had reserved the picnic shelter].
Fortunately, no one else had reserved the picnic shelter.

The reduced sentence is shorter and usually smoother.

We are thankful [that no one was hurt].
Thankfully, no one was hurt.

Note: Unfortunately, the similar use of *hopefully* has become a bone of contention and is best avoided. "Hopefully, it won't rain at the picnic."

Clear Relationships Between Sentence Ideas

Ideas are sometimes expressed in simple sentences, but often they are combined into more complicated sentences. Either way, there is frequently a need to show how the ideas are related to each other. Connective words like *and, but, because, while, however,* and *for instance* express some of the possible logical relations between ideas. This section will help you find the connectives that you need in order to express meaning relationships accurately.

Connective Words

The following paragraph is well organized but contains no connective words at all. The sentences are numbered for later comparison with other versions.

No Connectives

[1]Sometimes a concrete sidewalk will crack. [2]A shifting soil base under the sidewalk can cause the cracks. [3]Random cracks on a sidewalk are noticeable and unattractive. [4]Something can be done to prevent this problem. [5]Grooves can be cut in the wet concrete. [6]The finished walk will be relatively weak at these grooves. [7]Any cracks will occur in the grooves. [8]The cracks will be less noticeable in the grooves.

The paragraph is perhaps clear enough, but it is not very interesting. It sounds overly simple because it has no connecting words. Every clause in it stands by itself as a simple sentence. Since the sentences are fairly short and very much alike, the paragraph also sounds choppy and monotonous.

In the following sections the sample paragraph is improved in various ways. The same superscript number will be with the same clause each time to help you see the improvement.

Coordination and Subordination

Coordination

One way of joining ideas is to use coordinating conjunctions like *and, but,* and *or.* The conjunctions reduce the number of sentences and give us some variety between simple and compound sentences. Notice the result of applying this method to the sample paragraph found in the previous section.

[2]Sometimes the soil base under a sidewalk shifts, and [1]the concrete cracks. [3]Random cracks on a walk are noticeable and unattractive, but [4]something can be done to prevent this problem. [5]Grooves can be cut in the wet concrete. [6]The finished walk will be relatively weak at these grooves, and [7]any cracks will occur in them. [8]There the cracks will be less noticeable.

Subordination

Another way to point out the logical relations is to change some of the clauses into dependent clauses.

[1]Sometimes a concrete sidewalk will crack [2]because the soil base shifts under it. [3]Although random cracks on a sidewalk are noticeable and unattractive, [4]something can be done to prevent this problem. [5]Grooves can be cut in the wet concrete [6]so that the finished walk will be relatively weak at these grooves. [7]Then any cracks will occur in the grooves, [8]where they will be less noticeable.

Again we note an improvement in our sample paragraph.

Subordinating words have two advantages. First, they are sometimes the clearest way to express certain relations between sentences. In addition, they subordinate (make less prominent) the ideas that they introduce; thus they allow other ideas to stand out as more important. The bold numbers in this paragraph appear before the independent clauses. Notice that these clauses are among the more important ones for the paragraph.

Faulty Subordination

It often makes a difference which clauses are made independent and which ones dependent. For example, we can take the sample paragraph and reverse which sentences are dependent and independent. Even though the meaning relationships can be kept fairly accurate, the paragraph suffers. Notice the paragraph using faulty subordination.

[2]Sometimes the soil base shifts under a concrete sidewalk, [1]while the concrete cracks. [3]Random cracks on a sidewalk are noticeable and unattractive, [4]although something can be done to prevent this problem. [5]If grooves are cut in the wet concrete, [6]the finished walk will be relatively weak at these grooves. [8]Cracks will be less noticeable in the grooves, [7]where they will now occur.

Read the independent clauses in this version, as indicated by the bold numbers. Notice that these are not the most important ideas in the paragraph. This paragraph is an example of faulty subordination: the wrong ideas have been subordinated.

A Balanced Approach

Most good paragraphs use both coordination and subordination of clauses. Usually (though not always) the most important ideas should be expressed in the independent clauses.

Here is one final version of the paragraph, the one that uses both coordination and subordination. This paragraph works the best.

> [1]Sometimes a concrete sidewalk cracks [2]because the soil base shifts under it. [3]Random cracks on a sidewalk are noticeable and unattractive, but [4]something can be done to prevent this problem. [5]Grooves can be cut into the wet concrete [6]so that the finished walk will be relatively weak at these grooves. [7]Then any cracks will occur in the grooves, [8]where they will be less noticeable. [9]This simple procedure will result in a much better sidewalk.

Again, read the independent clauses and notice that they include the most important ideas. A final simple sentence has been added to make clear that simple sentences too have a place in good writing. Not every relationship between ideas needs to be expressed.

Ideas of Equal Importance

Ideas of equal importance should usually have equal status in the paragraph. They can stand side by side in simple sentences, or they can be joined in a compound sentence.

The top part of the table below shows the three usual relationships between ideas of equal importance: similarity and association, contrast, and choice. Listed on the table are a number of words and phrases that may express these ideas—mainly coordinating conjunctions and conjunctive adverbs. Use the table to help you achieve greater variety in expressing these ideas.

Ideas of Unequal Importance

In any paragraph some ideas are more important than others. Writers often do well to subordinate the ideas that are less important in a passage. As a rule, less important ideas are best expressed in adjective clauses or adverb clauses.

The second part of the table below shows various meaning relationships between ideas of unequal importance. Usually these meaning relationships are expressed by subordinating conjunctions or other transitional words. Use the table to help you find a variety of ways to express the meanings you intend.

Ways of Expressing Certain Relations Between Ideas

The following table shows how certain areas of meaning can be translated into various sentence structures using appropriate transitional words. It is divided from top to bottom into categories of meaning, and it is divided from left to right according to types of grammatical structure. Within the table boldface words are perhaps the most commonly used words for their categories; they are not necessarily better than the other words given.

	Coordinating Conjunctions	Subordinating Conjunctions	Other Transitional Words and Phrases (Mostly Conjunctive Adverbs)
COORDINATE IN MEANING (IDEAS OF EQUAL IMPORTANCE)			
Similarity and association	**and,** both—and, nor, neither—nor		also, besides, furthermore, likewise, in addition, in the same way, equally important, moreover, similarly, then too, too
Contrast	**but,** yet	whereas, while	**however,** instead, nevertheless, on the contrary, on the other hand, still, by contrast, though
Choice	**or,** or else, either—or		otherwise, alternatively, instead
NONCOORDINATE IN MEANING (IDEAS OF UNEQUAL IMPORTANCE)			
Cause or reason	for	**because,** since, for the reason that	
Result or consequence, or logical conclusion	and so, so		**therefore,** accordingly, consequently, hence, thus, as a result, as a consequence

Purpose		**so that,** so, in order that, lest	in order to (infinitive phrase), to (infinitive phrase)
Simple condition		**if,** only if, on condition that, under the condition that, provided that	
Negative condition		**unless**	
Concession		**although,** even if, even though, regardless of the fact that	
Same time		**as,** while, when, whenever	at that time, at the same time, meanwhile
Sequence of time		**after,** since, **before,** until	**then,** next, later, at last, finally, **first,** earlier, already
Place		**where,** wherever	there, in that place, in that direction, nearby, far away
Example			**for instance,** for example, that is, to illustrate
Logical ordering			first, in the first place, second, next, finally, in conclusion, in summary, to sum up
Manner		as, however, in whatever way	
Greater degree			indeed, even, in fact, as a matter of fact

Parallel Structures

Parallel structures are used for concepts of the same type. The structures are parallel when they have the same form and are joined by a coordinating conjunction.

Advantages of Parallel Structures

Using parallel structures can help you improve the "sound" of your writing as well as show the relationship between certain ideas. For instance, we can start with these acceptable sentences:

> This year Jack had good success in growing tomatoes. Even his watermelons did well, and so did his cantaloupes.

Then we can improve them by using parallelism.

This year	| |	in growing tomatoes		
Jack had	| |			
good success	| |	and even		
	| |	in growing	| |	watermelons
			| |	and
			| |	cantaloupes.

Because the second version puts similar things together, it is both shorter and easier to read. For a second example, we start with these sentences:

> To Joyce the dress appeared almost antique.
> However, her sister thought it was right in style.

Revision produces a single sentence with parallel structures.

The dress	| |	to Joyce		
appeared	| |		| |	as almost antique
	| |			
	| |		but	
	| |			
	| |	to her sister		
	| |		| |	as right in style.

The use of parallel structures can be overdone. However, the occasional use of parallel structures can be a very useful way to improve the clarity and even the rhythm of your writing.

Using Parallelism Only for Parallel Ideas

Parallelism is a very useful device, but it should be used only for ideas that are truly of the same type.

ILLOGICAL PARALLELISM	The Bible portrays Ruth as faithful, industrious, and fairly young.
CORRECTION	The Bible portrays Ruth as faithful and industrious.

The comment about Ruth's age does not fit in with the two character traits, and so it is removed from the parallel construction.

The next example illustrates the problem of having one item that is either more general or less general than the others.

ILLOGICAL PARALLELISM	We bought seeds for lettuce, carrots, and garden vegetables.
CORRECTION	We bought seeds for lettuce, carrots, and other garden vegetables.

Inserting the word *other* avoids here the logical problem of having one item that includes other items in the series.

In our final example the writer actually did have in mind two parallel ideas, but something else ended up being expressed in the parallel construction.

ILLOGICAL PARALLELISM	My sister has had six college roommates, including those living with her last year and living with her now.
CORRECTION	My sister has had six college roommates, including those living with her last year and those living with her now.

The correction properly draws the parallel between two groups of people rather than two activities of one group.

Using the Same Part of Speech

Sentence parts joined by coordinating conjunctions must be of the same grammatical type. Most important, they must represent the same part of speech.

NOT PARALLEL	Adj. Adj. N She is intelligent, pleasant, and a good neighbor.
CORRECTION	Adj. Adj. Adj. She is intelligent, pleasant, and neighborly.

Adj.   TrV

NOT PARALLEL   A good friend is faithful and helps you.

Adj.   Adj.

CORRECTION   A good friend is faithful and helpful.

The second nonparallel example could be interpreted as coordinating the two verbs *is* and *helps*. However, with any form of *be* we usually expect the coordination to be on the more important word that follows, in this case *faithful*.

Using the Same Type of Structure

Parallel elements should represent not only the same part of speech but also, when possible, the same type of structure.

Same Kinds of Words or Phrases

Certain kinds of phrases should not usually be joined to other types of words or phrases.

N   N   Ger. phrase

NOT PARALLEL   I enjoy novels, short stories, and daily reading of the newspaper.

N   N   N

BETTER   I enjoy novels, short stories, and the daily newspaper.

Adj.   Prep. Phrase

NOT PARALLEL   The ad was too wide, of excessive length, and possibly

Adj.

too late.

Adj.   Adj.   Adj.

BETTER   The ad was too wide, too long, and possibly too late.

Same Kinds of Verbals

Gerunds, participles, and infinitives should not be mixed in the same construction.

NOT PARALLEL   At their ceremonies, American Indians liked

Ger. phrase   Inf. phrase

smoking peace pipes and to perform ritual dances.

                       Ger. phrase   Ger. phrase

CORRECTION . . . liked smoking peace pipes and performing ritual dances.

or

                       Inf. phrase   Inf. phrase

. . . liked to smoke peace pipes and to perform ritual dances.

Same Kinds of Clauses

A phrase and a clause should not normally be joined by a coordinating conjunction.

                               Noun phrase

NOT PARALLEL The report showed *an improvement in average*

                               Dep. clause

attendance but [that average grades had dropped].

                               Dep. clause

CORRECTION The report showed [that average attendance had

                               Dep. clause

improved] but [that average grades had dropped].

                               Noun phrase

EVEN BETTER The report showed *an improvement in average*

                               Noun phrase

attendance but *a drop in average grades.*

An independent clause and a dependent clause should never be joined by a coordinating conjunction.

                  Indep. Clause   Dep. clause

NOT PARALLEL It was a hard game, and [which we could not have won without you].

                               Dep. clause

CORRECTION It was a hard game, [which we could not have won without you].

or

        Indep. clause   Indep. clause

It was a hard game, and we could not have won it without you.

Placing Correlative Conjunctions Correctly

Correlative conjunctions are pairs like *both—and, either—or, neither—nor,* and *not only—but also.* Correlative conjunctions can be very useful; however, they must be used carefully.

The sentence element that immediately follows the first correlative conjunction must be of the same type as the element that immediately follows the second correlative conjunction.

	TrV	DO

NOT PARALLEL   Egyptian hieroglyphics *both* included phonetic symbols
    DO
    and symbols that represented words.

		DO

CORRECTION   Egyptian hieroglyphics included *both* phonetic symbols
    DO
    and symbols that represented words.

The incorrect sentence has different elements after the two conjunctions. The problem can be corrected by moving the first conjunction.

	LV	PA

NOT PARALLEL   A phonetic symbol could *either* be alphabetic (for a
      PA
    single sound) *or* syllabic (for a whole syllable).

		PA

CORRECTION   A phonetic symbol could be *either* alphabetic (for a
      PA
    single sound) *or* syllabic (for a whole syllable).

So far, the corrections have been made by moving the first conjunction. However, other adjustments may also be possible.

	Aux	S	Verb

NOT PARALLEL   *Not only* has this third of the Al Murrah tribe continued
          Verb
    with camel herding, *but also* faced the inhospitable
    deserts to care for the herds.

CORRECTION   Not only has this third of the Al Murrah tribe continued
    with camel herding, *but* it has *also* faced the inhospitable deserts to care for the herds.

Adding a subject and an auxiliary makes the two parts parallel as independent clauses.

This kind of parallelism error is very easy to make, but usually it is also very easy to correct. Just be aware of the problem and look for the location of the correlative conjunctions.

Clarifying Parallelism

Sometimes in a written sentence the reader cannot be sure just what sentence parts are intended to be joined by the conjunction. To clarify such a sentence, try one of these methods:

1. Using correlative conjunctions
2. Repeating a key word
3. Reordering the joined elements

The first remedy, correlative conjunctions, is discussed in the previous section.

A second way to make the parallelism clear is to repeat a key word such as a preposition, an auxiliary, or the sign of the infinitive. (If you do repeat a key word, be sure to use it at the beginning of every item in the series.)

PARALLELISM UNCLEAR	In relations with the queen, work arrangements, and judicial matters, the Lovedu people practice cooperation. (in relations with work arrangements?)
IMPROVED	In relations with the queen, in work arrangements, and in judicial matters, the Lovedu people practice cooperation.
PARALLELISM UNCLEAR	A new missionary to the Lovedu should learn to speak their language accurately and understand their culture thoroughly.
IMPROVED	A new missionary to the Lovedu should learn to speak their language accurately and to understand their culture thoroughly.

A third way is to reverse the order of the confusing elements, putting the simpler element first.

PARALLELISM UNCLEAR	The people's method of governing themselves and their religion are closely related. (governing themselves and their religion?)
IMPROVED	The people's religion and their method of governing themselves are closely related.

Sentence Logic

Sentences can seem illogical because either the grammatical constructions or the meanings do not fit together quite right. In this section you will find ways to correct and improve the logic of your sentences.

Saying Things Directly

Do you take too many words to say what you could say in fewer words? Many times, nouns can be formed from simpler words; these are called "built nouns." Many sentences that have built nouns can be simplified by taking them back to an original part of speech. For example: *appointment* is formed from the verb *appoint, discovery* is formed from the verb *discover, sadness* is formed from the adjective *sad.*

> **TOO DENSE** Mme. Curie's *discovery* of radium happened because of her *persistence* in the *investigation* of natural radioactivity.

Who did what to what? Madame Curie discovered radium. Here the built noun *discovery* is peeled back to its root verb, *discover*. The sentence contains two other built nouns, *persistence* and *investigation*. Find the verb in each of these and ask yourself who did the action.

> **REVISED** Mme. Curie discovered radium because she persistently investigated natural radioactivity.

When a noun is built on an adjective, try asking what that adjective describes.

> **TOO DENSE** Great *difficulty* was involved in the *separation* of radium from pitchblende.

What was difficult? The separation of radium from pitchblende. And what about *separation*—can we use it in the form of a verb or a verbal?

> **REVISED** Separating radium from pitchblende was very difficult.

Saying What You Mean

It is important to say exactly what you mean.

1. Do your subjects and verbs work together logically?

> **ILLOGICAL PREDICATION** Using a good dictionary can be a guide for spelling.

> **CORRECTION** A good dictionary can be a guide for spelling.

The dictionary, not the using of it, is the guide.

ILLOGICAL PREDICATION	People who hold tickets issued by the now-bankrupt airline will be honored by other airlines.
CORRECTION	Tickets issued by the now-bankrupt airline will be honored by other airlines.

It is the tickets that will be honored, not the people. Looking for the sentence pattern elements will help you become aware of this kind of problem.

2. Are your examples really examples?

ILLOGICAL EXEMPLIFICATION	While the men of the tribe hunt, the women collect food in the area, **such as** picking berries or going to the beach and digging clams.
CORRECTION	While the men of the tribe hunt, the women collect food in the area, **such as** the berries that they pick or the clams that they dig on the beach.

The phrase *such as* tells the reader that the examples will follow. Therefore, in what comes next, the examples should be the main words.

Other kinds of illogical sentences are possible, of course. Correct all such sentences by looking for the main sentence elements and making them work together logically.

Saying Things Consistently

In conversation it is not uncommon to begin a sentence with one construction and then mistakenly end it with a different one. In writing, though, we want to catch that kind of problem.

MIXED CONSTRUCTIONS	In the Middle East, herding no longer has *the* important part *as* it once had.
POSSIBLE CORRECTIONS	In the Middle East, herding no longer has *the* important part *that* it once had. *or* In the Middle East, herding no longer has *as* important a part *as* it once had.

Usually there are two possible corrections for a sentence with mixed constructions. Sometimes one of the two is more formal than the other.

MIXED CONSTRUCTIONS	That is one problem *for which* we have found no answers *for.*

MORE FORMAL CORRECTION	That is one problem *for which* we have found no answers.

LESS FORMAL CORRECTION	That is one problem that/which we have found no answers *for.*

Making Clear and Logical Comparisons

When two similar things are being compared with reference to some quality, the comparison should be stated in a clear and logical way. Most obviously, the comparative and superlative degrees of adjectives and adverbs must be used correctly. The comparative, of course, is for two things being compared, and the superlative is for three or more things being considered together at once.

Comparing Separate Things or Groups

Things to be compared must be separate. That is, one cannot be part of another.

FAULTY COMPARISON	Our yard is bigger than any yard on our street.

The comparison is illogically stated because "our yard" is one of the yards on the street and as such cannot be compared with itself.

CORRECTION	Our yard is bigger than any *other* yard on our street.

The word *anyone* is often found in faulty comparisons.

FAULTY COMPARISON	He played better than anyone on his team.

CORRECTION	He played better than anyone *else* on his team.

Did you notice—the first version had him playing better than himself (since he is on the team). The word *else* solves the problem.

Comparing Things of the Same Type

The things to be compared must be things of the same type.

FAULTY COMPARISON	Spanish vowels are simpler than any other European language.

Spanish vowels should be compared with other vowels, not with "any other European language."

CORRECTIONS	Spanish vowels are simpler than the vowels of any other European language.
	Spanish vowels are simpler than those of any other European language.

The second correction, which has the advantage of brevity, uses *those* to stand for *the vowels.*

Comparisons using *same* or *different* also must involve things of the same type.

FAULTY COMPARISON	A young girl's role is different from any other aged woman's role.

This comparison, using *other,* is illogical because the young girl's role is not a subtype of the aged woman's role.

POSSIBLE CORRECTIONS	A young girl's role is different from any other female role.
	or
	A young girl's role is different from an aged woman's role.

The choice between these corrections would depend on what the writer wanted to say.

Making the Second Element Clear

Sometimes the last part of a comparison can be understood from the context.

He plays hymns more than classical music. (more than *he plays* classical music)

She has taken more math than Mary. (than Mary *has taken*)

It is acceptable, even advisable, to leave out the part that is not needed. However, nothing should be left out that is needed for clarity.

UNCLEAR	He calls Paul as much as Nate.

Here *Nate* could be intended as either the subject or the direct object of the understood verb *calls.* The sentence should be clarified.

POSSIBLE CORRECTIONS	He calls Paul as much as Nate does.
	or
	He calls Paul as much as he calls Nate.

Completing the Construction Before Or

Some comparisons state that one of the things may be *either* equivalent *or* superior with regard to some quality. In such a construction, *as* is needed after the first adjective or adverb.

INCOMPLETE CONSTRUCTION   My little brother plays as well or better than I do.

CORRECTIONS   My little brother plays as well as or better than I do.
My little brother plays as well as I do, or better.

The corrections work the same way for an adjective like *tall* as for the adverb *well.*

INCOMPLETE CONSTRUCTION   Probably by next year he will be as tall or taller than I.

CORRECTIONS   Probably by next year he will be as tall as or taller than I.
Probably by next year he will be as tall as I am, or taller.

Using Noun Clauses When Needed

A sentence sounds odd when one of the words in it is used as the wrong part of speech. Similarly, using the incorrect clause may throw a whole sentence off course.

Noun Clause, Not Adverb Clause

When the sentence construction calls for a noun or noun clause, do not substitute an adverb clause. (In standard written English, clauses that begin with subordinating conjunctions like *because* are always adverb clauses.)

ADVERB CLAUSE AS SUBJECT   Just because you want something does not mean that you will get it.

CORRECTION   The fact that you want something does not mean that you will get it.

ADVERB CLAUSE AS PN   The reason you received a poor grade is because you did not study.

CORRECTION   You received a poor grade because you did not study.

Also, the definition of any noun must be a noun phrase, a gerund, or a noun clause—not an adverb clause.

ADVERB CLAUSE AS PN	Success is when everyone who worked on something is happy.
CORRECTION	Success is the achievement of what was attempted.

Dependent Clause, Not Independent Clause

Never use an independent clause as the subject of a sentence. Instead, convert the independent clause to a noun clause (or to some other noun equivalent), or revise the sentence entirely.

INDEPENDENT CLAUSE AS SUBJECT	I studied hard this time was the reason I passed.
CORRECTIONS	The fact that I studied hard this time was the reason I passed. I passed because I studied hard this time.

Similarly, a direct question must be changed to an indirect question if it is to be used as a noun clause.

DIRECT QUESTION AS SUBJECT	How well do they adjust is the question.
CORRECTIONS	How well they adjust is the question. More important is how well they adjust. Here is the main question: How well do they adjust?

Word Placement in the Sentence

An important way to link sentences together, creating a natural flow from one to the other, is to make wise use of certain strategic positions in the sentence. Wise use of the end of the sentence will also help you highlight ideas that are important.

Managing the Sequence of Subjects

The subjects of a series of sentences or clauses should fit together well. Within a paragraph, do not jump around needlessly from one topic to another.

POOR PARAGRAPH WITH SUBJECT SHIFTS	One of the world's most common species is the spider. Spiders can be found from the Arctic to the Antarctic. The tropics, however, are where they are the most abundant. We picture them as brown or black; but green, yellow, red, and white are also spider colors. Insects are

their main food source, but wasps are their greatest enemy. Although people like spiders for killing bugs in the garden, we do not appreciate them in our homes.

IMPROVED   Spiders are one of the world's most common species. Spiders can be found from the Arctic to the Antarctic. They are, however, most abundant in the tropics. We picture them as brown or black, but spiders can also be green, yellow, red, or white. They feed mainly on insects, but they fear their enemy the wasp. Although spiders are good for killing bugs in the garden, we do not appreciate them in our homes.

Ending Sentences with New Information

Often in good writing, the end of one sentence introduces a new idea that is taken up toward the beginning of the next. The next sentence is thus linked to it by the repetition. This kind of link is not always possible, but it is sometimes a good way to tie sentences together. There are several ways to get the new information to the end of the sentence.

1. Reverse the subject and the predicate noun.

   Bergamot is another kind of flower that hummingbirds like. *Bergamot* is also called bee balm.

   Another kind of flower that hummingbirds like is *bergamot. Bergamot* is also called bee balm.

2. Move other things out of the way at the end of the sentence.

   Bergamot flowers may be red or white or *pink,* and somewhat ragged-looking. *The pink-flowered bergamot* grows well in shady places, but the others prefer sun.

   The somewhat ragged-looking flowers of the bergamot may be red or white or *pink. The pink-flowered bergamot* grows well in shady places, but the others prefer sun.

3. Change active to passive or vice versa.

   Reddish bracts *surround* the flowers of our red bergamot. The bracts look like small brightly colored leaves.

The flowers of our red bergamot *are surrounded* by reddish bracts.
They look like brightly colored leaves.

Certainly not every pair of sentences should be tied together in this way. However, at times this technique will provide just the link needed.

Ending in Strength

Partly because the final impressions are lasting impressions, it is good to end sentences strongly.

Important Information

Psychologically it is often natural to move in the sentence from familiar information to new information, and from less important to more important. Even our normal pronunciation of the sentence puts the greatest stress (emphasis) on its last significant word. Good writing usually follows this tendency by putting the important information last.

If you find the important information buried in the middle of your sentence, you can usually move other things away from the end of the sentence. If the important information is stranded at the beginning of the sentence, you can often move it out of the subject and into the predicate.

Solid Words

Just as we expect to find important information at the end of most sentences, we also prefer sentences that end with solid words. Weak wording can weaken a strong idea.

> **WEAK** His ideas may be brilliant, but they are rather hard *to get hold of.*

> **STRONG** His ideas may be brilliant, but they are rather hard *to grasp.*

Compared with the solid word *grasp, of* is a rather weak word. Verbs are nearly always more solid than prepositions. Now compare an adverb and a noun:

> **ADEQUATE** A key sentence should end *strongly.*
> **STRONGER** A key sentence should end *in strength.*

The adverb *strongly* is perfectly acceptable, but the noun *strength* gives the ending a special solidity. The most solid nouns are often those that are derived from other words.

Derived Noun	Source Word
strength	strong

solidity	solid
discussion	discuss

Sometimes, then, we can give greater force to a sentence by ending it with a more solid word. The more solid words seem to be those with full and definite meaning. For example, *thing* is less solid than *tractor,* and *was* is less solid than *parked*.

Below is a ranking of some common parts of speech according to how solid or how flimsy they tend to be.

Solid

↑
↓

Flimsy

- Nouns, especially derived nouns
- True verbs
- Adjectives and adverbs
- Prepositions, adverbs that sound like prepositions (like *in*), pronouns, and other minor parts of speech

Do not feel that you must change the ending of every sentence. It is probably best to use this information for two purposes:

1. To improve a sentence that ends with an especially weak word

2. To give special strength to a key sentence

Biased Language

The Christian writer must be especially careful to avoid giving unnecessary offense. The most common offense in writing is the stereotype. A **stereotype** is an oversimplified generalization usually founded on either ignorance or malice. Generalizations based solely on gender, race, cultural background, age, or physical characteristics have no place in a Christian's spoken or written vocabulary.

STEREOTYPE The woman driver in front of me slowed down and caused me to skid.
(The problem was carelessness, not gender.)

CORRECTION The careless driver in front of me slowed down and caused me to skid.

STEREOTYPE All-you-can-eat buffets appeal to obese Americans.
(Not all obese Americans enjoy all-you-can-eat buffets, nor are all who enjoy them obese.)

CORRECTION All-you-can-eat buffets appeal to many people.

STEREOTYPE   Like most preachers' kids, Robert was disruptive in Sunday school.
(Robert's being a preacher's son is irrelevant to his behavior in Sunday school.)

CORRECTION   Robert was disruptive in Sunday school.

STEREOTYPE   Elderly shoppers should take advantage of the motorized shopping carts.
(The sentence implies that all or only elderly shoppers need motorized shopping carts.)

CORRECTION   Shoppers needing special assistance should take advantage of the motorized shopping carts.

"The words of a wise man's mouth are gracious" (Eccles. 10:12). Using stereotypes evidences both faulty reasoning and insensitivity.

Research Skills

Part of education is knowing how to find the information you need and then knowing how to use it. The first sections of this chapter will help you find information, and the rest will help you use that information in a research paper.

Using the Dictionary

An ordinary desk dictionary contains a wealth of helpful information—more than you may realize.

Finding the Word

The **entry words** are those in boldface type set slightly to the left of the text column. Whether the entry is one or more words, it is alphabetized according to each letter throughout the whole boldface entry.

pronunciation

parts of speech

inflected forms

fleet[1] (flēt) *n.* **1.** A number of warships operating together under one command. **2.** A group of vessels or vehicles, such as taxicabs, owned or operated as a unit. [ME *flete* < OE *flēot* < *flēotan,* to float. See **pleu-***.]

verb types

synonym

fleet[2] (flēt) *adj.* fleet·er. fleet·est. **1.** Moving swiftly; rapid or nimble. See Syns at **fast**[1]. **2.** Fleeting; evanescent. *–v.* **fleet·ed, fleet·ing, fleets.** *–intr.* **1.** To move or pass swiftly. **2.** To fade out; vanish. **3.** *Archaic.* To flow. **4.** *Obsolete.* To drift. *–tr.* **1.** To cause (time) to pass quickly. **2.** *Naut.* To alter the position of (tackle or rope, for example). [Prob. < ON *fljōtr.* V. < ME *fleten,* to drift, float < OE *flēotan.* See **pleu-***.] **–fleet'ly** *adv.* **–fleet'ness** *n.*

definitions

etymology

Guide words help you determine which words are on a specific page. A pair of guide words appears at the top of each page, in boldface type, opposite the page number.

Even if you are unsure about the exact spelling of a word, you should be able to find it in the dictionary by guessing at its likely spelling. If your dictionary has a table of correspondences between sounds and spellings, you can use the table to help you think of other ways the word might be spelled.

Understanding the Entry

Pronunciation

The pronunciation usually appears just after the entry word. Some of the symbols used in the pronunciation may be unfamiliar to you. The pronunciation symbols are given in the pronunciation guide at the bottom of the page and in a fuller table in the front of the dictionary. Some words have two (or more) noticeably different acceptable pronunciations. In one popular dictionary, the first pronunciation is more common when the second is preceded by *also;* the two are equally common when they are joined only by a comma. If your dictionary follows a different system, you will find it explained in its introductory material.

The pronunciation also shows syllable divisions and stress. An accent mark indicates which syllable is emphasized, or stressed, when the word is pronounced. Some words have more than one accent mark because more than one syllable is pronounced with stress. The largest or heaviest accent mark indicates the strongest stress in a word.

Parts of Speech

All the parts of speech of each entry word are listed along with the definitions. For example, the word *aloof* can be either an adjective or an adverb.

Because the meaning of a verb may vary according to whether it is transitive or intransitive or linking, dictionaries usually classify verb meanings into two groups. Transitive verb meanings are labeled *tr.* (or *v.tr.* or *vt*). Intransitive and linking verb meanings are both labeled *intr.* (or *v.intr.* or *vi*). Every verb has at least one of these labels along with its meanings.

Inflected Forms and Related Words

The inflected forms of a word are forms that differ from the main entry because of the addition of suffixes or because of other changes to the word. Usually included are the irregular plurals of nouns, certain verb forms, and the suffixed comparative and superlative forms of adjectives and adverbs.

At the end of the entry there may be additional words in boldface type, words that are derived from the entry words by certain common suffixes.

Variant Spellings

Some words can be spelled two ways. In general, the spelling listed first is more common if the second is preceded by *also.* The two are equally acceptable if they are joined by *or.*

Definitions, Idioms, and Synonyms

A word may have several **definitions.** Each of these will be listed and numbered. If one definition includes closely related meanings, these are labeled a. and b. and c. rather than with new numbers. Depending on the dictionary, the first definition may be the most central or basic meaning, the most frequent meaning, or the earliest meaning still in use. The introductory material in your dictionary will tell which ordering system it uses.

Dictionaries also list the various idioms used with a word. An **idiom** is an expression whose meaning we learn individually; its meaning is not the same as the usual meaning of the words by themselves. For example, *let alone* (meaning "not to mention") has little to do with letting or with aloneness.

For certain words there is also a list of **synonyms** (words with the same or similar meaning) with the relevant distinctions of meaning.

Capitalization

The correct capitalization of a word is found in a dictionary entry, even for words like *alpine* that are capitalized for one meaning and not for another.

Miscellaneous Information in Entries

A dictionary usually provides such additional information as the scientific names for plants and animals, special usage notes, illustrations, and cross references. The introduction to a dictionary lists and explains these and any other types of information it provides.

Etymology

The etymology of a word is the word's life history—where it came from and sometimes where it has been at various stages. Instead of starting at the beginning, though, dictionary etymologies start with the recent past and work backward in time.

Some words, like *almost,* are **native words**—words that have always been English words. Other words, like *alms* and *aloft,* we call **borrowed words,** because they came from other languages. The abbreviations for languages and their historical stages are explained in the front of your dictionary.

Usage Labels

Each dictionary applies usage labels to certain entry words. These labels may differ somewhat from one dictionary to another. Check the introduction to your dictionary to find the meaning of the terms it uses. Here are some commonly used types of labels.

Field labels point out definitions that apply to a special area such as music, physics, or sports.

Geographic labels limit usage to a particular region. Some examples of geographic labels are *regional, dialect, New England,* and *chiefly British.*

Stylistic labels limit a word or a definition to a particular usage level. Unlabeled words are standard usage. Here are some examples of common stylistic labels.

- *nonstandard/substandard* (words or expressions generally not used by the educated)
- *informal* (words acceptable in conversation but generally not used in formal writing)
- *slang* (showy or humorous words, often faddish and short-lived)
- *vulgar/obscene* (words that violate standards of decency)
- *archaic/obsolete* (words that were once common but are now rarely seen except in old writings)

A Christian would certainly not want to use words that are labeled as vulgar or obscene. The worldly associations of some slang expressions should also cause us to avoid their usage. If you are unsure of a term or expression, find out its usage level and its meaning or associations. This information can help you decide whether or not to make it part of your own vocabulary.

Using the Library

The name *library* comes from the Latin word for *book,* but today's libraries contain much more than books—they often contain magazines, newspapers, and audio-visual materials too. You can attend classes, listen to lectures, or view displays on a variety of topics at many libraries. Some public libraries even offer free access to the Internet. Today's libraries provide a broad selection of information and tools for you to use. Before you can use these tools, however, you need to know where to find them.

Libraries usually are organized into several sections. These sections may be separate rooms or merely separate sections of shelves set apart from the other shelves. Each section contains a different type of library material.

The largest section holds books arranged on shelves called stacks. The stacks are usually divided into fiction and nonfiction sections.

The **periodical** section contains materials published at regular intervals, such as magazines and newspapers. Because they are published regularly, periodicals are an excellent source for current information about a variety of topics.

The **reference** section contains nonfiction books and other materials that are noncirculating. In other words, they cannot be checked out of the library. A capital letter *R* or the abbreviation *REF* on a book's spine indicates that the book belongs in the reference section.

Audio-visual materials include audiocassettes and CDs, videocassettes, works of art such as paintings and sculptures, or even puppets and games for young children. These materials are usually marked with the letters *AV.*

Most libraries place the books and other materials for **children** and **young adults** in a separate section. This section usually contains both circulating and reference materials. The letters *J* (for juvenile) or *YA* (for young adult) indicate that the materials belong to this section of the library.

The Arrangement of Books

Fiction

A fiction book, regardless of its topic, is shelved alphabetically according to the author's last name. If two or more authors share the same last name, their books are arranged alphabetically by the authors' first names. If a library has more than one book by the same author, that author's books are arranged alphabetically according to the first words of the titles (not including *A, An,* or *The*). The list below shows the order in which these books would appear on a library shelf.

> Richard D. Blackmore, *Lorna Doone*
> Anne Brontë, *The Tenant of Wildfell Hall*
> Charlotte Brontë, *The Professor*
> Charlotte Brontë, *Shirley*
> Emily Brontë, *Wuthering Heights*
> James Fenimore Cooper, *The Deerslayer*

Some libraries separate certain kinds of fiction books from the rest of the fiction collection. For example, a library may have separate shelves marked *mystery fiction* or *science fiction.* In addition, the book spines are usually marked with the letters *MYS* for mystery fiction or *SCI* for science fiction. Many libraries separate the paperback fiction books from the hardcover books. Paperback books are usually marked with the letters *PB*.

Nonfiction

The Dewey Decimal System

Many libraries use the Dewey decimal system to classify and arrange nonfiction books. The American librarian Melvil Dewey (1851-1931) devised this system to give every nonfiction book a number according to its subject matter. This number appears on the spine of the book and is the key to finding the book on the shelves. Here are the ten large classifications in the Dewey decimal system.

000-099	General works
100-199	Philosophy and psychology
200-299	Religion
300-399	Social sciences
400-499	Languages
500-599	Natural sciences and mathematics
600-699	Applied sciences and technology
700-799	Fine arts
800-899	Literature
900-999	History and geography

The Dewey system is called a decimal system because of its repeated divisions by ten. Each division can be divided by ten as long as needed. For instance, one division of 600 (science) is 630 (agriculture), which includes the subdivision 634 (orchards, fruit, and forestry). Further levels of subdivision use a decimal point: 634.3 indicates citrus fruit (a subdivision of 634) and 634.31 indicates oranges (a subdivision of 634.3).

Under a book's Dewey decimal number is a number that identifies the book by its author or perhaps by one or more letters of its title. The Dewey decimal number and the author number (known as the Cutter number) together make up the **call number** of the book.

The Library of Congress System

Some large libraries use the Library of Congress system rather than the Dewey decimal system. Instead of using only numbers, the Library of Congress classification system uses a combination of letters and numbers. There are twenty-one basic categories in the Library of Congress system.

A	General works	**K**	Law
B	Philosophy, psychology, and religion	**L**	Education
		M	Music
C	Auxiliary sciences of history (e.g., archaeology, genealogy, biography)	**N**	Fine arts
		P	Language and literature
D	World history	**Q**	Science
E	American history	**R**	Medicine
F	Local American history	**S**	Agriculture
G	Geography, anthropology, and recreation	**T**	Technology
		U	Military science
H	Social sciences	**V**	Naval science
J	Political science	**Z**	Library science

A typical Library of Congress number is CB245.K28, for *The Western Heritage,* a history of Western civilization. The first letter is C because the book is a broad work of history, and B245 further specifies the subject. After the period, K28 identifies the main author, Donald Kagan.

The Library Catalog

The library catalog is the most important key to finding information in a library. Traditionally, libraries used card catalogs as tools to help people find the books they wanted. Today many libraries have converted their card catalogs to online computer catalogs. Both kinds of catalog contain the same information in approximately the same format. Computer catalogs, however, offer more ways to search for information.

The Card Catalog

A **card catalog** is a cabinet with small drawers filled with cards containing information on each book in the library. There are three types of cards: the author card, the title card, and the subject card. These cards are usually alphabetized together, although some libraries have a separate file for the subject cards. Each kind of card has a different top line: the author card starts with the author; the title card starts with the book's title; and the subject card starts with the subject of the book. Each card includes the title, the author, the place of publication, the date of publication, the publisher, the number of pages, and the call number (for a nonfiction book).

To use the card catalog, you need to know the author or the title or the subject of the book you want. Perhaps you want a book by a particular author, but you are not sure of the title. Find the author card, which is filed alphabetically according to the author's last name. Title cards are arranged alphabetically according to the first word in the title (not including *A, An,* and *The*). If you do not know the titles or authors of nonfiction books on a subject that interests you, look for subject cards. There may be more than one subject card for some books.

The Computer Catalog

Instead of individual filing cards, a computer catalog contains electronic records for each book. Each record includes the same information you would find on an author, title, or subject card in the card catalog. In fact, a computer catalog may contain more information than a card catalog. For instance, some computer catalog records include a summary of the book. The summary can help you decide whether the book will be helpful to you. In addition, most computer catalogs contain information about each book's status. In other words, the computer catalog can tell you whether a book is available or already checked out. If the book is already checked out, the catalog may tell you when it is due to be returned.

Using the computer catalog is similar to using the card catalog. First, you need to know the author, the title, or the subject of the book you want to find. Next, type the information you know into the computer, according to the instructions on the screen. The computer will begin to search for the book you need by comparing the words you typed to the information in its database. When it finds a match, the computer screen will display the record for that book. If the information you typed was not specific enough, the computer screen will display a list for you to choose from. For instance, if you type the subject rather than the title, the screen will list several books about that subject. To see the record for an individual book, simply type or click on the number displayed next to that title on the list. If you want more information about the book, you may need to type an additional command, such as *F,* for *full title record.*

MATERIAL: Book

CALL NUMBER: 394.26 Sw12

AUTHOR: Swahn, Jan Ojvind

TITLE: Maypoles, crayfish and Lucia: Swedish holidays and traditions / Jan Ojvind Swahn; [translation by Roger Tanner].

PUBLICATION: Stockholm: The Swedish Institute, 1994.

DESCRIPTION: 47 p.: ill. (some col.), music: 24 cm.

NOTES: Lyrics of songs in Swedish.

NOTES: Bibliography: p. 47.

SUBJECT: Holidays—Sweden.

SUBJECT: Sweden, Social life and customs.

Labels: city of publication · publisher · date of publication · height of book's spine · special contents · contains illustrations · number of pages

The computer catalog at one library might be somewhat different from the computer catalog at another library. Be sure to ask the librarian for help if you do not know how to use your library's computer catalog.

The Periodical Indexes

Most library catalogs will help you find books and audio-visual materials on your subject, but they will not help you find articles in magazines or newspapers. To find these articles, you need to consult a **periodical index.**

The most generally useful periodical index is the *Readers' Guide to Periodical Literature.* Articles from over two hundred magazines are listed in it by subject and by author. Soon after publication, articles are listed in one of the twenty-one issues during the year. At the end of each year, all of these are combined and reissued in the single large volume.

To find an article about a particular subject, look up the key word. Under many subject headings, you will find "see also" entries to suggest other related subject headings. Each individual entry will tell you the article's subject, its title, its author, the magazine in which it appears, the issue number or date of the magazine, and the page numbers where you can find that particular article. The listing uses a number of abbreviations, explained in the front of each volume.

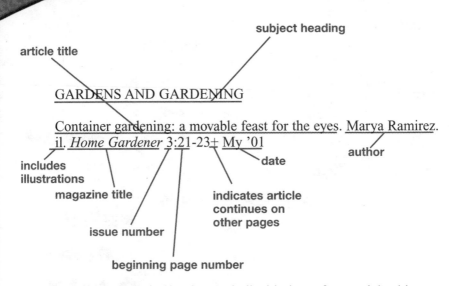

subject heading

article title

GARDENS AND GARDENING

Container gardening: a movable feast for the eyes. Marya Ramirez.
il. *Home Gardener* 3:21-23+ My '01

author

date

includes
illustrations

magazine title

indicates article
continues on
other pages

issue number

beginning page number

You may want to check other periodical indexes for special subjects. Examples of other indexes include the *Social Sciences Index* and the *Humanities Index,* both of which cover scholarly journals in certain fields of study. The *New York Times Index* lists articles that have appeared in that newspaper. However, it can help you find information in back issues of other newspapers as well as the *New York Times,* since it will help you discover the dates of newsworthy events.

Today many libraries have online database versions of some periodical indexes. Check with the librarian for information about the resources available in your library.

Special Reference Tools

Several special reference tools can be useful when you are researching a topic. Many of the reference tools discussed here are also available online or as software for personal computers. Check with a librarian for more information about online reference tools.

Almanacs and Yearbooks

Both **almanacs** and **yearbooks** supplement encyclopedias by giving current information about statistics and recent events. Most almanacs, and all yearbooks, are published every year. You can find the information you need by looking in the almanac's index, which may appear at the front of the book like a table of contents. Yearbooks tend to concentrate on special subjects. For instance, the *Statesman's Year-book* gives information about the governments of countries around the world.

Atlases and Gazetteers

Atlases are books of collected maps. Most atlases also contain information about weather, geography, population, and other statistics. Every atlas has an index that lists the page number of the various maps. **Gazetteers** are indexes of place names. Some gazetteers include additional information for each place listed.

Bible Commentaries and Concordances

Commentaries are explanations of the Bible, going through part or all of the Bible, verse by verse or section by section. Some commentaries cover individual books of the Bible; longer works cover the entire Bible.

Bible concordances are alphabetical indexes to the words of the Bible. They are helpful for locating a passage and sometimes for studying a subject through the Bible. Some concordances include the Greek or Hebrew word from which the English word was translated.

Biographical Sources

Besides book-length biographies of particular people, the library contains a number of sources for more concise biographical information. People living today appear in such works as *Current Biography, Contemporary Authors,* and the various *Who's Who* biographical dictionaries. Persons no longer living are described in sources such as the *Dictionary of American Biography* and the British *Dictionary of National Biography.*

Dictionaries

In addition to desk dictionaries, libraries also contain various larger dictionaries and special-purpose dictionaries. Large unabridged dictionaries contain several hundred thousand words. The most complete dictionary in any language is the *Oxford English Dictionary,* which contains a full history of nearly every word used in England since 1150. Special-purpose dictionaries include dictionaries of synonyms, Bible dictionaries, foreign language dictionaries, and dictionaries of subjects like sports or the sciences.

Encyclopedias

Encyclopedias contain articles that are arranged alphabetically to give brief introductions to many subjects. Guide words at the top of each page tell you the topic of the first article on that page, somewhat like the guide words in a dictionary. The index lists all the pages that contain information on a particular subject. Some sets of encyclopedias have an index in each separate volume; others have a separate volume (usually the last volume) that is the index for the entire set. Many encyclopedia articles list cross-references to other related articles under a heading such as "See also."

Indexes

Indexes are listings that make it easy to find information. Most useful are the periodical indexes such as *The Readers' Guide to Periodical Literature.* Other indexes include *Book Review Index, Essays and General Literature Index,* and books of quotations such as *Bartlett's Familiar Quotations.*

Thesaurus

A thesaurus is a treasury of synonyms and antonyms. Some thesauruses list the main words alphabetically, while others group all words by meaning, directing you to the meaning groups from a detailed index in the back. In either case, you choose a synonym included in the words you find listed. A dictionary and a thesaurus are often well used together—the thesaurus to help you think of a word and the dictionary to confirm that the word is in fact the one you need.

Researching a Topic

Let's assume that you need to write a research paper. After you choose your topic, how should you begin researching it?

Exploratory Reading

A useful first step when you begin researching a topic is to go to the library and to do some exploratory reading. If you know almost nothing about your topic, look in a general source like an encyclopedia. Some general knowledge about the subject will help you proceed more intelligently. Next, find out what other information your library contains and where it is. Now you are ready to make a working bibliography of the sources that you may use.

The Working Bibliography

A **bibliography** is a list of sources. A working bibliography is a list of sources that you believe will be helpful in your research. Your finished research paper will include your final bibliography, a list of the sources you actually used in the writing of your paper.

As you find likely-looking sources, record all the information you will need later for your final bibliography. (Details about bibliography form appear on pages 261-68.) You should also include the complete call number of every book so that later you can easily locate the book.

In addition, you should add a note about how helpful the book or article seems to be. These notes will help you later when you begin taking notes for your paper.

Initial Planning

After you locate some possible sources, you will be ready for the planning stage. Even though your paper will be based on research, the planning stage is essentially the same as the planning stage described in Chapter 13. Your plan may change, but having one can save you wasted effort as you take notes.

Note Taking

Most of the information you use in your paper will come from the notes you take from your sources. When you take notes, remember that you are looking for information—not necessarily how someone else worded that information. There are three basic note-taking methods: summary, brief phrases (to help you paraphrase), and quotation. Usually you should take down the information in your own words.

SUMMARY	Summarize when you need only the general idea from a passage, not the examples or details. Be careful to use your own wording. If you need to include a phrase of the author's, you must put quotation marks around it.
BRIEF PHRASES	Use brief phrases when you need specific facts from a passage. To keep from just copying the author's words, take notes in your own brief phrases rather than in whole sentences. Remember to use quotation marks if you include any of the author's exact words.
QUOTATION	Use quotation sparingly. If you quote a phrase or a sentence for its special emphasis or its special effectiveness, copy it accurately (the words, spelling, and punctuation) and enclose it in quotation marks.

Whether you use note cards, notebook paper, or a personal computer for your notes, keep track of all the facts. At the top of each note, write a **slug,** a brief phrase telling its contents. If you have already written a tentative outline, try to use the points on the outline as slugs on your note cards. At the beginning or end of the note, identify clearly which source and which pages you are using. You can identify the source by title and author or by a temporary numbering system, using a different number for each note.

Acknowledging Sources

The Purpose of Source Notes

Anyone writing a research paper makes use of some facts or ideas that he found in doing his research. Unless a fact is common knowledge—something mentioned by nearly everyone who writes about the subject—you should tell where you learned it. Use source notes to give credit to your sources. Source notes serve two main purposes.

- Source notes preserve the honesty of the writer.

  Do not make it appear that you discovered the facts yourself; instead, give the source.

  Do not make it appear that someone else's words are your own; instead, put them inside quotation marks and then give the source.
- Source notes also make it easy for the reader of your paper to find out more about the subject. If you note your sources adequately, your reader will know where to look for more information about any part of your paper.

Failure to use source notes correctly could result in plagiarism. **Plagiarism** is intentional or unintentional dishonest use of your sources. You can avoid plagiarism by being careful to credit the facts and ideas that you get from others and by using quotation marks as part of crediting the wording you get from others. When you summarize or paraphrase (put something into your own words), be sure to do so completely—use your own words, your own sentence structure, and your own ordering of ideas.

THE ORIGINAL MATERIAL   Niagara Falls actually consists of two waterfalls, the Horseshoe Falls and the American Falls. The Horseshoe Falls is on the Canadian side of the border in the province of Ontario. The American Falls is on the United States side in the state of New York. (Macinko, George. "Niagara Falls." *The World Book Encyclopedia.* 1994 ed.)

ACCEPTABLE PARAPHRASE (CHANGE IN WORDS AND STRUCTURE)   The Horseshoe Falls in Ontario and the American Falls in New York make up Niagara Falls.

UNACCEPTABLE PARAPHRASE (PLAGIARISM OF WORDS AND STRUCTURE IN ITALICS)	*Niagara Falls actually consists of* more than one water-fall. *On the Canadian side of the border* is the Horseshoe Falls and *on the United States side* is the American Falls.
ACCEPTABLE PARAPHRASE OF PART AND QUOTING OF PART	Niagara Falls, which "consists of two waterfalls, the Horseshoe Falls and the American Falls," spans the border between Ontario and New York.

Parenthetical Citations in the Text

In literature and languages particularly, and in other humanities as well, the system most often used for documenting sources is the MLA system, published by the Modern Language Association. MLA style for research papers is based on Joseph Gibaldi, *MLA Handbook for Writers of Research Papers,* 5th ed. (New York: Modern Language Association, 1999).

Basics

Parenthetical citations give source information in very brief form inside parentheses in the text itself. These brief parenthetical source notes give the essential information at the point where it is relevant.

High atop the Peruvian mountains, explorer Hiram Bingham explored the wonders of Machu Picchu (Tagliapietra 122-23).

This parenthetical citation tells the reader that the information about Bingham came from pages 122 and 123 in a work by Tagliapietra. To learn more about this work, the reader can turn to the list of works cited and find the complete bibliographic information for that source.

Tagliapietra, Ron. *The Seven Wonders of the World.* Greenville, SC: Bob Jones UP, 1999.

Parenthetical citations must clearly identify specific sources. If you use two or more works by the same author, add the title (either shortened or complete) after the author's name and a comma:

Stones for the Incan refuge were transported 1500 feet straight up the mountainside (Tagliapietra, *Seven Wonders* 125).

Keep parenthetical citations as brief as possible by not repeating information that is already in the sentence. For example, if you mention the author's name or other information in the sentence, do not repeat it in the parenthetical citation.

> In *Seven Wonders* Tagliapietra points out that the stones were hewed and the city built "without the benefit of machinery or even iron tools" (125).

Placement

Place the parenthetical citation at the end of the sentence or at a natural pause in the sentence, keeping it as close as possible to the material being acknowledged. The parenthetical citation comes before the punctuation needed at that spot in the sentence (with the exception of closing quotation marks).

> In Mabie's literary interpretation book, Samuel Johnson is described as having "resolute Saxon bluntness" (Dodd, Mead and Company 31).

> Many scholars, such as Sweet (v-vii), point out the problem with studying Middle English before mastering Old English.

> Is it any wonder that God used McCheyne to bring revival to Scotland (Stewart 80-82)?

If you need to quote an excerpt of more than four typed lines of prose or three typed lines of poetry, the entire quotation is indented one inch and no quotation marks are added. In this case the parenthetical citation comes after the closing punctuation and a blank space; no punctuation follows it.

> Probably the most famous passage in *Julius Caesar* is Mark Antony's funeral speech, which begins with these words:

>> Friends, Romans, countrymen, lend me your ears;
>> I come to bury Caesar, not to praise him.
>> The evil that men do lives after them;
>> The good is oft interred with their bones.
>> So let it be with Caesar. (3.2.74-78)

Special Matters

If your source names no author, identify the source by its title. You can shorten the title, but be sure to include its first word so that it can be located alphabetically in the list of sources.

Hamilton suggests making Scripture memory a priority (*Feeding on Ashes,* 36).

If an organization is named as the author, use that name.

Several characteristics can indicate high quality in a doctoral nursing program (American Association of Colleges of Nursing 200).

When you parenthetically cite an editor (perhaps quoting from the editor's introduction to an edited work), simply give the editor's name without the abbreviation *ed.* The list of works cited, which comes at the end of the paper, will clarify his role as editor.

If you repeatedly quote a well-known literary work, you may use its common abbreviation in parenthetical citations. Examples are *JC* for *Julius Caesar, SL* for *The Scarlet Letter,* and *Beo.* for *Beowulf.* It is usually best to introduce the abbreviation the first time you refer to the work.

In *Julius Caesar (JC),* Shakespeare creates a work of art from historical events.

Then use that abbreviation when you refer to act, scene, and lines: (*JC* 3.1.1-3) Notice that the numbers used are arabic and that periods with no spaces are used to separate the divisions. If your teacher prefers Roman numerals, use those instead for the act and scene numbers (III.i.1-3).

Similarly, you may use the common three- or four-letter abbreviations for the books of the Bible whose names are longer than four letters (e.g., Gen., Exod., Matt., Gal., Rev.).

A voice from heaven will thunder, saying, "Alleluia: for the Lord God omnipotent reigneth" (Rev. 19:6).

A foolish man thinks that his own actions are wise (Prov. 12:15).

Normally you quote original sources, not someone else telling about the original. If you do need to cite an indirect source, use the abbreviation *qtd. in* for "quoted in."

Tindley describes his father as poor but "rich in the grace of God" (qtd. in Sidwell 79).

Notes for Supplementary Information

Even though you use parenthetical documentation, you may still use footnotes or endnotes for supplementary information that would interrupt the body of the paper. There are two types of possible supplementary notes: content notes and reference notes.

Content notes can clarify or support what you have written in the body of the paper. Be careful here—usually such information is either important enough to include in the text itself or unimportant enough to leave out. Use a note only if the material is important but would interrupt the flow of your explanation or argument.

Reference notes can give evaluative comments about sources, such as their bias or accuracy. Reference notes can also cite multiple sources, enabling you to avoid interrupting your sentence or paragraph with a long string of names and pages.

If you use a supplementary note, link it to the sentence or phrase in the text by using a superscript number. The note itself follows a matching superscript number at the bottom of the page (for a footnote) or at the end of the text (for an endnote). The first line of a note is indented one-half inch, and the following lines come to the left margin.

Endnotes begin a new page just after the body of the paper with the centered heading *Note* or *Notes* typed an inch from the top of the page. The heading has no underline and no quotation marks. Everything is double-spaced: the body of the paper, the headings, the endnotes, and the list of works cited. (Only footnotes are single-spaced, with a double space between them; but few papers today contain footnotes.) Here is an example of an endnote.

[1]This view of Hamlet's dementia is sometimes referred to as the "White Castle Interpretation."

The List of Works Cited

The final section of your paper is the alphabetical list of works cited. The works cited are the works to which you have referred at least once in a parenthetical citation in the body of your paper.

The list begins on a new page with the centered heading *Works Cited* one inch from the top of the page. The first double-spaced entry is two spaces below the heading. Each entry begins at the left margin, and any following lines are indented one-half inch. This arrangement makes it easy to search for a source alphabetically.

The author's name should appear in full as it is in the work. The author's (or first author's) last name comes first for the purpose of alphabetizing. When alphabetizing by the author's names, ignore first names unless the last names are identical.

Williams, Reginald

Williamson, Arthur B.

Williamson, Blake S.

Also ignore spaces and punctuation within last names.

Dabney, Michael

D'Agostino, Frederick

Two works coauthored by the same person are further alphabetized by the second authors' last names.

Rathbun, Renton, and April Masters

Rathbun, Renton, and Bruce A. Pryor

When no author is known, alphabetize by the title, ignoring beginning articles *(A, An, The)*. For example, *The Authorized Biography of Wilberforce Fitzgerald* would appear under *A* rather than *T*.

If two or more works have the same author, give the name in the first entry only. After that, use three hyphens followed by a period. However, if the person was an editor, translator, or compiler, use a comma instead of a period and follow it with the appropriate abbreviation.

Smith, Carole. *Five Twentieth-Century Poets.* Austin: U of Texas P, 1985.

—, ed. *Robert Frost: Early Critical Essays.* Boston: Little, 1979.

—. *T.S. Eliot's Christian Symbolism.* New York: Barnhart, 1995.

Works by the same author are alphabetized by title.

Books

General pattern for a book

Author(s). *Title.* Place of publication: publisher name, year.

Book by one author; subtitle after a colon

Williams, Joseph M. *Style: Ten Lessons in Clarity and Grace.* 6th ed. New York: Longman, 2000.

More than one author

Leonard, Arthur Willis, and Claude Moore Fuess. *Practical Précis Writing.* New York: Harcourt, 1929.

More than three authors (alternate forms)

Day, Randal D., Kathleen R. Gilbert, Barbara H. Settles, and Wesley R. Burr. *Research and Theory in Family Science.* Pacific Grove, CA: Brooks/Cole, 1995.

Edition number

Stageberg, Norman C. *An Introductory English Grammar.* 4th ed. Orlando: Holt, 1981.

Organization as author

Langenscheidt Editorial Staff, ed. *Langenscheidt's German-English English-German Dictionary.* 3rd ed. New York: Pocket Books, 1970.

Publisher's imprint

Elliot, Elisabeth. *Quest for Love.* Grand Rapids, MI: Revell-Baker Book, 1996.

[Fleming H. Revell is one of the imprints, or special group names, used by Baker Book House; so the imprint and the publisher are joined by a hyphen.]

Volume in a series

Brophy, Elizabeth Bergen. *Samuel Richardson.* Twayne's English Authors Ser. 454. Boston: Twayne-Hall, 1987. [Number 454 in the series. Twayne Publishers is a division or imprint of G. K. Hall.]

No author or editor given (alphabetized by title)

Webster's New Geographical Dictionary. Springfield, MA: Merriam-Webster, 1988.

Editor, compiler, or translator (ed., comp., trans.)

Sidwell, Mark, ed. *Faith of Our Fathers: Scenes from Church History.* Greenville, SC: Bob Jones UP, 1989.

Introduction, preface, foreword, or afterword

White, E. B. Introduction. *The Elements of Style.* New York: Macmillan, 1979. xi-xvii. [Use Arabic numerals for body text or pages numbered with that form: 11-17.]

Article in an edited or compiled book

Panosian, Edward M. "More Evidences of His Gracious Hand." *Faith of Our Fathers: Scenes from Church History.* Ed. Mark Sidwell. Greenville, SC: Bob Jones UP, 1989. 43-46. [inclusive page numbers for the article]

Unsigned article in a familiar reference book

"Falchion." *The American Heritage College Dictionary.* 3rd ed. 1993.

[Familiar reference works are identified only by edition and year; for others give full publication information. If articles are arranged alphabetically, omit the volume and page numbers.]

Signed article in a familiar reference book

Reznicek, Anton A. "Goldenrod." *The World Book Encyclopedia.* 1994 ed.

Previously published article reprinted in a collection

Hungerford, Harold R. " 'That Was at Chancellorsville': The Factual
Framework of *The Red Badge of Courage.*" *American Literature* 34 (1963):
520-31. Rpt. in *Stephen Crane's Career: Perspectives and Evaluations.* Ed.
Thomas A. Gullason. New York: New York UP, 1972. 205-16.

Republished book

Stover, Jo Ann. *They Didn't Use Their Heads.* 1960. Greenville, SC: Bob Jones
UP, 1990.

Missing information

Fullerton, W. Y. *F. B. Meyer: A Biography.* London: Marshall, n.d.

[Besides *n.d.* for "no date," other abbreviations are *n.p.,* used when there is no
place of publication (used before the colon) or no publisher given (used after
the colon), and *n. pag.* for "no pagination," used at the end of the entry to explain why citations lack page numbers.]

Multivolume work, using two or more volumes

Schaff, Philip. *History of the Christian Church.* 8 vols. Grand Rapids:
Eerdmans, 1995.

Multivolume work, using one volume only

Schaff, Philip. *History of the Christian Church.* Vol. 4. Grand Rapids:
Eerdmans, 1995.

[Because you have given the volume number, your parenthetical citations in the
text need give only page numbers.]

Government publications, with and without author

Heliker, Christina. *Volcanic and Seismic Hazards on the Island of Hawaii.* US
Geological Survey. Washington: GPO, 1992.

[*GPO* represents the Government Printing Office, the publisher of most federal
publications.]

United States. Cong. Joint Committee on the Investigation of Pearl Harbor
Attack. *Hearings.* 79th Cong., 1st and 2nd sess. 32 vols. Washington:
GPO, 1946.

[The ordering before the title is from greater to smaller divisions: the United
States government, the Congress, the Joint Committee.]

Scholarly Journals

General pattern for a journal article

Author(s). "Article title." *Journal Title* volume.issue-if-paged-by-issue (year):
inclusive pages.

Journal article

Nickell, Pat. "The Issue of Subjectivity in Authentic Social Studies Assessment." *Social Education* 63 (1999): 353-55.

More than three authors

Lifford, Jean, et al. "Reading, Responding, Reflecting." *English Journal* 89.4 (2000): 46-57.

Author not stated in the source

"Guidelines for Literary Analysis." *Journal of Dramaturgical Studies* 7 (2000): 211-16.

Article in a journal paged by issue

Scott, Judith L. "Journey into Cyberspace." *Voices from the Middle* 7.2 (1999): 24-26.

[volume 7, number 2]

Other Periodicals

General patterns for newspaper and magazine articles

Author(s). "Article Title." *Newspaper title* date: page(s).

Author(s). "Article Title." *Newspaper title* date, edition: page(s).

Author(s). "Article Title." *Magazine title* date: inclusive pages.

Newspaper article

Szobody, Ben. "For the Sake of Art." *Greenville News* [SC] 29 March 2000, City People: 5.

Unsigned newspaper article

"Running for Mayor: Somebody's Gotta Do It." *City Life* 1 November 2000: A1.

Letter to the editor

Martz, Brad. Letter. *Centre Daily Times* [PA] 14 June 1999, final ed.: B7.

Magazine article

Kadlec, Daniel. "A Biotech Wreck." *Time* 3 April 2000: 93.

Magazine editorial

Lippy, Elsie. "Preparing for the Final Year." Editorial. *Evangelizing Today's Child* Nov.-Dec. 1998: 4.

[A newspaper editorial is done similarly, with the word *Editorial* after its title.]

Electronic Publications

General patterns for online journal articles and online books

Author(s). "Article title." *Journal, newsletter, or conference title* volume.issue-or-file-number (date): number of pages or paragraphs (if they are numbered). Date accessed <Network address>.

Author(s). *Book title.* Name of editor, compiler, or translator (if relevant). Publication information (Date and organization if online only; city of publication: publisher, year if from an original print version). Date accessed <Network address>.

Online journal article

Boston, Tim. "Exploring Anti-Environmentalism in the Context of Sustainability." *Electronic Green Journal* issue 11 (December 1999). 5 April 2000 <http://egj.lib.uidaho.edu/egj11/boston1.html>.

Online book

Austen, Jane. *Emma.* 5 Apr. 2000 <http://www.bibliomania.com/Fiction/Austen/Emma/index.html>.

The Merck Manual of Medical Information—Home Edition. Whitehouse Station, NJ: Merck, 1997. 5 April 2000 <http://www.merck.com/pubs/mmanual_home/sec5/58html>.

Article in an online book

"Exercise and Fitness." *The Merck Manual of Medical Information—Home Edition.* Whitehouse Station, NJ: Merck, 1997. Sec. 5, Ch. 58. 5 April 2000 <http://www.merck.com/pubs/mmanual_home/sec5/58.html>.

General pattern for public online postings (newsgroups, bulletin boards, forums, etc.)

Author(s). "Title of posting." Online posting. Date posted. Newsgroup or forum. Date accessed <Network address>.

Public online posting

Rose, Bruce. "1740s London: A Divine Poem and Earthquakes." Online posting. 22 Feb. 2000. C18-L. 25 Feb. 2000. <http://www.personal.psu.edu/special/C18/c18-l.htm>.

General pattern for electronic texts of literary and historical documents

Author(s). *Title of the text.* Publication information for the printed source. Title of the project or database if relevant. Name of the editor of the project or database if available. Electronic publication information (version number, date, name of the sponsoring organization or institution). Date accessed <Network address>.

Electronic text of a literary document

Shakespeare, William. *Macbeth. The Complete Works of William Shakespeare.* [1623]. MIT. 25 Feb. 2000. <http://the-tech.mit.edu/Shakespeare/works.html>.

Wodehouse, Pelham Grenville. *Something New.* The Project Gutenberg Etext of *Something New,* Etext no. 2042. Jan. 2000. 6 Apr. 2000. <ftp://metalab.unc.edu/pub/docs/books/gutenberg/etext00/smtnw10.txt>.

General pattern for material accessed from an online database

Author(s). "Title." *Database title.* Name of the editor of the database if available. Electronic publication information (version number, date of electronic publication, name of sponsoring organization). Date accessed <Network address>.

Information from online database

"USA Counties 1998." *Statistical Abstract of the United States.* No. 01. 19 Jan. 2000. 6 Apr. 2000. <http://www.census.gov/statab/USA98/01/001.txt>.

General pattern for material from a periodical portable database (CD-ROM, diskette, magnetic tape)

Author(s). Title and publication information for the printed source. *Database title.* Publication medium (CD-ROM, diskette, or magnetic tape). Name of the vendor if relevant. Electronic publication date.

Print-source article from a CD-ROM periodical database

Selding, Peter B. de. "Arianespace Prepares for Changes in Market." *Space News* 8 Jan. 1996: 1. *Space News 1994-96.* Record 7/1524. CD-ROM. Army Times. 1997.

Information from a CD-ROM periodical database, no print source evident

"Goddard, Robert H." *Compton's Interactive Encyclopedia.* 1996 ed. CD-ROM. Compton's-Tribune. 1995.

General pattern for material from a nonperiodical portable database (CD-ROM, diskette, magnetic tape)

Author(s). Title of the part of the work, if relevant, underlined or in quotation marks. *Title of the product.* Name of the editor, compiler, or translator. Publication medium (CD-ROM, diskette, or magnetic tape). Edition, release, or version if relevant. Place: publisher, year.

Information from a CD-ROM nonperiodical database

"Dickinson, Emily." *The Concise Columbia Encyclopedia. Microsoft Bookshelf '95.* CD-ROM. 1995 ed. Redmond: Microsoft, 1995.

"Bark." *The Oxford English Dictionary.* 2nd ed. CD-ROM. Oxford: Oxford UP, 1992.

MacArthur, Douglas. "On Landing on Leyte." 17 Oct. 1944. *Bartlett's Familiar Quotations.* Boston: Little, 1992. CD-ROM. Expanded multimedia ed. New York: *Time,* 1995.

"Seattle Aquarium/Pier 59." *AAA Map 'n' Go.* CD-ROM. Ver. 3.0 American Automobile Assn., 1997. Yarmouth, ME: DeLorme, 1997.

Audio-visual Materials
General pattern for audio-visual material
Person of interest if applicable. *Title.* Other persons and groups as applicable. Medium. Producer or manufacturer, date.

Compact disc
Kerry Baggett. *Consider Your Ways.* CD. Perfect Peace Publications, 1999.

Selection on a compact disc
Kerry Baggett. "Order My Steps." *Consider Your Ways.* CD. Perfect Peace Publications, 1999.

Audiocassette
Bonam, Rebecca. *How Firm a Foundation.* Audiocassette. SoundForth, 1998.

Selection on an audiocassette
Luther, Martin. "A Mighty Fortress." *How Firm a Foundation.* Audiocassette. Rebecca Bonam. SoundForth, 1998.

Videocassette
Christiana. Ken Anderson Films. Videocassette. 1989.

Videocassette series
The Story of English. Narr. Robert MacNeil. 9 PBS programs. 5 videocassettes. MacNeil-Lehrer/BBC, 1986.

Unpublished and Oral Communications
Letter, memo, or e-mail
Jacoby, Brighton L. Letter to the author. 21 Apr. 2001.

Reagan, Nancy. Letter to Josefina Martinez. 6 Feb. 1999.

Hall, Kimberly R. "Modifying Nouns Revisited." E-mail to the author. 20 Dec. 2000.

Interview that you conducted
Quayle, Dan. Telephone interview. 15 July 1999.

Turner, Jamie L. Personal interview. 18 Sept. 2001.

Public address

Thomas, Rebecca. "Jefferson Davis's Mistake." Missouri Assn. of Christian Schools Convention. Timberlake Christian School, St. Louis. 7 Jan. 2001.

Robinson, Todd J. "So Great a Salvation." Sermon. Crossroad Community Fellowship, San Rafael, CA. 12 Oct. 1999.

Sample Research Paper

Brown 1

Gerald Brown
Mr. Trenton
English 11B
14 November 2001

Once Every Seventy-Six Years

The year Mark Twain was born it paid the earth a visit. The United States, Europe, Japan, and Russia will all spend millions of dollars to study it—about every seventy-six years (Maran 35). Scientists have called it a "dirty snowball," but it has showered fame upon a variety of people, from scientists to the German farmer who was the first person to spot its 1758 appearance. What is this hero-maker and scientific marvel? It is none other than the famous Halley's Comet.

Halley's Comet has many of the same characteristics as other comets. Like other comets, it has two main parts, a head and a tail. The solid nucleus of the head is very small, probably just a few miles in diameter ("Comet"). The tail of any comet is created by the tiny dust particles and gases that have melted away from the head of the comet as it neared the sun. A comet's tail can become millions of miles long when the comet comes close to the sun. However, the tail contains little material—less than in the purest vacuum man can achieve on earth (Brown 68). Also like other comets, Halley's Comet has a definite orbit. All comet orbits are either short-period or long-period. Short-period comets have orbits that take less than one or two hundred years to complete. Halley's Comet, of course, is a short-period comet.

Halley's Comet has some characteristics, though, that set it apart from other comets. Unlike many short-period comets, Halley's goes around the sun in the opposite direction from the planets ("Comet"). Halley's is also the brightest of the short-period comets (Oppenheimer and Haimson 58). Furthermore, because of its brightness, Halley's Comet has been traced back in

Brown 2

history as far as 240 B.C. (Brown 31-32). Finally, Halley's Comet received its name in an unusual manner. Generally, it is a comet's discoverer who gives his name to it. Halley's Comet, though, received its name instead from the man who first calculated that its orbit is about seventy-five to seventy-six years in length. This astronomer, Edmund Halley, based his concept of the predictability of a comet's orbit on Isaac Newton's book *Principia*. This scientific masterpiece discusses the law of gravity and the laws of motion governing the movement of heavenly bodies.[1] Using this information and using some historical accounts of the comet's past appearances, Halley predicted that the comet would return in 1758. Although Halley died in 1742, when his comet returned on schedule scientists unanimously gave it his name (Oppenheimer and Haimson 58-59).

The reactions to Halley's Comet have been mixed and often surprising. The ancient philosopher Seneca once exclaimed, "When one of these fiery bodies . . . appears . . . [men] know not whether to wonder or tremble" (Oppenheimer and Haimson 55). Mark Twain thought that since he had come in with Halley's Comet he might as well go out with it. So he did, dying in the year of its 1910 appearance. When Halley's Comet came in 1910, some were even afraid that it would poison the inhabitants of the earth, or that it would hit the North Pole and electrocute everyone, or that it would eliminate earth-dwellers with laughing gas (Oppenheimer and Haimson 59-60).

Each time Halley's Comet returns, people may both wonder and tremble at this ball of ice and rock that speeds through space and appears in our skies every seventy-six years. We can certainly agree with Newton that such precision and order "could only proceed from the counsel and dominion of an intelligent and powerful Being. . . . This Being governs all things, not as the soul of the world, but as the Lord of all" (qtd. in Turnbull).

Brown 3

Notes

[1]Halley was so convinced of the value of Newton's *Principia* that he paid to have it published (Oppenheimer and Haimson 58).

Brown 4

Works Cited

Brown, Peter Lancaster. *Comets, Meteorites and Men.* New York: Taplinger, 1974.

Maran, Stephen P. "Getting Ready for Halley." *Natural History* 90 (1981): 32-39.

Oppenheimer, Michael, and Leonie Haimson. "The Comet Syndrome." *Natural History* 89 (1980): 55-60.

Roemer, Elizabeth. "Comet." *Encyclopedia Americana Online.* vers 2.0. 2000. Grolier. 5 April 2000 <http://ea.grolier.com/cgi-bin/build-page>.

Turnbull, Herbert Westren. "Principia." *Encyclopedia Americana.* 1976 ed.

Glossary of Terms

Absolute comparative and superlative   The comparative or superlative degree used without any intention of comparison to other things.

Absolute phrase   A phrase that only loosely modifies the rest of the sentence. Because the phrase has no close connections with any other part of the sentence, it is called "absolute." Often an absolute phrase consists of a noun modified by a participle or participle phrase.

Abstract noun   A noun that refers to mental, nonmaterial things.

Action verb   A verb that expresses action. It is not necessarily either transitive or intransitive.

Active voice   The verb forms which signal that a subject acts or is identified or described. All the basic sentence patterns incorporate active verbs.

Adjective   A word that modifies a noun or pronoun; most adjectives can be compared using *er/est* or *more/most*. Any word that fits both blanks in this test frame sentence is an adjective: The _____ thing (person) is very _____. (See also **Determiner.**)

Adjective clause   A dependent clause that modifies a noun or a pronoun. Also called an "adjectival" clause or a "relative" clause. Most adjective clauses contain relative pronouns.

Adverb   A word that modifies a verb, an adjective, or another adverb. Adverbs answer the questions *where, when, why, how, to what extent* about those words. (See also **Qualifier.**)

Adverb clause   A dependent clause that modifies a verb. Also called an "adverbial clause." Adverb clauses are introduced by subordinating conjunctions.

Antecedent   The word or word group that a pronoun replaces. The antecedent nearly always appears before the pronoun.

Appositive   A word or phrase that renames a preceding noun or pronoun. The appositive usually comes right after the word renamed.

Article   An adjective that shows whether a noun is being used in a definite or an indefinite sense.

Auxiliary   A "helping verb" that may join the verb in making the complete verb of a sentence or clause.

Case   The form of a noun or a pronoun that reflects the way the word is used in the sentence. Pronouns have three case forms—subjective, objective, and possessive.

Clause   A group of words that has both a subject and a predicate.

Close appositive   A short appositive that is necessary to identify the word it follows. A close appositive can also be called a restrictive appositive.

Collective noun   A noun that refers to a group.

273

Comma splice Two sentences incorrectly joined by only a comma.

Common noun A general word for a person, place, thing, or idea. A common noun is the opposite of a proper noun.

Comparative degree The form of an adjective or adverb that shows comparison of two things. It is formed by adding *er* or *more* to the positive form of the word.

Complement A "completer" of any of the sentence patterns. Complements include predicate nouns, indirect objects, and so on. Both simple predicates and verbals can have complements.

Complex sentence A sentence made up of one independent clause and at least one dependent clause.

Compound noun A noun formed by joining two or more words to make a new word. Also called simply a "compound."

Compound sentence A sentence made up of two or more independent clauses.

Compound sentence element Two or more items of the same kind of sentence element joined by a coordinating conjunction. For example, a sentence may have a compound subject.

Compound-complex sentence A sentence made of two or more independent clauses and at least one dependent clause.

Concrete noun A noun that refers to physical, material things.

Conjugation A systematic listing of all forms of a verb.

Conjunction A connecting word that joins words or groups of words in a sentence.

Conjunctive adverb An adverb that modifies the verb in an independent clause and serves as a meaning-link to another independent clause.

Coordinating conjunction A connecting word that joins sentence parts of the same type.

Coordination The joining of sentence elements on an equal basis.

Correlative conjunctions A separated pair of words used to join equal sentence parts together.

Count noun A common noun that can be made plural.

Dangling modifier A modifier that has nothing in the sentence that it can logically modify.

Demonstrative pronoun A pronoun that points out the position of something. A demonstrative pronoun acts as an adjective when it precedes a noun.

Dependent clause A clause that cannot stand alone as a sentence. A dependent clause has a subject and a predicate but is subordinate to an independent clause.

Determiner   A type of adjective that points out, or limits, the following noun. In general, a determiner signals that a noun is coming in the sentence. Determiners come before any descriptive adjectives that may modify the same noun.

Direct object   A word in the predicate that receives the action of the verb. Except when the direct object is a reflexive pronoun, the direct object names something different from the subject of the sentence.

Expletive   A word in the sentence that is a mere "placeholder" for the subject, which comes later. Two English words can be expletives: *it* and *there*.

Fragment   An incomplete sentence wrongly punctuated as if it were a complete sentence.

Function   What a word or phrase does in the sentence; how it is related to other parts of the sentence.

Fused sentence   Two sentences incorrectly joined with no punctuation and no conjunction.

Future perfect tense   A verb expressing action that will be completed before a certain time in the future.

Future progressive tense   A verb that expresses continuing action that will take place in the future.

Future tense   A verb expressing what is going to happen in the future.

Gender   The classification of third-person singular pronouns into masculine, feminine, and neuter.

Gerund   A verbal noun: a verb form ending in *ing* that performs one of the functions of nouns.

Indefinite pronoun   A pronoun that refers to persons and things in general terms. It refers to a large category, without definitely specifying the particular individual or the particular part.

Independent clause   A clause that can stand alone as a sentence.

Independent possessive   A possessive word or phrase that by itself is used like a noun phrase (for instance, as a subject or a direct object).

Indirect object   A word or phrase that (without a preposition) tells to whom or for whom an action is done. It appears before the direct object.

Infinitive   A phrase made up of *to* and a following verb. Infinitives may modify nouns or verbs, or they may perform the functions of nouns.

Intensive pronoun   A pronoun ending in *self* or *selves* that emphasizes some noun or pronoun already in the sentence. Grammatically it functions as an appositive to the noun emphasized.

Interjection   A word that can stand alone, punctuated as a sentence, or can appear along with a regular sentence in which it takes no real part. It is not a necessary part of any regular sentence. Interjections express strong feeling, agreement or disagreement, greetings, politeness, and hesitation or introduce a subject.

Interrogative adverb   An adverb that asks a question.

Interrogative pronoun   A pronoun that asks a question; the answer would be a noun or pronoun.

Intransitive verb   A verb that occurs in the pattern *S-InV*. An intransitive verb does not require anything to complete it (that is, it is an active verb without a complement).

Linking verb   A verb that appears in either pattern, *S-LV-PN* or *S-LV-PA*. A linking verb is something like an equal sign, linking the subject with a predicate noun or a predicate adjective.

Misplaced modifier   A modifier whose position makes it seem to modify the wrong word in the sentence. The sentence should be revised so that the modifier is by the word it modifies.

Modifier   A grammatical relationship in which one word is dependent on another. In meaning, a modifier describes whatever is named by the word it modifies.

Modifying noun   A noun that modifies another noun.

Noncount noun   A common noun that cannot be made plural (cannot be counted).

Nonrestrictive modifier   A modifier that adds extra information but is not necessary for identification of the particular item described.

Noun   The name of a person, place, thing, or idea. Most nouns can be made plural or possessive or both.

Noun clause   A dependent clause that functions in the sentence as if it were a noun. Also called a "nominal clause." Most noun clauses are introduced by the subordinating conjunction *that*.

Noun of direct address   A noun that identifies the person being addressed.

Number   The classification of personal pronouns into singular and plural. Also, the singular and plural forms of nouns.

Object of preposition   The word or phrase that the preposition relates to the rest of the sentence. The preposition and its object together with any modifier make up the prepositional phrase.

Objective case   The form of a pronoun when it is an object: direct object, indirect object, object of preposition. Words with certain other functions may also be in the objective case.

Objective complement   A word or phrase that comes after the direct object and either renames or describes it. An objective complement completes the information about the direct object as a result of the action of the verb.

Parallel elements   Words or phrases that have the same grammatical form and are joined on an equal basis (usually by a coordinating conjunction).

Part of speech   One of the kinds of words (noun, verb, preposition, etc.) that we use to make sentences. The parts of speech are recognized most reliably by their form and the typical ways they are used in sentences, but they also tend to express certain areas of meaning.

Participle   A verbal adjective. A participle, made from a verb, modifies a noun. Many participles end in *ing, en,* or *ed.*

Passive voice   The verb forms which signal that the subject is acted upon. Only transitive verbs can be made passive.

Past perfect tense   A verb expressing action that was completed before a certain time in the past.

Past progressive tense   A verb expressing continuing action that took place in the past.

Past tense   A verb expressing action that has already happened.

Personal pronoun   One of the groups of pronouns that is distinguished by person, number, and sometimes gender. The personal pronouns are *I, he, she, it, we, you,* and *they,* along with their other case forms.

Personification   A literary figure of speech in which inanimate objects exhibit human characteristics.

Phrase   A word group that does not contain both a subject and a predicate.

Possessive   A word that expresses ownership or some other kind of "belongingness." Most possessive nouns and pronouns function as adjectives, modifiers of nouns.

Possessive phrase   A group of words that contains a possessive noun and shows ownership. When a possessive phrase modifies a noun, it does so as a unit, acting as a single adjective.

Predicate   The part of the sentence that asserts something about the subject. The complete predicate consists of a verb (the simple predicate) and usually other words.

Predicate adjective   An adjective in the predicate that describes the subject.

Predicate noun   A noun (or noun-substitute) in the predicate that renames or identifies the subject.

Preposition   A word that relates its object (normally a noun or a pronoun) to another word in the sentence.

Prepositional phrase   A preposition and its complete object (a noun phrase).

Present perfect tense   A verb expressing action that has been done within the present time period.

Present progressive tense   A verb expressing action going on (action in progress) in the present.

Present tense   A verb expressing action that normally happens (in the general present), or a present state of affairs.

Principal parts   The three basic forms of a verb from which all other forms of that verb can be made.

Pronoun   A word that substitutes for a noun or for an entire noun phrase.

Pronoun reference   The relation of a pronoun to its antecedent, an earlier word or phrase.

Proper noun   A specific name for a certain person, place, or thing. Proper nouns must be capitalized.

Qualifier   A special kind of adverb that modifies an adjective or an adverb, either strengthening or weakening the idea of the adjective or adverb. (See also **Adverb.**)

Reciprocal pronoun   A pronoun that expresses a mutual relationship among the persons mentioned in the subject. There are two reciprocal pronouns, *each other* and *one another.*

Reflexive pronoun   A pronoun ending in *self* or *selves* that is used as an object to refer to the same person or thing as the subject.

Relative adverb   An adverb that modifies the verb in a dependent clause, introducing the clause and relating the clause to the rest of the sentence. (A relative adverb introduces an adjective clause that modifies a noun of time, place, or reason.)

Relative pronoun   A pronoun, in a dependent clause, that relates the dependent clause to the rest of the sentence. The relative pronoun has a function such as subject or direct object in its own clause.

Retained object   A direct or indirect object that is retained in object position when an active sentence is made passive.

Sequence of tenses   How the tenses of two clauses work together to relate the times of two events.

Simple sentence   A sentence made of one independent clause only.

State verb   A verb used to describe a state or condition. It is not necessarily a linking verb.

Subject   The word or phrase that the sentence is about. It may refer to the doer of the action or to the person or thing described or identified by the predicate.

Subject-verb agreement   Correct use mainly of singular subjects with singular verbs and of plural subjects with plural verbs. The first word of the complete verb agrees with the person and number of the subject.

Subjective case   The form of a pronoun when it is a subject. Words with certain other functions may also be in the subjective case.

Subjective complement   A word or phrase in the predicate that either renames or describes the subject. The two kinds of subjective complement are the predicate noun and the predicate adjective.

Subordinating conjunction   A conjunction that joins a dependent clause (a subordinate clause) to an independent clause. A subordinating conjunction is part of the dependent clause, but its only function in that clause is to introduce it in a fitting way.

Subordination   Changing certain independent clauses to dependent clauses to express the relations between clauses and to make the paragraph flow more smoothly.

Superlative degree   The form of an adjective or adverb that shows comparison of three or more things. It is formed by adding *est* or *most* to the positive form.

Tag question   A phrase like *didn't he* or *would you* that is "tagged" to the end of a sentence to make it into a question.

Tense   Forms of a verb that indicate time, continuing action, or completed action or state of being. (Strictly speaking, tense has to do only with time: past, present, future. For convenience, though, we usually speak of the progressive and perfect forms as being tenses too.)

Test frame   A formula used to determine the part of speech. There is a test frame for verbs and one for adjectives.

Transitive verb   A verb that appears in any pattern that includes a direct object, such as *S-TrV-IO-DO*. Only a transitive verb can be made passive.

Two-way modifier   A modifier that is unclear because it stands between two sentence elements that it could modify.

Verb   A word that expresses action or state of being. A verb can be identified by form: it can take the *ing* suffix, and in the present tense it has a change in form for the third-person singular. It can also be identified by the use of the test frame.

Verb-adverb combination   A verb and a following adverb used to express a single meaning. The adverb is movable, appearing right after the verb or after the direct object.

Verbal   A verb whose form allows it to be used in a way other than as a simple predicate. There are three types: infinitives, participles, and gerunds.

Voice   The verb-form differences that signal the role of the subject in relation to the verb. English has two voices: active and passive.

Glossary of Usage

A/an   *A* is used only before words that begin with a consonant sound. *An* is used before words beginning with a vowel sound. —*She lit **a** candle. She searched with **an** anxious heart.*

Accept/except   *Accept* is a verb that means "to receive"; it is never a preposition. *Except* is a preposition that means "not including." —*I **accept** your gift. Everyone is going **except** me.*

Affect/effect   *Affect* is usually a verb meaning "to influence." *Effect* is usually a noun meaning "the result of some action." *Effect* can also be a verb meaning "to cause or bring about." —*Randall's decision did not **affect** me. The **effect** of his decision was minimal. His decision **effected** great changes in the system.*

Ain't   *Ain't* is a nonstandard contraction for *am not*. Replace *ain't* with *am not, is not, are not, have not, has not,* or an accepted contraction, such as *isn't, aren't, haven't,* or *hasn't.*

Alot/a lot   *Alot* is not a word; it is a misspelling of *a lot*. —*I like having **a lot** of friends.*

Alright/all right   *Alright* is not a word; it is a misspelling of *all right*. —*He is doing **all right** now.*

Altar/alter   *Altar* is a noun meaning "a religious place." The verb *alter* means "to change." —*The pastor has an **altar** call after he preaches. Will you **alter** my suit?*

Anyway/anywhere/nowhere/somewhere   Do not add *s* to these adverbs. Adding *s* makes an incorrect word.

Bad/badly   *Bad* is the adjective and *badly* is the adverb. —*Benton would have felt **bad** if he had performed **badly** in the concert.*

Beside/besides   *Beside* is a preposition meaning "at the side of." *Besides* is a preposition meaning "in addition to." —*__Besides__ you, no one will be sitting **beside** me.*

Between/among   *Between* is a preposition generally used to compare just two items. *Among* is a preposition used to compare three or more items or people. —*He divided the money **between** the two boys. The students in the class divided the work **among** themselves.*

Between you and me   Pronouns that follow any preposition must be in the objective case. Therefore, it is correct to say "between you and me" and not "between you and I."

Borrow/lend/loan   *Borrow* is a verb meaning "to receive something on loan." *Lend* is a verb meaning "to provide something temporarily." Some dictionaries also accept *loan* as a verb, a synonym for *lend*. In informal speech this usage is acceptable. Although *lend* is preferred in general usage, especially for more formal writing, *loan* is commonly used as a noun in the business world. —*I need to **borrow** some money. Would you **lend** it to me? I promise to repay your **loan** tomorrow.*

Bring/take   *Bring* implies movement toward the speaker or listener whereas *take* refers to movement away from the speaker or listener. —*Please **bring** your homework to me. When you are finished, **take** the garbage to the curb.*

281

Calvary/cavalry   *Calvary* is the hill outside Jerusalem where Jesus was crucified. *Cavalry* means "troops trained to fight on horseback." —*Jesus was led up **Calvary** to die for me. The **cavalry** fought for an entire day before retreating.*

Capital/capitol/Capitol   A *capital* is a town or city that is a center of government. A *capitol* is the building where a state legislature meets. The *Capitol* is the building in Washington, D.C., where the U.S. Congress meets. —*Did you know that St. Paul is the **capital** of Minnesota? Cass Gilbert designed its **capitol** with its large marble dome. He also designed the Supreme Court Building near the **Capitol** in Washington, D.C.*

Desert/dessert   *Desert* can be used as a noun to mean "a wasteland" or as a verb to mean "abandon." *Dessert* is a noun indicating a dish, usually sweet, served as the last course of a meal. —*Have you ever visited the Mojave **Desert**? Only a coward would **desert** his comrades. Chocolate ice cream is my favorite **dessert**.*

Different from   When a noun or pronoun object follows, use *different from*, not *different than*. —*How is soccer **different from** football?*

Double negative   Avoid the use of two negative words together. Also remember unusual negative words like *scarcely* and *hardly*. Some examples of double negatives are *can't hardly, not no,* and *hardly no*. For these examples the correct forms are *can hardly, not any,* and *hardly any*. —*I **can hardly** believe that there are **not any** empty seats.*

Etc.   *Etc.* is the abbreviation of *et cetera,* meaning "and others." Because *etc.* includes the meaning "and," it is never correct to say *and etc. Etc.* (and *et cetera*) should not be used in formal writing. They are generally appropriate only in informal writing or in technical or business writing. Substitute an English phrase such as *and others* when needed, or else introduce the list with *such as*. —*My uncle grows **such** vegetables **as** carrots, lettuce, and onions.*

Fewer/less   *Fewer* is used with plural count nouns (items that can be counted). *Less* is properly used with noncount nouns. —*Margo had **fewer** papers to take home than Cecil. Jacob had **less** time for soccer practice because of his work.*

Good/well   *Good* is the adjective, and *well* (except when referring to a person's health) is the adverb. —*I feel **good** about doing **well** on the test this morning. However, I am not feeling **well**.*

Hear/here   *Hear* is a verb meaning "to receive sound by the ear." *Here* is an adverb meaning "at or in this place." —*From our apartment we can **hear** the traffic. Wait **here** while I close the window.*

Hisself/theirselves   These words are the incorrect forms of the pronouns *himself* and *themselves*. —*He wanted to hear the news **himself**. They are doing the work **themselves**.*

How come/why   *How come* is an informal expression for *why* and does not belong in academic writing. *Why* is an adverb meaning "for what purpose, reason, or cause." —***How come** we're wearing our blue jerseys for the game? **Why** the hummingbird can fly is one of the great scientific mysteries.*

Infer/imply   *Infer* means "to draw a conclusion." *Imply* means "to suggest indirectly." *—From her expression, Jerome **inferred** that his mother was pleased with his idea. In his remarks the speaker **implied** that he was conservative.*

Its/it's/its'   *Its* is the possessive of *it,* and *it's* is the contraction of *it is* or *it has. Its'* is not a word. *—**It's** odd that the committee has not announced **its** decision.*

Learn/teach   The verb *learn* means "to get knowledge by study or experience." *Teach* means "to give knowledge or skill to another person or animal." *—We **learn** by listening. Darla **is teaching** her students to paint.*

Leave/let   The verb *let* means "to permit." The verb *leave* means "to go away from or to cause to remain." *—He **let** her go to the game. I did not want her to **leave.***

Lie/lay   The verb *lie* means "to recline." As an intransitive verb, it never has a direct object. Its principal parts are *lie, lay, lain. Lay* is normally a transitive verb that means "to put or to place." *Lay* is normally a transitive verb and has a direct object. The principal parts are *lay, laid, laid. —The children are **lying** down; they usually **lie** down after lunch. The book is **lying** on the shelf; it **lay** there yesterday. In fact, it has **lain** there all week. Ken is **laying** the book on the shelf; he **laid** it there yesterday. In fact, he has **laid** it there before.*

Like/as   Both *like* and *as* have a variety of uses, but only one causes problems: the use of *like* as a subordinating conjunction. Although this use has a long history, you would be wise to stick with *as,* not *like,* as the subordinating conjunction. Instead of "he did it like he should have," say "he did it as (in the way that) he should have." *—Sherry made the pie **as** the recipe suggested. Little Billy acted **as if** he had never heard of table manners.*

Loose/lose   The adjective *loose* means "unfastened." The verb *lose* means "to misplace or not to win." *—Her **loose** shoelace caused her to trip. Did you **lose** your jacket? Maureen was relieved that she did not **lose** the race.*

May/can   The auxiliaries *may* and *can* are often used interchangeably; however, *may* usually means "to be allowed or permitted to," and *can* generally means "to have the capacity to do something." *—You **may** go to the ball game after supper. You don't need to get a ride; you **can** walk to the park.*

Might could   In standard English only one modal auxiliary is used in a single complete verb. Use *might be able to. —I **might be able to** come to your house today.*

Of instead of *have*   Expressions like *could of, might of,* and *would of* may sound all right to the ear, but they are incorrectly written. The correct form uses the auxiliary *have.* For example, the correct contraction for *could have* is *could've. —Tonya **could have** helped you if you had told her sooner.*

Pain/pane   A *pain* is an unpleasant physical sensation. A *pane* is a piece of glass used in a door or window. *—The **pain** in his side could be a symptom of appendicitis. The softball broke the upper **pane** of the neighbor's front window.*

Passed/past   The past tense of *pass* is *passed,* meaning "moved ahead." *Past* can be used as an adjective that means "no longer current" or as a noun that means "before the present." —*We passed several restaurants before we selected one. Past vacations have required us to eat at various restaurants. In the past Dad has not enjoyed Mexican food.*

Peace/piece   *Peace* means "harmonious relations." A *piece* is a part of a whole. —*The two countries are finally at peace. Now both nations have a piece of the disputed territory.*

Plane/plain   The noun *plane* can refer to an airplane or to a flat surface. The adjective *plain* usually means "ordinary" or "obvious." —*Dora's uncle flies a plane in an airshow. The wings of the aircraft are long planes designed to lift the craft off the ground as air passes around them. He usually wears a plain uniform when he flies. Although he would not brag, the plain facts about his flying record show him to be a careful pilot.*

Pray/prey   *Pray* is a verb that means "to make an earnest request." *Prey* can be used as a verb to mean "to hunt" or "to victimize" or as a noun to mean "an animal that is hunted" or "a victim." —*We all need to pray that we can be better witnesses. The bear preyed on the small animals. The lion hunted his prey.*

Precede/proceed   The verb *precede* means "to come before." The verb *proceed* means "to go forward or to continue." —*Please proceed with the meeting. Prayer will precede the rest of the meeting activities.*

Principal/principle   *Principal* can be used as a noun to mean "a person who holds the highest rank" or as an adjective to mean "main or most important." *Principle* is always a noun that means "a basic truth or guiding policy." —*Does the principal hire the new teachers? Who has the principal role in the play this year? Do you understand the principles of government?*

Profit/prophet   *Profit* can be used as a verb to mean "to benefit or earn" or as a noun to mean "a gain or income." *Prophet* is a noun that means "a predictor" or "the interpreter through whom God speaks." —*The Israelites profited by listening to the prophets.*

Quiet/quite   *Quiet* is an adjective meaning "silent." *Quite* is an adverb meaning "completely." —*Jack stayed quiet for the whole sermon. His grandparents were quite impressed by his maturity.*

Rain/reign/rein   *Rain* is a type of precipitation. The verb *reign* means "to rule." The noun *rein* is a type of restraint for a horse or other animal. —*Don't get wet by walking in the rain. Our God will set up His kingdom and will reign forevermore. Use the reins on the horse to guide it gently.*

Rise/raise   *Rise* means "to go up." As an intransitive verb, *rise* never takes an object. Its principal parts are *rise, rose, risen. Raise* is a transitive verb that usually means "to make something go up." Its principal parts are *raise, raised, raise.* —*The balloon is rising now; it rose yesterday; it has risen before. Al is raising the window; he raised it yesterday; he has raised it before.*

Role/roll   *Role* is a noun that means "a part or position that an individual plays." *Roll* can be used as a noun to mean "a register or list" or "a portion of bread" or as a verb to mean "to turn over." —*He is playing the title role in the production. Is your name spelled correctly on the class roll? Roll the bowling ball toward the pins.*

Scene/seen *Scene* is a noun meaning "a view." *Seen* is the past participle of the verb *see.* —*The **scene** from the top of the mountain was breathtaking. I **have** never **seen** such a sight before.*

Sit/set *Sit* usually means "to be in a seated position," and it usually does not take an object. Its principal parts are *sit, sat, sat.* *Set* is normally a transitive verb that means "to put or to place." Its principal parts are *set, set, set.* —*The baby **is sitting** up; he **sat** up yesterday; he **has sat** up before. Adrian **is setting** the vase on the shelf; she **set** it there yesterday; she **has set** it there before.*

Shall/will *Shall* and *will* are two auxiliary verbs that sometimes give students trouble. In older styles of English, such as the English of the King James Bible and of Shakespeare, *shall* and *will* often had different meanings. Today *will* usually indicates the future. *Shall* has two main uses, both with the first-person pronouns *I* and *we:* in a question of preference or in a formal statement. —***Shall** we go now? **Shall** I find you a seat? We **shall** strive to make your stay a pleasant one. I **will** attend the concert tonight. Jordan **will** accompany me. You **will** meet us afterwards, won't you?*

Stationary/stationery *Stationary* is an adjective that means "unmoving." *Stationery* is a noun that means "writing paper." —*The large saw at the mill is fastened to a **stationary** stand. My aunt sent me a letter on her beautiful **stationery.***

Than/then *Than* is a conjunction used to introduce the second part of a comparison. *Then* is an adverb usually indicating time. —*Is Tim older **than** Paul? Hit the ball and **then** run around the bases.*

There/they're/their *There* is an adverb meaning "in that place." *There* is also an expletive serving as a "placeholder" for a delayed subject. *They're* is a contraction for "they are." *Their* is a possessive pronoun. —***There** is a game tonight. The opposing players are training over **there**. **They're** working out getting ready for **their** big game.*

This here (that there, these here, those there) Instead of "this here book," for example, say "this book" or "this book here." The same applies to *that there, these here,* and *those there.*

This kind, these kind Although *these kind* and *those kind* are often heard in conversation, they are illogical and incorrect. The safe rule is to never mix the singular and the plural. Say "this kind" and "these kinds."

Threw/through *Threw* is the past participle of the verb *throw. Through* is a preposition meaning "by way of." —*I **threw** the ball **through** the hoop.*

To/two/too *To* is a preposition often indicating direction. *Two* is a number word often used as an adjective. *Too* is an adverb that means "also" or "very." —*Are you going **to** the store? Yes, I need **two** onions for this recipe. Please buy me a banana **too**. You can't have **too** much fruit in your diet.*

Used to could Instead of *used to could,* use *used to be able to* or *once could.* —*I **used to be able to** run a mile in under five minutes.*

Wear/where *Wear* is a verb that means "to have on" or "to damage." *Where* is an adverb indicating place or position. —*Did you **wear** your coat? Long use will **wear** out these shoes. **Where** is the shoe store?*

Were/we're *Were* is the third-person plural form of the past tense of the verb *be*. *We're* is a contraction of *we are*. —*We **were** late for school yesterday. **We're** not going to be late today, however.*

Who/whom *Who* is a subjective pronoun. *Whom* is an objective pronoun. —***Who** is here today? I am not sure for **whom** you are looking.*

Your/you're *Your* is a possessive form of *you*, and *you're* is the contraction of *you are*. —***You're** not coming to **your** own party?*

Sentence Diagrams

Sample diagrams are given under the following major headings:

Subject and verb, with simple modifiers and appositives

1. Subject, complete verb (S-InV)
   Christ is coming.

2. Understood subject of imperative, prepositional phrase
   Rejoice in the Lord.

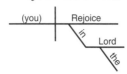

3. Modifiers (adjectives and adverbs)
   The most faithful Bible characters prayed very confidently.

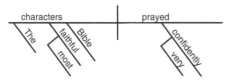

4. Possessive phrase
   The man of God delights in his Lord's Word.

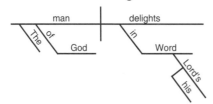

287

5. Appositive with modifiers

David, a man after God's own heart, meditated daily in the Scriptures.

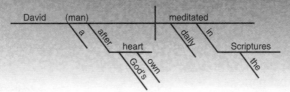

Sentence patterns with complements

6. Predicate noun (S-LV-PN)

David is the author of many psalms.

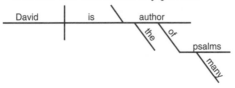

7. Predicate adjective (S-LV-PA)

The Bible is faultless.

8. Direct object (S-TrV-DO)

God's Word reveals His will.

9. Indirect object (S-TrV-IO-DO)

God gave Moses the law.

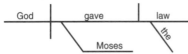

10. Adverbial after *be* (S-*be*-Advl)
    God's truth is there.

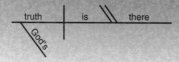

11. Prepositional phrase as adverbial after *be* (S-*be*-Advl)
    His commandments are in its pages.

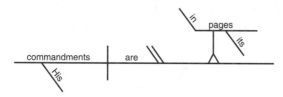

12. Adjective as objective complement (S-TrV-DO-OC)
    Bible study makes the Christian wise.

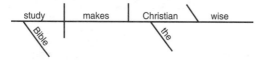

13. Noun as objective complement (S-TrV-DO-OC)
    God renamed Jacob Israel.

14. Retained object (passive of S-TrV-IO-DO)
    Moses was given the law.

15. Predicate adjective with passive (retained objective complement)
    The Christian is made wise by Bible study.

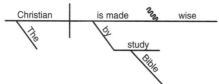

16. Predicate noun with passive (retained objective complement)
    Jacob was renamed Israel.

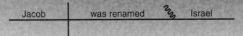

Compound sentence elements

17. Compound subject, compound predicate
    Both the best students and the best teachers listen attentively and communicate ideas clearly.

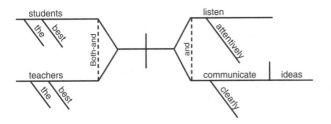

18. Compound verb with a shared auxiliary and adverb and a shared direct object
    Tom, Jack, and Barbara have already read and understood that assignment.

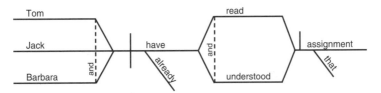

19. Compound adjectives, compound direct object with shared modifier
    An effective and dedicated Christian teacher bases his values and philosophy on the Bible.

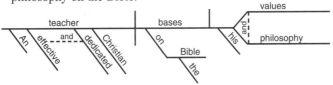

20. Compound adverbs
    Modern office machines operate faster and more reliably.

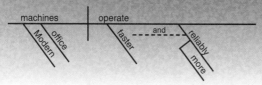

Independent sentence elements

21. The subject substitutes (expletives) *there* and *it*
    There is time now for your homework.
    It is good to study early.

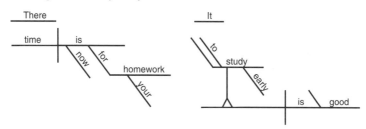

22. Interjections
    Oh, sure, I still have plenty of time.

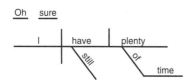

23. Noun of direct address
    Joan, have you finished yet?

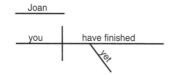

24. Absolute phrase (with and without participle)
    Her work being complete, she slept peacefully.
    Her work complete, she slept peacefully.

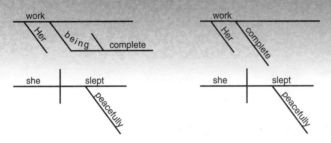

Verbals and verbal phrases (Participles)

25. Participle
    We once saw the flooding Amazon River.

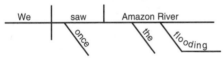

26. Participle phrase
    The Amazon, placidly crossing four countries, almost follows the equator.

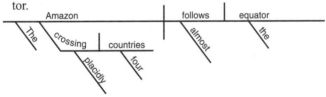

(Infinitives)

27. Infinitive phrase as subject
    To live on the Amazon requires a boat for transportation.

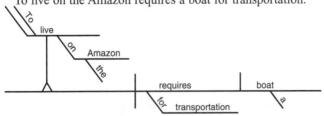

28. "Subject" of the infinitive
    We asked the pilot to fly over some large islands.

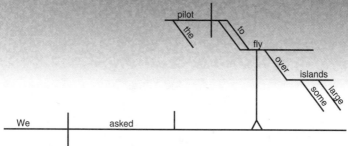

29. Infinitive phrase as object of the preposition, sign of the infinitive understood
    In that area people can do nothing except travel by boat.

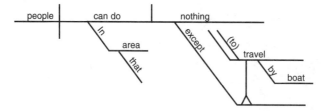

30. Adverbial infinitive phrase
    Roads are now being built to decrease the area's isolation.

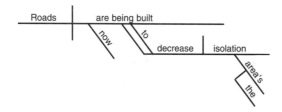

31. Infinitive modifying predicate adjective
    A road through that jungle would be hard to build.

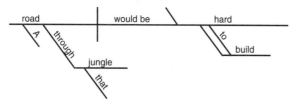

(Gerunds)

32. Gerund as subject
    Running is good exercise.

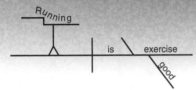

33. Gerund phrases as direct object and object of preposition
    Paul compared living for Christ to running a good race.

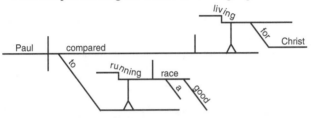

34. Gerund phrase as appositive, possessive "subject" of the gerund
    The Christian life, our running of the race, requires obedience to Christ.

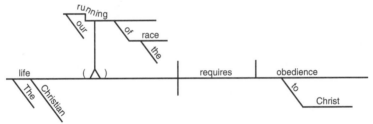

Dependent clauses/complex sentences
(Adjective clauses)

35. Adjective clause
    The coach who wants the best for his athletes teaches them self-discipline.

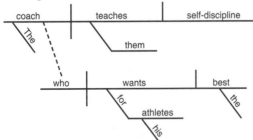

36. Adjective clause containing *whom* as direct object
    Such coaches will patiently instruct their athletes, whom they can help a great deal.

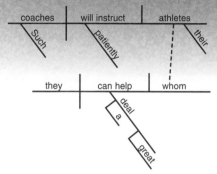

37. Adjective clause with understood relative pronoun
    The lazy student is not the kind they want on their teams.

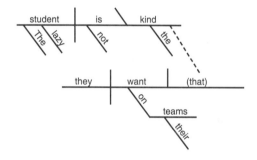

38. Adjective clause with relative adverb *when*
    I can hardly remember a time when the coach was so happy with our effort.

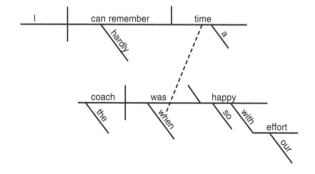

(Adverb clauses)

39. Adverb clause modifying the verb
    The coach rejoiced because we won the sportsmanship trophy.

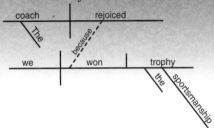

40. Adverb clause of comparison modifying the comparative word
    The star player is six inches taller than the coach.
    The coach is more experienced than he is.

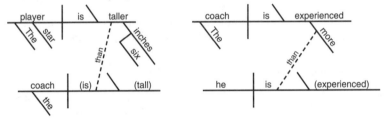

41. Adverb clause of comparison modifying *as*
    The coach deserved as much credit for our victory as we did.

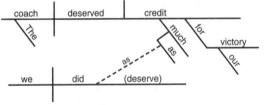

(Noun clauses)

42. Noun clause as subject (introduced by subordinating conjunction *that*)
    That the Pony Express quickly failed has not lessened its impact on
    American history.

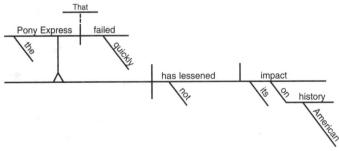

43. Noun clause as direct object (introduced by the indefinite relative adverb *how*)

    Have you ever studied how the Pony Express was formed and financed?

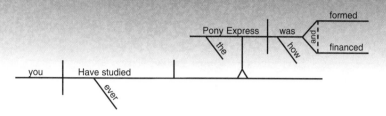

44. Noun clause as object of preposition

    The investors were stunned by how much money they lost.

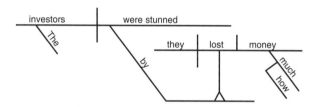

45. Noun clause as appositive

    The owners' idea that they could succeed financially died with the establishment of the telegraph.

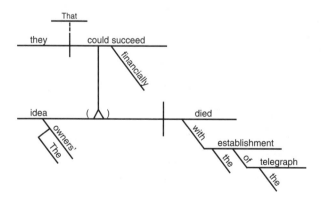

Compound and compound-complex sentences

46. Compound sentence with conjunction
President Franklin Pierce was from the North, but he denounced the antislavery movement of his day.

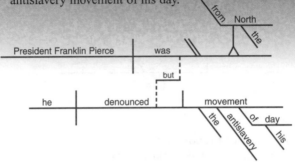

47. Compound sentence with semicolon instead of conjunction
His decisions and policies as President accomplished little; consequently, his party did not nominate him for re-election.

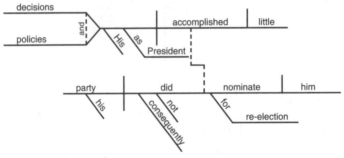

48. Compound-complex sentences
Above all, he wanted to avoid a civil war; and in later years he strongly criticized President Lincoln, whom he saw as the instigator of that conflict.

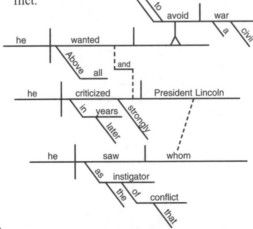

A